Social work in a cha

Europe is changing. The fall of the Iron Curtain, German unification, the rise of nationalism and fascism – all are having a
profound and unexpected impact on European integration. Walter
Lorenz, who has wide experience of social work in various European countries, believes that social work has a vital role to play in
promoting effective European integration – above all by helping to
eliminate racism.

Lorenz gives a descriptive overview of the current state of social
work in Europe, taking into account the historical and conceptual
origins of social work in different countries. This provides the
reader with a critical yardstick with which to assess the significance
of differences in practice. The author deals extensively with the role
of social work under the Nazi regime and the recent shift from multicultural to anti-racist education, and emphasises the important part
social work has to play in the development of a civil society that
integrates cultural diversity and personal identity. He argues that,
to do this effectively, social work must confront racism at all levels
and participate critically in the transformation of welfare structures
towards user-controlled services.

Social Work in a Changing Europe draws on the rich diversity of
European social work traditions to inform readers about the variety
of approaches available across Europe and to consider future
developments. It will be invaluable reading for all lecturers, students
and professionals in social work and social policy, as well as to
youth and community workers and staff in care management and
administration.

Walter Lorenz has wide experience of social work in various parts
of Europe and is currently Lecturer in Social Work at University
College, Cork, Ireland.

Social work in a changing Europe

Walter Lorenz

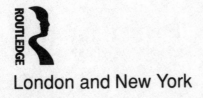

London and New York

First published 1994
by Routledge
11 New Fetter Lane, London EC4P 4EE

Simultaneously published in the USA and Canada
by Routledge
29 West 35th Street, New York, NY 10001

© 1994 Walter Lorenz

Typeset in Bembo by
Ponting–Green Publishing Services, Chesham, Bucks
Printed and bound in Great Britain by
Mackays of Chatham PLC, Chatham, Kent

British Library Cataloguing in Publication Data
A catalogue record for this book is available from the
British Library.

Library of Congress Cataloging-in-Publication Data
Lorenz, Walter, 1947–
    Social work in a changing Europe/Walter Lorenz.
    p. cm.
    Includes bibliographical references and index.
    1. Social service–Europe.
    2. European federation.
    3. Nationalism–Europe.   I. Title.
    HV238.L75   1994
    361.94–dc20   93–3483
                                                        CIP

    ISBN   0–415–07807–5 (hbk)
    ISBN   0–415–07808–3 (pbk)

To my European family

Contents

Preface

The writing of this book marks a point on a long continuing journey, a journey through intertwining biographical and political events. I encountered moments of 'social work in Europe' at various stages: I left Germany for the UK in 1971, just at the time when social work training in both countries underwent major changes; since my move to Ireland social work education there has differentiated itself even further from British models and is striving towards a wider European orientation. But in my search for 'European social work' I had to learn to live with an elusive aspiration. On closer acquaintance all models seem to be in constant flux and the contradictions irreconcilable.

By comparison, 'Europe' seemed a relatively stable entity, at least as far as my own and the dreams of many Germans of my generation were concerned: it would grow into an almost organic reality once the vestiges of nationalist thinking which had been the source of so much evil and suffering in Europe, had finally disappeared. Europe, the exotic mix of cultures, the vastness of its possibilities, the removal of archaic borders which never correspond to lifestyles, friendship patterns and cultural interests promised reference points for a new kind of identity which we simply could not find in the national context of West Germany. The divided country symbolised a broken, uneasy relationship with the German past and I, like many of my friends, refused to settle for a 'new German identity' while the nation which offered it did so little to face up to its awful past and to atone for it by surrendering all nationalist aspirations. Europe was the multicultural framework into which I was prepared to fit my identity and also my understanding of 'multicultural social work'. I only needed a few more details to fill in and complete the picture.

But looking at the Europe of today with my post-war sensitivities, after German unification and the fall of the Iron Curtain, makes me feel homeless again. The economic bastion, ready to adopt a concerted military role, turning against refugees and migrants who seek a tangible share in its values and wealth, driven by the power interests of the centre which extend their colonial tentacles to the furthest corners of 'the periphery', compares poorly to our dreams. What are the chances of a transformation?

The recent developments have had a sobering effect, disorienting though they might be. The sense that old concepts, historical certainties and the fundamental principles of society are in a state of flux might open up new ways of seeing and shaping Europe and social work alike. I have come to realise that we cannot get to the essence of social work by abstracting from its historical origins and contextual ties and that we have to understand social work, the many different versions of social work, as intrinsically historical processes. For Europeans as for social workers this means first of all facing up to our past, and working on this book for me has been an important personal piece of *Vergangenheitsbewältigung* (coming to terms with the past). This has given me the confidence to face up to the present and to recognise hopeful signs in the present confusion.

Part of that historical reflection was the realisation of how much the various social work traditions in Europe have in common. This alone has convinced me that 'Europe' is not a remote, optional factor for social workers today, a kind of private preoccupation for those with an inclination to travel and learn foreign languages. Europe *is* the horizon within which everyday social work actions and decisions take place, just as the nation state provided the taken-for-granted framework for earlier forms of social work. But the history of all forms of social work as bounded by nation states also cautions against taking this horizon for granted. Only by recognising our historical contingency as social workers can we begin to transcend and transform it, just as there are reflective social movements at work which transcend and transform national and European boundaries. Social workers do have a choice between fitting into a given agenda of exclusion and segregation whose racist implications are manifesting themselves ever more clearly today, and grounding their work on principles of social rights and social solidarity. It is in this sense that Europe, as a metaphor for the co-existence of a diversity of cultures, interests and political concepts, has relevance in highly localised contexts, just as it has relevance in a global context.

While everything seems in flux, there are themes and continuities which come across loud and clear, not least from the darker side of social work's past. It has been my objective to articulate some of these themes, not to give a definitive picture of the state of social work in Europe. Being able to communicate across all the obstacles and barriers that divide us in our different national contexts has been a most gratifying experience in itself, and I would like to thank the many colleagues and friends who have been, and hopefully will continue to be, partners in this wider European dialogue which is so vital in order to keep social work tuned to the changing demands. Listing all those partners in dialogue who have helped to ease my confusion would amount to presenting my c.v., but for their help in clarifying issues for this book I would like to thank in particular Annamaria Cavallone, Robert Constable, Lena Dominelli, Peter Gstettner, Franz Hamburger, Hans Pfaffenberger, Maurizio Pollo, Fernanda Rodriguez, Ulla Schröder, Friedrich Seibel, Hans Tuggener, Øvind Tutvedt and Isidor Wallimann.

Walter Lorenz
Cork, April 1993

Introduction

A map of the world that does not include Utopia is not even worth glancing at, for it leaves out the one country at which Humanity is always landing.

Oscar Wilde

Europe, like social work, is not a fixed entity. In contrast to most other continents it has no clear geographical boundaries that would settle the question of its identity unambiguously, just as social work's professional boundaries are no match for the boundaries surrounding the 'established' professions, which are more clearly imprinted on the public's mind. While Europe's western boundaries might be precisely defined by the Atlantic, and most of its southern outreaches of land are at least sufficiently firmly connected to the central land mass, its expanse to the north is already somewhat blurred by the insular existence of several countries some of whose inhabitants still speak of 'entering Europe' when travelling to the continent. As to how far Europe extends to the East, this has once more become a crucial historical (and not merely geographical) question since the early 1990s.

Europe is therefore more a project, the construction of an object, a vision not yet realised. There are several versions of the 'vision of Europe'. At a cultural level the ideal of a common heritage has periodically been a rallying call for the renewal of self-confidence of nations and people buffeted by political and historical disasters. The affirmation of Greece as the cradle of 'Western Civilisation', of Rome as the standard-bearer of administrative and legal clarity and of Christianity (though emanating from Asia!) as the source of spiritual values and the emanci-

pation from 'pagan darkness' were strong elements in the arts –
from the Renaissance to the Romantic Movement and post-
modern architecture – in the shaping of civil society according to
the principles of the Enlightenment and in the ethical and social
concepts of the emerging nation states. Yet the actual unity and
consistency of such cultural patterns exists mainly as an ideological fiction, to be activated in the face of internal or external
opposition.

The cultural tapestry of Europe is far too complex to lend
legitimacy to any one exclusive picture of cultural identity and
the selective (mis-)use of single elements is a primary tool of
racist propaganda and colonialist chauvinism – Europe owes
much of its 'cultural heritage' to non-European influences
(Nederveen Pieterse 1991: 4). Even in attempts to 'deconstruct'
the implied elitism of such fictions – as exemplified by the
grandiose 1991 exhibition in Venice on Celtic civilisation – the
fiction of the unifying force of a common cultural heritage
prevails as expressed by the chairman of the organising committee who pronounced that the exhibition 'was conceived with
a mind to the great impending process of the unification of
western Europe, a process that pointed eloquently to the truly
unique aspect of the Celtic civilisation, namely its being the first
historically documented civilisation on a European scale'
(*Guardian* 18 October 1991: 25).

The economic ideal of a 'Europe without frontiers' gained
rapid momentum in the early 1990s with the further expansion
of the trade privileges negotiated between the countries of the
original EEC, and indeed the inclusion of European Free Trade
Association (EFTA) countries. This development follows the
principles of a 'free market economy' which hold that national
frontiers are impediments to the free movement of goods,
capital and labour and thereby to its logic of efficiency. Free
trade arrangements have historically been the source of prosperity and political power since trade came to constitute the
economic foundation of modern empires. However, free trade
arrangements require more than economic legitimation inasmuch as the unregulated logic of the market might actually
make the differences between regions of the EC and between
different parts of the general population more pronounced. This
was indeed the case under the original *laissez-faire* principles of
the Treaty of Rome: in the 1960s regional variations between

central and more remote regions became more pronounced, and
people with disabilities, women, younger and older workers and
migrants became more disadvantaged (Shanks 1977: 4). The
threatening inefficiencies themselves, and the 'costs of growth',
quite apart from the political agenda of a 'united Europe',
resulted in social policy issues finally being put on the EC
agenda, culminating in the so-called Social Action Programme,
approved by the Council of Ministers in 1974. Social policy at
EC level is therefore very much an afterthought of the EC, a
mopping up of social costs, with the market economy remaining
the prime mover of developments. The adverse 'side effects' were
anticipated in view of the creation of the single internal market
in 1993 when the EC Commission warned 'of social exclusion
and marginalisation and the . . . appearance of new forms of
poverty' (quoted in Room 1990: 6). It is the mutual dependency
between the economic principle of free trade and the political
aim of unification, with the promise of a lessening of differentials between 'core' and 'periphery', which necessitates compensatory political measures.

Politically, the fall of the Berlin Wall in 1989 became the
source of renewed hopes and possibilities of an ending of the
ideological and political divisions which had rent modern
Europe apart. For the citizens of war-torn central Europe this
hope had found its first tangible expression in the rapproche-
ment between France and West Germany in the 1950s, which
formed the nucleus of the movement from which the EC was to
emerge. Quite apart from the more sinister function of this
political move in the context of the Cold War, the sponsorship
of youth exchanges and other collaborative projects within this
'friendship pact' offered the immediate post-war generation of
Germans the opportunity to re-orient themselves away from the
discredited confines of nationalism towards a European identity
'in the making' that would give them new objectives. Cultural
bonds transcended the links that had always been present in the
'high culture' of classical music and literature as popular culture
transmitted music and lifestyles regardless of boundaries.

As with cultural unity and economic integration, the ideals of
the political unity of Europe stand in stark contrast to the reality
facing the countries of Europe, particularly after the fall of the
Iron Curtain as an intra-European dividing line. With the
establishment of political freedom and self-determination in the

East, greater numbers of immigrants and refugees are reaching the West, and nationalism and racism have made a renewed appearance in unofficial and official politics. The European integration project has met with developments that run counter to its aims and promises, in terms of both political unity and social unity. The evidence of the everyday reality of homelessness in inner-city areas, of overcrowded refugee camps, ghettos of migrant workers under virtual siege, and de-populated rural areas of the 'periphery', to say nothing of the open war in former Yugoslavia, adds up to a picture of disintegration.

The 'vision of a united Europe' therefore does not command wide acclaim; it reveals itself as a complex, contentious and often contradictory set of assumptions and principles full of hidden agendas. Questions have been raised as to whether the intended unity will be at the expense of traditional differences and minority interests, and whether it will introduce new divisions within Europe, or indeed globally as the 'Fortress Europe' asserts itself in a super-league of dominant world nations. The European nation states of the nineteenth century did not form in a vacuum, but as they consolidated their internal cohesion, they gave rise to explosive external confrontations cumulating in two devastating world wars this century. As European states move towards political integration at the end of the twentieth century, confrontation with other power blocs, and indeed with the nations of the developing world, looms large.

What has all this to do with social work? Traditionally, social work's place and function in society centres on the creation of internal social peace, to be established not primarily by coercive means but through the considered, informed and professional negotiation of differences and inequalities. Social work has a 'dual mandate' for these negotiations, from individuals and from society at large, either through state agencies or through non-governmental organisations. It was originally not just a private, charitable movement but an organised, systematic activity which took account of the overall societal context in which it operated and developed. Broadly speaking, social work's origins coincide with the formation of modern Western nation states and are directly related to the internal stability that these states needed. But it is not a creation of the state in the sense that employment agencies or social insurance schemes are products of defined state policies. Social work belongs to the realm of civil society, to the self-regulatory structures of modern society which mediate between individual and state. It did at times become an instrument of the state or come to serve the interests of the state very explicitly and with terrible consequences, as the review of social work under Fascism will show. But on the whole it at least preserved the appearance of being 'in the hands of the people', even if those people were largely the dominant social class. Social work expanded dramatically in all West European countries in the era after the Second World War, mainly due to governmental funding even where the bulk of social services, as in Germany or the Netherlands, has traditionally been in the hands of non-governmental organisations. What is more, this increase was generally sustained or the employment level at least maintained, even when right-wing governments began to implement cuts in social expenditure and to criticise social workers for reneging on their social control duties. The relationship between the state and social work is a complex mixture of autonomy and dependency, of necessity and convenience, of extending the influence of the state and rolling back the state.

The services of social work in creating stability are again being enlisted in the project of European integration, directly and indirectly. Increasingly, social workers employed in projects dealing with youth training or rural community development, in initiatives to combat poverty, in information and education centres run by women's groups or by people with disabilities are financed partly from EC moneys, from funds established with the explicit aim of achieving the social integration of groups that would be in danger of further marginalisation as a result of EC economic policies. But 'more traditional' areas of work are also affected by transnational developments such as emigration, unemployment and homelessness. And finally social workers deal with migrant workers and their families, both from inside and outside the EC, with asylum-seekers and refugees, and with gangs of youths who attack foreign nationals. This is the problem side of European integration, which is more tangible for the majority of users of social services than the beneficial side enjoyed by well-to-do citizens – the wider choice of goods, the freedom to travel without border restrictions, and easier currency transactions.

But social work is affected in an even more profound way by

'Europe', because parallel to the political problems at European level of bringing diversity into balance with unity, the same problems manifest themselves at the national level, and more specifically at the level of the welfare state. The political consensus that the welfare state was basically a good way of expressing solidarity between the social classes can no longer be taken for granted. A complex restructuring is taking place in all European welfare states which amounts to a partial retreat of the state and a revival of voluntarism. Interest groups are voicing their own demands or launching their own new initiatives and monetarist public finance restrictions are heightening conflicts between user groups and introducing a private market of services, so that commercial, professional and political interests intersect and clash. Social workers find themselves at the centre of those divergent trends, too, having to balance demands for greater choice and immediacy of services with the maintenance of universal, professional standards of care.

These developments have not been caused by 'Project Europe', but there is an affinity between the construction of a European entity and the restructuring of national entities; a juxtaposition of the two processes may allow the underlying dynamics and principles of both to be seen more clearly. And this is the purpose of this book: to give social workers caught up in these confusing changes some guiding perspectives which might make it easier to understand what is going on, where the connections lie and, especially, how to overcome the confusion. The assumption made is that social work can better come to terms with these divergent trends when it faces up to the full diversity of its own field, its different organisational settings, its varying ideological starting positions, its multiplicity of professional titles and its uncertain professional status. Or, to put it bluntly, insecurity, ignorance and the inability to integrate conflict in the encounter with cultural, ideological or ethnic diversity activate racist responses. An anti-racist approach to social work must also confront the power and discrimination implied in the 'model building' of social work methods, in the professional differentiation of various training traditions and in policies on access to the profession. Current forms of practice and the current shape of the profession in the various countries are historical products, products of discourses in which a variety of interests assert and conceal their power. In order to lay bare those processes the following explorations frequently refer to earlier historical events, not as facts that determine subsequent developments, but more as illustrations of the interplay of forces that are still at work today. A better historical understanding of the nature of its own diversity and the development of forms of practice which acknowledge and fully use this diversity without discrimination, might also leave social work better equipped to make a contribution towards developing Europe as a non-repressive society.

Since some of that rather confusing variety of different forms of social work already exists within any one country, widening the perspective to the whole of Europe gives the opportunity of seeing one's own national diversity in proportion. These international cross-references constantly beg the question: is this still social work, is social work the right title for this activity? No attempt at a definition of social work will be made since all such definitions are bound to be either so vague as to be all-encompassing and meaningless or so subjectively biased as to omit crucial details.

A few illustrations might stake out the outer perimeters of the field where it perhaps merges with other social occupations and activities, without making the claim that these practices are in any way typical of social work in that country:

- Social work students specialising in *inrichtingswerk* (working in day and residential settings) might find themselves sharing their course with prison officers since 'social training' became a requirement for Dutch prison staff.
- Adult literacy workers in a community education project in Scotland prepare an exhibition on welfare benefits with their students which is linked to a benefit uptake campaign.
- A youth worker in a voluntary project in an industrial city of Germany helps a group of children, most of them of Turkish nationality, with their homework.
- Volunteers, members of a Romany community, settled travellers who live in a confined district of a Hungarian town, are being coordinated from a social service centre which also offers shelter for homeless people, alcoholism treatment and welfare benefits advice.
- A Swedish occupational social worker, employed as part of a team by a major industrial firm, gives a course on stress

management, for which she was contracted by another company that does not employ social workers.
- The local shareholders of a community-owned limited company, trading in local craft products and managing holiday cottages in the West of Ireland, are being called to a shareholders' meeting by the community worker who is one of the directors of the company.
- A sociologist who, employed as a social worker chairs a multidisciplinary community health team in a town in Northern Italy, draws up plans for emergency accommodation for newly-arrived migrant workers from Africa.
- Mothers discuss the possibility of setting up a toy library at their children's nursery with the professional nursery educator in charge of a church-financed project in Portugal.
- Voluntary assistants organise sports and recreational activities at a Greek summer camp for city children under the supervision of a social worker.
- A youth employment project, financed by the local council of an Austrian city, deliberates with its members and social work team the range of ecological products they could manufacture.

But even the assumed 'core' of social work is very varied and hard to summarise other than by giving very general details like 'work with children and families', 'work with offenders', 'counselling and therapy'. Some countries and languages identify the worker by the activity ('educator', 'animator'), others by the field of work ('youth worker') or by the agency ('probation officer'), and different titles co-exist everywhere, albeit often in a hierarchical order. Descriptions of activities, titles, curricula, job contracts, and user views all present different sides of social work without capturing its essence.

What are the factors that determine the varying, changing, evolving identity of social work? Is social work 'in essence' an activity determined and necessitated by the contradictory nature of welfare in modern market economies? Or is it a professional activity that follows (or will one day follow) the logic of its own scientifically established principles of practice and just happens to have its predominant field of practice in the arena of public welfare? Is it a professional field of practice that should not exist at all and should make way as soon as possible for people solving their own problems?

These are the questions that guided the organisation of the following chapters. They are an attempt to make the diversity of European social work accessible from basically three perspectives:

1 social work's relationship with different dominant ideologies and political programmes as mediated by different types of welfare states and welfare regimes (Chapter 1), by organisations and movements of civil society (Chapter 2) and under the totalitarian incorporation of all organisations of civil society by National Socialism (Chapter 3);
2 social work's relationship with different intellectual traditions in social science, psychology and pedagogy as an escape from ideologies (Chapter 4);
3 social work's potential relationship with service users and social movements (Chapter 5).

These three dimensions are not ranked in any order of priority. Instead, the intention is to raise the possibility of integrating all three in such a way that they constantly criticise and relativise each other. In other words, it is assumed that the essence of social work cannot be found in any one of the three factors in isolation and that whenever social work's identity was too closely identified with one of them it made social work a potentially very dangerous enterprise. Social work as the tool of the state with no redress to independent professional or consumer-led checks and balances represents the denial of welfare. Social work as the exercise of internally regulated professionalism, answerable only to itself, becomes oppressive. Social work in the hands of separate private and voluntary initiatives with no reference to legally backed equality and without statutory powers promotes inequality.

These latter considerations lead to the final two chapters, which are not so much about 'another field of social work', i.e. multicultural work and anti-racism, but rather about social work as such. The way social work becomes involved in and defines its role in relation to societies that are in the process of greater diversification tests the profession's ability to integrate the three perspectives. The possibility of basing social work on anti-racism will depend crucially on how political responsibilities, professional skills and competences and the subjective interests voiced by service users can be brought together without resorting to fixed, dogmatic certainties. By reflecting thoroughly and critically on the past history of their profession and on theoretical assumptions, and above all by tuning in to the dynamics and messages of social movements, social workers may gain important reference points for tackling confusing dilemmas in everyday practice.

With this practical purpose in mind, Chapter 1 explores the difference it might make for social workers to be working under different welfare regimes. The types of welfare state that developed in Europe after the Second World War can be usefully distinguished as the Scandinavian model, aimed at full employment and universal social services; the residual model, which preserves a dual approach to welfare where the state fills gaps left by private provisions; the Bismarckian model, relying heavily on social insurance contributions and more generally on a corporatist organisation of society where 'subsidiarity' prioritises private initiatives; and finally the rudimentary model, where the division of state and private welfare responsibilities follows no overall agreed pattern. The effects of those differences on social work are subtle, since social work in all cases has to differentiate between private and public responsibilities in borderline situations. But in doing that, social work practice interprets and makes manifest the nature of solidarity that prevails in a particular society and the level of citizenship reached. A look back at social work under communism shows that those regimes had a great tendency to 'pathologise' social problems and that a veiled form of social work had a legitimating function. The decentralisation of state services, and in particular of health and social services, in several European countries made the role of social work in 'narrowing the gap' between state and citizens even more evident, but those measures could not prevent the 'crisis of the welfare state' becoming acute. This crisis, in essence a crisis of citizenship, puts renewed pressure on social workers everywhere to define their role independently of the official policies of the state.

Chapter 2 goes back to the organisations and movements of civil society which gave rise to the development of social work and social work education, each reflecting a particular value position on the nature of welfare in society. Christianity in most countries plays a prominent role in welfare; many schools of social work started as church foundations and remain under church management today. While charity might be seen as a timeless characteristic of Christianity, its translation into organised welfare occurred under the impact of secularisation. As in philanthropy, the value position expressed by religious charitable projects has a distinctly rational flavour and makes statements about welfare as a public concern. These traits furthered the secularisation of social work education and the merging of ideological positions in an 'instrumental rationality' which makes the actual practice of social workers often hard to trace back to 'principles' and 'convictions' which remain a private matter. The women's movement, a decisive influence on social work, moves in the opposite direction. Women developed their personal dissatisfaction and grievances into political demands and brought questions of values and principles more sharply into focus in the process, although, again, the type of feminism that had the greatest impact on early forms of social work was generally prepared to accommodate itself to given political limitations. But the emancipatory agenda set by women and the manner of conducting politics developed by the movement are of lasting importance to social work. Significantly, the labour movement left no space for social work, and where social work training did arise from socialist politics, as in the city of Vienna, it shared many of the features of its bourgeois counterpart. This says as much about the middle-class bias of the whole notion of 'personalised welfare' as about the blind spot in socialism in relation to the politics of the personal sphere.

The readiness of all those value positions and organisations of bourgeois civil society to adjust to National Socialism is the topic of Chapter 3. The fascist take-over occurred just at the time when social work was building international links and, through these, seeking to gain greater independence from the state. But the profession also has to face up to the very disquieting observation that many of its members welcomed the arrival of Nazi ideology and the powers and 'solutions' it put at their disposal. Fascism makes insidious use of instrumental rationality and was able to exploit precisely that step towards scientifically based, more efficient forms of intervention which a whole range of professions had taken. The regime relied heavily on the assessments made by welfare personnel for its instruments of racist discrimination and it was clear right from the beginning that discrimination would end in extermination. The answer formulated by the UN and specifically by the British and American governments to Germany's precarious ideological position after the defeat was 're-education' towards democracy in all aspects of life, and social work played an important part in this programme. Many German social workers in enforced exile had in the meantime further contributed to the international exchange of ideas and concepts; the models of social work, differentiated into the methods of case work, group work and community work, which became the new 'international standard' after the Second World War, reflect some of those influences. But the concern for democratic rules and 'value neutrality' set the scene for the new beginning in European social work, although earlier traditions gradually became re-activated. Social work at all times remained involved in state politics even under its assumed neutrality.

Chapter 4 investigates the various attempts to ground this neutrality and autonomy in distinct intellectual traditions. However, the requirements of practice, which constantly straddles personal and structural dimensions, made it difficult for social work to become aligned with any one academic discipline. Social science was an early choice in the British tradition, but it was always a very selective encounter since to social scientists structural changes obviate most social work functions. Psychology, especially in the form of psychoanalytic psychology, for a long time appeared as a better fit, and despite the conservative reputation that case work came to acquire, the potential for political change contained within psychoanalysis has been nowhere near fully exhausted. Least known in the English-speaking world is the paradigm of education or 'pedagogy' which in many continental European countries has been a mainspring of intellectual development in social work. The chapter therefore goes into considerably more detail on this tradition in order to make pedagogy accessible as an approach that conceptualises simultaneously the personal and the structural side of change and development. Schools as the 'seat' of education are only one of many locations where these processes apply, where society reproduces itself culturally and where social solidarity and historical continuity have to be reconciled with personal identity and authenticity. The entire project of modern civilisation, state formation and individuation can in a sense be understood as an educational project promoted through many different agents, social work among them. 'Educators', in English often referred to as 'care workers', therefore have a very important place in this tradition and demonstrate also that theory is formed out of, and is contained in, 'everyday living with people'. The critical educational tradition which refuses to become incorporated into agencies and structures experienced a revival among the late twentieth-century social movements to which the professional branch of 'animation' is directly related.

And this marks the shift in both politics and intellectual traditions from structures to movements, which Chapter 5 tries to come to terms with. New social movements can be regarded as the culmination of tensions that have been building up between individuals and the state due to the state's increasing encroachment on the private sphere. The movements demonstrated their impact most vividly in the historical events of 1989 that led to the fall of communism but had already become a force in Western societies, for instance in the form of feminism, the peace movement and the ecology campaigns. They are of particular relevance in relation to the crisis of the welfare state inasmuch as they challenge the divide between private and public concerns and signal the importance of grass-roots initiatives, self-help and self-advocacy groups as a corrective to welfare bureaucracies and their oppressive power. However, social workers view them with a great deal of ambivalence. The rise in voluntarism is not only a reminder of their pre-professional past but also a prime ally in the conservative politics of public cuts. The movements themselves are in danger of losing their autonomy and identity by becoming incorporated into official schemes and policies, and the alternative for social work is therefore not whether to go along with the new wave or to oppose it, but whether it is possible to extricate this critical component and to turn the tensions between service users and state provisions into an agenda over social rights. The reorganisation of community care in the UK is one of the arenas in which social work's ability to contribute towards the transformation of civil society in the direction of full participation and full citizenship is being put to the test.

But the issue of citizenship has become very much an international issue. As Chapters 6 and 7 argue, it would be wholly inconsistent to work towards the establishment of full citizenship among nationals while condoning the exclusion of non-national residents from citizenship. The manner in which European identity and the possibility of European citizenship will be defined depends crucially on how the question of immigration will be addressed. European policies show a basic ambivalence between liberal attitudes towards temporary migrant workers needed for economic expansion and increasingly harsher measures against immigrants, refugees and asylum-seekers. Rather than being the cause of racism and other renewed signs of xenophobia, right-wing extremist groups merely exploit this ambivalence and attempt to take the political initiative. Social workers in all countries and in all fields of work are again directly implicated in this process, since their skills and expertise with other forms of 'deviance' suggest that they might have a useful role to play in the 'adjustment' of foreign nationals. The behaviour of immigrants, refugees and asylum-seekers therefore becomes processed and labelled as deviant or substandard, and even in the more critical approaches to 'multicultural work' there is still a tendency to work from a position of dominant norms. A 'multicultural' reference point for social work practice is as flawed in the European context as it has been shown to be in the national context of countries with a tradition of immigration. The actions and interventions of social workers signify inclusion and exclusion, and the racism that has established itself or is about to establish itself in those practices needs to be confronted if social workers do not want to find themselves in a situation similar to those who became implicated in the fascist manipulation of welfare.

Social work in Europe, like Europe itself, faces many uncertainties. Old certainties have vanished or become questionable, and new certainties assert themselves often more with brute force than with reasoned argument. Identities are under threat and new identities are but a vague outline on the distant horizon. But social work has a history of uncertainty and of continuously changing identities. The historical context of the last decade of the twentieth century is a good moment to re-appraise the past and the diversity in which the profession presents itself as a means of facing the tasks ahead more competently.

Chapter 1

Social work within different welfare regimes

It used to be generally assumed that, as social work has become a more or less fully professionalised activity, its forms of practice are largely the result of theoretical positions and methods elaborated in the academic context of training. These methods centre on the welfare of clients or client groups, on their personal experiences of social problems and on scientifically established ways of alleviating and resolving them. This professionalism should make the competence easily transferable into other countries and their different legal and political contexts, provided that the substance of training programmes and hence of the qualifications awarded is broadly compatible. The first European Directive on mutual recognition of higher vocational qualifications (89/48/EEC) operates on this principle that a qualification which entitles the holder to practise in the country of origin would be recognised as valid in any host EC country, subject to the migrant professional making up any deficits that a national recognition body identifies (Lavan 1991: 3).

But is social work really that 'client-centred' or is it not in fact a 'state-centred enterprise' (Harris 1990: 205)? A superficial glance at the main social work employers in different European countries shows immediately that there are pronounced variations between countries where they are mainly state agencies (e.g. Finland, Ireland, Norway, Sweden, UK) and countries where they are predominantly non-governmental (e.g. Germany or the Netherlands). But social work is represented in both sectors in all countries and non-governmental agencies are sometimes publicly financed and may carry out statutory duties, which relativises this distinction. Even references to the differences in the legal framework regulating the practice of social work have relative value in predicting the development of a particular form of practice, since most legislation does not actually detail the exact functions of social workers. For instance, an overview of responses to child abuse in the EC found that the legal model, prevalent in the UK, is not paralleled in all other countries although most now have detailed child protection legislation. The Dutch system of Confidential Medical Centres offers a centralised, multi-professional consultation and assessment service distinguished by total confidentiality so 'that the issue of criminal prosecution is marginalised with very infrequent recourse to the law' (Armstrong and Hollows 1991: 147).

It appears therefore that the tasks of social work, and to some extent also its forms of practice, are influenced by the social welfare system in a very complex fashion. Social work undoubtedly has a place in the welfare state but does not seem to be directly determined by it. Before examining the possible effects the various forms of the welfare state might have on social work, its position in relation to the state tradition as such warrants a closer look, given that the emergence of social work generally pre-dated the arrival of a state welfare system. Its forms of practice might reflect elements of particular cultural traditions of a country which were not directly mediated by the prevailing welfare regime (but which might have influenced the regime independently).

One of the fundamental dividing lines between different forms of social work relates to the handling of welfare benefits. Certainly with British social workers the handing out of money is highly unpopular (Becker 1987: 23) and the profession carefully avoided taking on official responsibilities in this regard in relation to the Social Fund (Stewart 1992: 123). But this clear separation has its only parallel in the Republic of Ireland; continental social workers do not find benefit assessment duties incompatible in principle with their professional mandate. The issue therefore relates not to a technical detail, but directly to the political significance of welfare benefits and to the way they symbolise the relationship between state and recipient.

CITIZENSHIP AND THE STATE

It is significant, for instance, that the concept of 'the state' in Britain is very little developed and used by comparison with continental Europe. As Dyson observes:

> The composite character of the English idea of parliamentary sovereignty, an idea that comprises King, Lords and Commons and represented an appeasement or settlement between these traditional powers, contrasts with the integrated 'public power' of continental Europe, a rationalist conception which was the product of the attempt to achieve peace by offering an explicit defence of public authority in abstract and impersonal terms.
>
> (Dyson 1980:19)

This means that the powers of the state in the continental concept are on the one hand more visible and manifest, and on the other hand they are more explicitly prescribed and in principle subjected to the scrutiny of 'the citizen'. The state, distant though its central seat of power might be in nations such as France, Ireland, Italy and, until recently, Greece, is an everyday reality with whose structures citizens interact visibly. It controls them, haunts them at times with the spectre of the police state, but is to an extent also controlled by them. The legal embodiment of this relationship is the notion of 'rights' enshrined mainly in the constitution of these countries (or in equivalent fundamental laws such as the German *Grundgesetz* ('Basic Law').

Continental notions of the state, far from being homogeneous, are themselves broadly differentiated between the Roman Catholic tradition of deriving authority from divine or natural law, which needs to pay less attention to securing the allegiance of and legitimation by the general population, and the Protestant tradition which holds those in authority to have a duty for the general well-being of the ruled and for the maintenance of a 'neutral' public order.

The state tradition in France, for instance, is characterised by a profound contrast between strong, rationally constructed central authority dating back to the late sixteenth century and the Edict of Nantes, when the state became accepted as the carrier of 'nationhood', and equally strong collective (emotional) societal movements which challenge this authority periodically (Jouhy 1984: 7). Consequently

> conceptions of nationhood and citizenship bear the stamp of their revolutionary origin. The nation, in this tradition, has been conceived mainly in relation to the institutional and territorial frame of the state: political unity, not shared culture has been understood to be its basis.
>
> (Brubaker 1989: 7)

The recent decentralistion of services in France in the wake of the unrest of 1968, which will be discussed below, is a further manifestation of this basic political tension and its 'settlement'.

The birth of many continental nation states is associated with the growth of capitalist industrialisation, which had the effect of 'commodifying' people through their labour power.

> In pre-capitalist societies, few workers were properly commodities in the sense that their survival was contingent upon the sale of their labor power. . . Stripping society of the institutional layers that guaranteed social reproduction outside the labor contract meant that people were commodified.
>
> (Esping-Andersen 1990: 21)

Loyalty to the state must therefore be based on principles different from those operating in the market, and 'social citizenship', the granting of welfare and security irrespective of the person's position in the market, came to be recognised as a most useful ingredient in building this solidarity, in the words of T.H. Marshall:

> Social integration spread from the sphere of sentiment and patriotism into that of material enjoyment. The components of a civilised and cultured life, formerly the monopoly of the few, were brought progressively within reach of the many, who were encouraged thereby to stretch out their hands towards those that still eluded their grasp. The diminution of inequality strengthened the demand for its abolition, at least with regard to the essentials of social welfare. These aspirations have in part been met by incorporating social rights in the status of citizenship and thus creating a universal right to real income which is not proportionate to the market value of the claimant.
>
> (Marshall and Bottomore 1992: 28)

But political citizenship, for instance through the extension of the franchise, was being realised only gradually and in a manner that reproduced inequalities, most notably of gender and property. Social citizenship was likewise extended very selectively and according to patterns which were to set the scene for the various types of welfare state. Whilst the broad outlines of the scope of social citizenship were decided by politics, from the very beginning social workers or their pre-professional ancestors came to be placed on the frontline of those micro-processes that decided on inclusion or exclusion from social citizenship and simultaneously on the commodification or de-commodification of people's needs. In all nascent welfare systems case-by-case assessments had to be made as to whether poverty, hardship and destitution could be overcome by 'reintegrating' the person affected into the labour market or only by granting public or private subventions.

STATE PATERNALISM IN WELFARE

While in Britain the tightening of the Poor Law in 1834 ruled out 'outdoor relief' and 'treated the claims of the poor, not as an integral part of the rights of the citizen, but as an alternative to them' (Marshall and Bottomore 1992: 15) the paternalist–conservative political culture of countries like Germany committed public funds more readily for such 'outdoor relief' but in turn expected the 'case assessor' to be answerable to the local authority. An early manifestation of the individualised application of public welfare obligations is the Elberfeld system of providing personalised financial assistance to the poor, on which public welfare in Germany came to be modelled. In Elberfeld, a rapidly industrialising town on the River Wupper in Germany, the middle-class citizens devised in 1853 a co-ordinated, efficient approach to alms distribution. The system divided the town into 252 districts or quarters and allocated to each a voluntary supervisor who had a 'case-load' of up to four families. Applications for support would be dealt with by the volunteers, who had a duty to assess the individual circumstances in great detail and according to guidelines laid down by the town administration (Wendt 1985: 121).

The significance of this systematised practice of poor relief for the future development of German social work derives from the fact that these proto-case-workers were not actually volunteers but had a public mandate. In those days all citizens entitled to vote also had to make themselves available to the town council for administrative duties, of which the supervision of paupers was but one type of commitment (regulations quoted in Sachße und Tennstedt 1980: 218). In Strasbourg in 1905 the Elberfeld system of combined care and public surveillance was further developed and adjusted to the conditions of rapid urbanisation by creating bigger districts, teams of volunteers and staffing the central administrative and decision making office with paid, and increasingly also trained, employees. A format became hereby established which combined and coordinated voluntary and statutory activities and which distinguished between, but subsumed under public control, central administrative functions as well as personalised service delivery (Sachße und Tennstedt 1988: 26).

In stark contrast to British nineteenth century liberalism, German conservatism was prepared to grant the state a much more comprehensive role. In his speech to a congress in 1872 which led to the founding of the 'Association for Social Policy', Gustav Schmoller, a member of the conservative group of national economists known as 'lectern-socialists', declared: 'The state is the most marvellous moral institution for the education of the human race'. Particularly in view of the unification of the until then independent German principalities into the German Reich, engineered by Bismarck, Schmoller advocated that the state take the initiative 'to call ever increasing portions of our people to participate in the cultural, educational and material wealth [of the nation]' (quoted in Wendt 1985: 181).

Bismarck's pioneering and 'pre-emptive' introduction of social insurance schemes in the 1880s was no yielding to socialist demands (he simultaneously declared the social-democratic party illegal) but a shrewd recognition that his strategy for the construction of a strong German nation required a carefully targeted portion of public welfare commitments for its legitimation and for the further strengthening of a paternalistic state tradition (Tampke 1981: 73). These political factors provided a framework for German social work in which public and private services, statutory and voluntary work, case orientation and policy concerns are very closely related.

When the Charity Organisation Society in Britain, influenced by the Elberfeld model, instituted its system of 'friendly visitors' and created an archetype for the interplay between the Poor-Law authorities and private charity during the last decades of the nineteenth century, the responsibilities of the 'visitor' differed in one fundamental detail. Octavia Hill, one of the pioneers of 'organised, individualised charity' in Britain, stated in 1874:

> The important difference between the Elberfeld and the Marylebone systems is that, whereas in Elberfeld the volunteers themselves decide on the parochial relief, our volunteers have no such authority committed to them. It would be a fundamental change of the gravest nature to throw any share of such responsibility on the visitor . . . The large discretionary power exercised by Guardians under our English Poor-Law (which contrasts with the very definite scale for outdoor relief in use at Elberfeld) would make it an additional difficulty to place the decisions as to grants in the hands of visitors.
>
> (Hill 1883: 73)

In the handling of welfare benefits, therefore, different state traditions and different approaches to citizenship manifest themselves, with 'methodological' differences being secondary.

The history of the Netherlands represents another type of state–society relationship. This nation state was shaped by a series of struggles for independence in which religion on the one hand and bourgeois liberal ideals on the other were important factors. The struggle strengthened the internal solidarity of the various factions and resulted in finely balanced compromises and relative tolerance between them (Ellemers 1984: 136). Since the late nineteenth century the state came to be regarded as resting on separate 'pillars' – collective yet sectionally divided structures representing civil interest groups (Catholic, Protestant, Jewish, socialist and humanist). The right to have not just schools and hospitals that reflect one's own religious or ideological 'sense of belonging', but also trade unions, political parties, newspapers and radio stations led to the 'sectorisation' or 'pillarisation' (*verzuiling*) of Dutch, and to a large extent also of Belgian public life and society (van Schendelen 1984; Roebroek 1989: 153; Branckaerts 1983: 144). In relation to welfare and particularly in relation to personal social services this principle meant that most organisations developed as 'sectoral', privately managed but mainly publicly financed initiatives (*par-*

ticulier initiatief), and the local authority would only set up its own services if no such initiative had taken root.

CITIZENSHIP AND THE WELFARE STATE

According to Marshall and Bottomore's classic analysis the welfare state represents the third step in a sequence from civil rights to political and social rights in the organisational differentiation of modern societies (Marshall and Bottomore 1992: 8).

> The modern welfare state is a European invention – in the same way as the nation state, mass democracy, and industrial capitalism. It was born as an answer to problems created by capitalist industrialisation; it was driven by the democratic class struggle; and it followed in the footsteps of the nation state
>
> (Flora 1986: XII)

This means that in the work of welfare personnel, complex sets of relationships between state and citizens are being acted out even where welfare workers are employed in the voluntary sector. The different forms of 'welfare regimes' (Esping-Andersen 1990) that developed in Europe correspond to the various types of state traditions only to a degree, and introduced additional independent variables affecting social work. Each type of welfare regime interprets the notion of social citizenship differently and extends it to a different range of people. 'The welfare state is not just a mechanism that intervenes in, and possibly corrects, the structure of inequality; it is, in its own right, a system of stratification. It is an active force in the ordering of social relations' (Esping-Andersen 1990: 23).

All typologies of welfare states are abstractions which cannot do justice to the complex historical relations that make up each national system, but the following signposts might help in the general orientation. By combining Esping-Andersen's analysis of 'welfare regimes' with Leibfried's typology (Leibfried 1992: 254) the post-war welfare states of Europe can be seen as broadly conforming with the following models.

The Scandinavian model

The universalism of the Scandinavian model is predicated on employment as a primary entitlement provided or at least sponsored by the state. If the bulk of 'welfare' can be secured through work the state needs to rely less on redistributory measures outside the labour market. 'The enormous costs of maintaining a solidaristic, universalistic, and de-commodifying welfare system means that it must minimize social problems and maximize revenue income. This is obviously best done with most people working' (Esping-Andersen, 1990: 28). This strategy is of particular benefit to women as it aims at actively facilitating their full participation in employment (while not thereby automatically eliminating gender inequality).

Within this model, most clearly exemplified until recently by Sweden, social workers are mainly employed by state agencies and are part of dense networks of multidisciplinary services which have taken over a considerable proportion of the informal caring functions traditionally associated with women in the family. According to the Swedish Social Services Act of 1980, social services exist to promote democracy and solidarity, and assistance is an entitlement. The structure and the resourcing of municipal social services allow and compel social workers to be directly involved in evaluating, adapting and developing the services in line with changing needs and in an integrated manner. The emphasis on public employment has led to a high participation rate by women in the job market, not least in the social services, and day-care services for children are a high priority. All this amounts to social workers enjoying a relatively high status in society and the stigmatising effects of their interventions being kept to a minimum.

The residual model

By contrast the residual model focuses on supportive measures outside the labour market, which makes the means test a pivotal device in ensuring both minimum subsistence levels and the willingness to work. Measured by its income maintenance system the UK conforms with this model 'because the new middle classes were not wooed from the market to the state' (Esping-Andersen 1990: 31). The universalism once envisaged by Beveridge has given way to the dualism of state and market in insurance, housing, education and now also in the privatisation of health and community care services.

Personal social services, as the 'fifth social service' in the

British welfare state, have experienced more than their fair share of the divisiveness characteristic of the residual model. Social workers' attention, in particular, remained focused almost exclusively on poor families and they inherited the last-resort image of the Poor Law as their mandate rarely extended to proactive, inclusive and universal initiatives. These remained the domain of the voluntary sector and of other professional groups such as youth workers. The recent preoccupation with child protection responsibilities has accentuated the social pathology orientation of British social work, which is itself perhaps the most direct result of the residual welfare concept within which it is made to operate, with statutory workers bearing the brunt of the political dilemma (Corby 1991: 102). They are not only made to draw the line between acceptable and unacceptable child rearing practices but also to weigh up the rights to citizenship between parents and children, without being able to command the resources that would secure the social rights of both. Thus the residual framework is conducive to a more pronounced polarisation of care and control. The state comes into evidence through controlling assessments and first-line interventive functions, while non-statutory services can provide the caring. British social work has born the brunt of public criticism over child protection decisions precisely because it is associated so directly with a state that plays very ambiguously with the boundaries of social rights, relying more on coercion than on endorsing civil and social rights for social cohesion.

The corporatist model

Compensation is the key principle of social insurance on which Bismarck built his strategy of national and social integration. The right to social security for people incapable of earning a living through labour is no longer a contested issue as the state presents itself as a 'social state', but this does not extend to a right to work. The state as a corporatist state may delegate welfare and above all insurance responsibilities to occupational, religious and other 'voluntary' organisations, thus preserving status differentials while safeguarding basic welfare rights. Exponents of this welfare regime are Austria, Germany, the Netherlands and Switzerland, with France and Italy also showing signs of this corporatist–statist legacy in Esping-Andersen's view (1990: 27).

'Subsidiarity', recently elevated to the rank of a catch-all formula for the salvaging of European integration, is the key to understanding the interplay between the statutory, the voluntary and indeed the informal sector of care in these models. Historically it resulted from the confluence of secular corporatist ideas about the 'organic' relationship between individuals, families, communities, interest groups and the state as one body with many parts, and Catholic social philosophy. The latter is embodied in the 1931 encyclical of Pope Pius XI, *Quadragesimo Anno* (referring back to the encyclical *Rerum Novarum* of 1871 with which the Catholic Church had sought to formulate its alternative to both socialism and liberalism); it states:

> just as it is wrong to withdraw from the individual and commit to the group what private enterprise and industry can accomplish, so too it is an injustice, a grave evil and a disturbance of right order, for a larger and higher association to arrogate to itself functions which can be performed efficiently by smaller and lower societies . . . Of its very nature the true aim of all social activity should be to help members of the social body, but never to destroy or absorb them . . . The State therefore should leave to smaller groups the settlement of business of minor importance, which otherwise would greatly distract it; it will thus carry out with greater freedom, power and success the tasks belonging to it alone, because it alone can effectively accomplish these: directing, watching, stimulating, restraining, as circumstances suggest and necessity demands. Let those in power, therefore, be convinced that the more faithfully this principle of subsidiary function be followed, the greater will be both social authority and social efficiency, and the happier and more prosperous the condition of the commonwealth.
>
> (Pius XI 1931: sections 79–80)

In Germany this principle forms the cornerstone of social policy. The priority it bestows on the powerful voluntary associations over state services was upheld by a decision of the constitutional court in 1967 and is reflected in all social legislation. This means that in terms of volume and of diversity of services the voluntary sector commands a leading position. Its six blocks, the welfare organisations of the Catholic, Jewish and Protestant religions, the Red Cross, the association of the labour movement and the independent association (*Paritätischer Wohlfahrtsverband*) are represented nationally and across all fields of services and can draw on public resources as well as mobilising voluntary assistance. For subsidiarity in Germany (in contrast to countries like Ireland which operate a 'rudimentary' version of subsidiarity consisting only of delegation of responsibilities) was always linked to the principle of solidarity: the 'smaller unit' can claim the support of the 'bigger unit' to fulfil its tasks appropriately, while retaining control over its activities. Only solidarity and subsidiarity in combination can form the 'social state' (*Sozialstaat*) which 'refers to a state whose legal, economic and social system is founded on the principle of social security (avoidance of material distress for the citizen), social justice and social equality (of opportunity)' (Dyson, 1980: 21). Social work in those countries has generally reaped the full benefits of this diversity of services, commanding sufficient resources for a professional quality of service and enjoying the stability of a statutory framework that extends over many functions in the voluntary field. 'Pillarisation' in the Netherlands consolidated the social work professions and made them flourish in their diversity (Nokielski 1987: 116). Their influence was such that the traditional interest groupings had to give way to functional, task-oriented 'social services' administered by professionals, based on social rights and entitlements rather than charity and geared towards the rational implementation of universal social policy aims (Brenton 1982: 69).

This leaves public social work services in corporatist countries encumbered with social control tasks and generally regarded as far less attractive. Furthermore, much of the 'competition' between different non-statutory agencies enhances creativity and innovation, often through specialisation and with ideological impositions derived from the distinct 'charity tradition' of the agency. Social workers get absorbed in 'sectoral responsibilities' which can easily reproduce and magnify social inequalities and which also make it difficult to develop a community approach. Specialisation can lead to relative inaccessibility, as was reported of the Dutch system before its more recent reorganisation (Roebroek 1989: 187).

The rudimentary welfare model

The class of rudimentary welfare states includes Portugal, Spain, Greece and also Ireland and some regions of Italy, inasmuch as they have instituted no, or only minimal, legal rights for social security (Leibfried 1992: 253). In these countries the development of social services has been patchy and often unco-ordinated. Full employment has never been a reality, with emigration offering an escape route politically and economically, while at the same time the promise of a future comprehensive welfare system remained a strong political factor in securing loyalty and staving off disaffection.

The employment situation of social workers in countries representing the 'rudimentary' welfare model is hard to quantify. In countries such as Ireland or Spain plans existed in the late 1970s for a decisive expansion and the full professionalisation of public social services, but they were thwarted by the economic crisis affecting public expenditure at the very moment when the expansion was set to take place. Nevertheless, most professionally qualified social workers in those countries are to be found in public employment, but because of the blurred distinction between informal and formal care the bulk of personal services is probably provided by the voluntary sector, which utilises numerous volunteers and professionals with other qualifications. The new Spanish constitution of 1978 declares Spain to be a 'democratic and social state based on rights' (Article 1) and details the social obligations of the state (Articles 39ff.), but in practice other laws making relatives primarily responsible for assisting family members in need (*alimentos entre parientes*) have had more effect (Zaragozà 1991: 32).

Particularly in the case of Ireland, where the state is openly reluctant to become involved in welfare provision (Peillon 1987: 207), social work skills must of necessity include imaginative wheeling and dealing for resources, negotiating with the informal sector for institutional places and generally 'keeping the balance' on behalf of society. Indeed, it was voluntary initiatives, set up by socially aware Roman Catholic bishops, that pioneered the idea of a generic and community based social service (Kennedy 1981). In articulating the needs of their service users these early centres had a major role in bringing social issues to the attention of a wider public and in rendering them an object of the state's attention. The result was that when regional health authorities were set up in Ireland in 1971 they included a limited form of social work provision, concentrating, however, on child care and family work and gradually taking over child protection functions from the Irish Society for the Prevention of Cruelty to Children, which had been in existence for decades (Gilligan 1989: 65).

Regardless of the particular model of the welfare state within which social work operates there are great similarities in the daily practice of social workers. In that sense, social work practice is a reflection of the welfare state as such:

> It is an intrinsic feature of the Welfare State as it was built and planned, through conflicts and compromises, that it implies both acknowledgement and displacement of needs, both support of social rights and new forms of social control through the enforcing of rigid regulations and the increasing power of professionals and bureaucrats.
>
> (Saraceno 1987: 61)

In no European country has social work become associated entirely with state services; indeed nowhere does it operate totally outside a statutory framework. This means that while the profession certainly carries out certain functions of the welfare system, and above all interprets the system by individualising its provisions, it also acts as a potential corrective in taking its mandate from the users of its services or from its own professional standards. All types of welfare systems, on account of both their logic and their inconsistencies, create a growing demand for social workers.

> Paradoxically, we might say that the more social rights are acknowledged, the more individuals and groups become aware of their partiality and ambivalence; not only because their private lives and responsibilities have been eroded by the state, but because through the state's acknowledgement of their needs they become able to develop a fuller and richer consciousness of themselves as subjects of rights and needs.
>
> (Saraceno 1987:61)

SOCIAL WORK UNDER COMMUNISM

The existence of social work during the period of state socialism in East European countries, albeit in a variety of disguises, is further evidence that a state, even a socialist totalitarian one, requires the assistance of additional 'steering mechanisms' in the form of welfare structure and personalised support. 'It was maintained that with economic growth based on socialist relations of ownership social evolution would soon get rid of all kinds of problems, such as delinquency, alcoholism or mental illness, poverty and even economic hardship' (Ferge 1979: 63). Officially, the concern for material subsistence had been taken care of by the state's centralised regulation of employment, housing, education, health and income maintenance. But even within the logic of this approach – leaving aside for the moment its feasibility – there remained the need for the 'fine-tuning' of state measures to the needs of individuals, or indeed the fine-tuning of individuals, their attitudes and abilities to the collective interest. This necessitated the growth of a stratum of workers, some employed in official or semi-official capacities and some working on a voluntary, unofficial basis, who dealt with issues of 'adjustment'.

Much of this work was referred to as 'rehabilitation' as use of the term 'social work' would have meant acknowledging the existence of social problems. Rehabilitation focused mainly on guiding people back to a productive life after physical illness or accidents and on 'conductive', physiotherapy-based education for young people with congenital disabilities; professional competences spanned the range of medical, physiotherapeutic, educational and counselling skills. But rehabilitation also extended to work with people suffering from addictions and to delinquents, where the parallels with western-type social work were even more apparent. Rehabilitation and education as conceptual (and ideological) reference points allowed for the emergence of explicit 'welfare workers' – particularly in Hungary, East Germany and Poland – who were employed in welfare centres advising parents on child-rearing problems, dealing with substitute care arrangements or with material hardship and coordinating the work of voluntary organisations (Ksiezopolski and Sienko 1988: 300). Georgy Konrad's veiled autobiographical account of such work in Budapest in his novel *The Case Worker* (Konrad 1977) highlights the universality of everyday dilemmas across the ideological state barriers.

At the same time, party and trade union officials also carried a mandate for some types of welfare work, particularly in relation to housing, job transfers, marital difficulties, alcoholism and minor forms of delinquency. This was partly in response to the desire to get away from the stigmatising effects of charity when support and insurance schemes handled by 'the people themselves' through their representatives were meant to under-line their emphasis on self-help and rights (Ferge 1979: 62).

The work of unofficial volunteers was organised mainly through the churches and their respective welfare organisations, whose assistance was officially disapproved of but in fact prevailed upon by official welfare workers, for instance in Poland (Medical Post-graduate Education Center in Warsaw 1978: 21). These organisations had often been re-constituted after their original ban with tacit government approval: an ideological sleight of hand which allowed for the utilisation of existing welfare networks without giving official approval to their continued existence and thereby publicly demonstrating the necessity for 'bourgeois' welfare support services.

Together these formal and informal welfare workers had to fill the gaps remaining between officially proclaimed and actual social rights. They could not publicly articulate the existence of these gaps and thus demonstrate the fundamental discrepancy between social rights on the one hand and civil and political rights on the other. 'By far the most important factor . . . which ultimately led to the downfall of these regimes, was that the real enlargement of social rights (even though unequally distributed among different groups in the population) was accompanied by a severe restriction of civil and political rights' (Bottomore in Marshall and Bottomore 1992: 62).

These latter considerations are of particular significance in the reconstruction of social policy and social services in formerly socialist countries under capitalist conditions. A similar rupture looms when market principles are introduced for both economic activity and social service delivery with the claim that these principles alone could take care of the steering processes of social development. Under that dictate social work will again be relegated to the secondary, auxiliary function of redressing imbalances, compensating for the lack of rights, and gate-keeping at the boundaries of entitlements, unless the emerging political systems aim for the comprehensive and simultaneous implementation of civil, political and social rights. The momen-tum for such a development can only be generated in a vibrant civil society, which asserted itself briefly and effectively in the overthrow of communism but which now requires support and stimulation through social work as community action. The following thoughts on the role of social policy in society, formulated during the dying years of the Polish communist regime, retain their validity in principle even after its eventual collapse:

> The state has an untransferable responsibility for the welfare of its citizens. This does not mean that the state should take over responsibility from the people but that conditions should be created to enable people to manage by themselves, in co-operation with the family, other citizens, local communities, social organisations and, of course, the state. People have to regain a subjective role in the creation of a social policy on all levels of the decision-making process as well as in the realisation of its goals. Without these changes it would be impossible to direct social policy towards awakening a feeling of affiliation with a community, towards promoting mutual aid or social work motivations.
>
> (Ksiezopolski 1987: 105)

SOCIAL WORK AND DECENTRALISATION

Fostering solidarity and endorsing formal democratic rights proved particularly difficult in European countries with highly centralised governmental structures. This weakness was exposed in the wave of protest movements which swept Europe (and much of the rest of the world) in the late 1960s. It is not surprising, therefore, to find that in some countries – for instance, France, Italy and Greece – the governments, in seeking to address the deficit in political credibility without wanting to yield power, changed over to accessible, community-based social and health services.

In Italy, the trend towards decentralisation had a variety of origins; mutual aid associations and particularly cooperatives had always been a strong feature of Italian life and the political demands for participation and greater immediacy arose from both radical sources such as Marxism and feminism and from Catholic social teaching. Italy's Law 833 of 1978, which heralded the radical reorganisation of health services, designated the local 'district' or borough (*comune*) as the political and administrative level for the provision of services. The over 8,000 *comuni*, with usually 20,000 to 50,000 inhabitants (but sometimes less than 1,000) set up local health units (*unità sanitaria locale*, USL) which combined health and social welfare responsibilities (Cigno 1985: 174).

The Italian achievements in terms of decentralising state services are considerable given the absence of a 'participatory culture' of shared and devolved decision-making, and in the context of a reliance on clientelism in that country. Local service committees confront politicians, who are proportionally represented on them, with the practical dilemmas caused by their policies (Cigno 1985: 178). But the initial agenda of *gestione sociale*, i.e. social accountability in management, simply aimed at a more direct representation of citizens; it failed to address their dependence on bureaucrats and professionals. Government backing for local initiatives often had the effect of 'demobilising' the social movements and burnishing the caring image of the state (Ergas 1982: 452).

Compared to the Swedish system of local social service committees, which are similarly composed but operate in a political context that emphasises the legal entitlements of service users, the Italian experience of decentralisation still tends to play into the hands of the old patronage system (*clientelismo*), which is deeply ingrained as a pattern of dependence (Ascoli 1987: 122). There are striking parallels in this regard with the situation in Greece, where clientelism is also very much part of the political culture. Stathopoulos (1991) describes the limited impact of recent legislation promoting decentralisation and citizen participation at local and regional levels (laws No. 1262 of 1982 and No. 1622 of 1986) in rural Greece. Political power remains concentrated in the hands of central government and political parties. The newly created participatory structures were quickly seized by members of national political parties seeking to 'promote their own party's interests at local level' (Stathopoulos 1991: 124). Consequently, local people tend to measure the usefulness of community workers by their ability to tap official funds, create channels of political influence and gain access to government. The political culture yields very slowly to the sense of empowerment that community workers seek to engender in the local population.

In France decentralisation officially came about in the early

1980s with a series of legislative measures by which the Mitterand government sought to radically alter the centralised structure of French government. But the path had been prepared through participatory initiatives in the 1970s, notably in the sphere of social services: well over a hundred social centres (*centres sociaux*) sprang up all over the country, financed out of both governmental sources and the French 'private' health funds, with the explicit brief of applying the principle of user participation in the management of the centres. Triggered by the political events in France this movement meshed with the typically French system of *caisses* – funds for old age, sickness and family welfare – which have consumer representatives. But it also activated new forms of social and cultural work which de-emphasised a problem orientation (Chamberlayne 1992: 15) and, through the method of 'animation', sought to encourage wider community participation. This facilitated interaction between workers and community representatives to identify the causes of need instead of concentrating solely on delivering state responses to these needs (Cannan 1991: 26; Cannan, Berry and Lyons 1992: 109). Democratic accountability to service users, however, was not enhanced by the dual responsibility of social service centres (to state and private organisations) and the generally more complex structure of local government. (Wallimann 1986: 1315).

The very fact that governments, in the context of their decentralisation policies, frequently called upon the services of social workers to 'make it work' reveals the ambivalence of decentralisation. It has been argued (for instance by Mayer and Müller 1984) that, overall, the 'enmeshment' of private lives with the institutions of the state has not been reduced. Instead, the growing complexity of these relations and the emphasis on cost effectiveness have diverted attention away from the state and the political arena towards economic and local management issues. Professionals like social workers, priding themselves on their autonomy, become pivotal in lending legitimacy to the resource allocations with their 'objective assessments'.

Whatever new levels and forms of decentralisation can be observed, they are part and parcel of a system growing in complexity. . . In many areas of health and social services the individual meets the State mediated through the professionals charged with the provision of care and services. It is ironic that the individual as client on whose behalf the whole system is said to be organised has so few opportunities of taking part in a more active sense.

(Nowotny 1984: 11)

As the UK embarks on a major restructuring of community care under the banner of choice and decentralisation, the experience of professionals in other European countries contains an ambiguous message. Decentralisation can, on the one hand, provide an opportunity for client participation and for questioning the entire basis on which welfare and welfare services are structured and organised in a society. The role of self-help movements and of general social movements in the 1980s will be examined in more detail in Chapter 5. On the other hand, it can lead to a more insidious form of control (Cannan, Berry and Lyons 1992: 114), a greater presence of the state and its agenda in the lives of citizens under the guise of participation. Shifting services from official agencies to voluntary groups, informal networks, 'the community' and indeed to 'the family' has a well-established place on the neo-liberal political agenda and may lead to new forms of capitalist exploitation and hegemony (Chamberlayne 1992: 14). There is therefore a clear need for social workers to assert their professional autonomy in the context of these developments, not in order to achieve a widening of their power position, but to provide a critical and independent reflection on the political consequences of their 'fitting into a given agenda', no matter how closely this agenda appears to meet the fundamental principles of client initiative and participation that underlie social work. The task of empowerment is not achieved merely by going through the motions.

THE RESTRUCTURING OF THE WELFARE STATE

The 'crisis of the welfare state' and the subsequent rise of New Right policies led West European countries into similar dilemmas. All four types of welfare regimes experienced this crisis at both a material and an ideological level. In fiscal terms, the Keynesian mechanism of public investments boosting economic expansion had exhausted itself under the increasingly costly burden of repayment commitments, which exacerbated the unemployment crisis. Full male employment as the economic basis of insurance-based welfare systems began to crumble and women started to question their marginalisation in the labour market, their increasing dependence on assistance and the lack of public and economic recognition of their care and domestic functions.

Unemployment and marginalisation associated with the fundamental restructuring of industrial and agricultural economies in the 1970s, combined with the demographic effects of an ageing population and a loosening of marital and family ties, simultaneously made heightened demands on welfare services. All this led to a redefinition of the relationship between insurance and assistance and of the boundary between self-help responsibilities (voluntary, private and commercial) and the responsibilities of the state. Assistance was made to cover risks and sectors of the population for which it was never intended. This in turn made the state's controlling functions in welfare matters more visible and added to the alienation experienced by recipients of welfare. At the same time the bifurcation of the labour market into those in stable, well-paid employment and those in marginal, temporary and discontinuous employment turned the mutuality principle of insurance schemes on its head, so that they became 'bastions of corporatist privilege from which the most vulnerable were increasingly excluded' (Chamberlayn 1992: 7). At the ideological level, the political left, with its traditional advocacy of institutional universal welfare measures, lost influence, even in Scandinavian countries and in Austria and began to woo the middle-class voters with an agenda dictated by the New Right rationale. In this climate the 'Swedish model' of relying largely on state services was curtailed as 'the national efforts to solve the economic problems seem to develop local social problems that create, in the long run, heavy structural costs for the public sector' (Nilsson and Wadeskog 1988: 37). The Italian attempts to move from a rudimentary to a more egalitarian, though still corporatist, welfare state experienced a 'jamming up' under bulging public expenditures and divergent consumer interests (Donati and Colozzi 1988: 97).

In the Netherlands, the dismantling of the traditional welfare

structure by the conservative–liberal government in the 1980s
coincided with the gradual disestablishment of social work just
as a comprehensive, pro-active, profession-led concept of welfare came within sight. The politics of retrenchment exploited
the growing demands for 'grass-roots democracy', which also
turned against the power vested in professional organisations
and extolled the virtues of the 'caring community' (*zorgsame
samenleving*, Nokielski 1987: 122). Nevertheless, the Netherlands remain an example of at least an attempt at a 'needs-led'
structuring of social services: local authorities grant-aid (albeit
according to measures of cost efficiency) private non-profit
making organisations (*stichting*) set up around particular fields
of need and social problems, notably in areas such as mental
health, family work, homelessness and drug addiction. Only one
project catering for a particular area of need receives assistance
per local authority and their performance is monitored annually.

The progressive erosion of the principle of equality in social
welfare heightened the crisis of legitimation experienced by the
nation states since the 1970s. Social workers are once more in
the front line of political pressures to maintain the appearance
of legitimacy by presenting a 'caring image' to society, by
mediating in the conflicts created by an increasingly vociferous
service-user population and by individualising or particularising
social resource allocation to selected 'vulnerable groups'. The
continued expansion of welfare expenditure and of social work
posts in all countries, as well as the rush in former communist
countries to establish social work services, testify to the continued need for the stabilising functions of social security and
personalised welfare.

The convergence of developments in all the various welfare
regimes towards a 'welfare mix' (Evers and Wintersberger 1988)
is a clear signal of the pre-eminence which market considerations
are beginning to assume in state and welfare politics. What is
more, this tendency is being amplified by the social policy
initiatives the EC itself is taking. Most of these initiatives are
geared towards enhancing the global market position of Europe
and of economically active individuals and groups within this
market. 'Historically a key component of continental state-
building processes, the "social dimension" of the EC remains
extremely rudimentary' (Leibfried and Pierson 1992: 333). The
main areas in which the EC becomes active in social policy terms

are the protection of the welfare rights of migrant workers, health and safety at work, and gender equality, the latter having affected national social policy practice perhaps the most profoundly. The underlying principles are re-affirmed in the Social Charter and the Protocols to the Maastricht Treaty, which deal only with employment-related issues and rights, apart from a mention of the entitlement of people with disabilities 'to additional concrete measures aimed at improving their social and professional integration' (Section 26, CEC 1990). In addition, the European Structural Funds provide a measure of compensation for the deregulation of the market through (re-)training programmes (ERGO, LEDA, ELISE, SYSDEM, LEADER, SPEC, etc.) and programmes for the integration of disadvantaged people (NOW, HORIZON, EUROFORM) (Baine, Bennington and Russell 1992: 61–2). Outside these funds three phases of 'Programmes to Combat Poverty' have operated since 1975, the most recent one, in 1989, involving thirty-nine projects in all the member states with an overall five-year budget of 55 million ECU (less than the annual budget of many UK social service departments, as Townsend points out (1989: 9)).

Social workers in all parts of the EC, but particularly in 'peripheral' countries and 'regions of industrial decline', work in projects financed through these programmes and have to tailor their project objectives to EC guidelines. This outlines a situation where opportunities for tangible EC citizenship in the EC are created or denied depending on the conditions of funding but also on the 'interpretation' of those conditions at the local level. 'In the short run, the structural funds appear to be competitors to any emerging focus on social citizenship' (Leibfried and Pierson 1992: 340), but the struggle for citizenship can be taken on, not so much by the professionals but by the users of services themselves. Networks are being set up across Europe between different user groups, which take self-advocacy right up to the level of lobbying EC institutions and MEPs. Their experience has been that the politics of the funding process no longer conform to the channels of local and national government structures but show an interesting propensity for 'shortcuts' directly to Brussels. 'Eurolink Age', for instance, maintains an office in Brussels while the Single Parent Action Network (SPAN) is forging cross-national links, as is FEANTSA, a Europe-wide campaign on homelessness (Baine, Bennington and

Russell 1992: 88–9). 'For the moment there is not a single civil right which is defended by the European Community. There is not a single basic right of citizens which has anything to do with the Treaty of Rome' (Dahrendorf 1992: 85). European integration confronts social workers once more, as in the history of each nation state, with the alternative of developing social services to compensate for the lack of social rights or as a vehicle for the full rights of citizenship. The decoupling of welfare benefits from market principles will be the single most crucial task to be achieved not by the EC bureaucracy, but by the nascent European civil society in which social work must become a driving force.

When Pinker, by way of calling on social workers to concentrate on personal issues, states that, 'it seems obvious – to me at least – that problems of a personal nature do exist and that people are quite capable of being the architects of their own misery' (Pinker 1990: 93), he misses the point that the political mandate given to social workers within all the welfare systems is to locate and define, first of all, the boundary between personal troubles and public issues. The dichotomy between case work and social action as two distinct methods treats that boundary as given, whereas the actual core skill of social workers lies in the ability to leave the choice – and the mix – of methods open and to give clients a say in the choice. It is the hallmark of modern societies that this boundary can no longer be regarded as fixed, that it has become problematic and the subject of political negotiations. The fact that every modern state has developed some system of public welfare and that the EC is being drawn, very reluctantly, into ever more expansive social policy areas bears ample witness to this. Society *is* implicated not just in people's lack of education, jobs or housing, but also in a case of fatal child abuse, in the death of a pensioner from hypothermia, and in the plight of a homeless person. In counselling people in their personal grief or outrage it is essential for social workers to open up the official, taken-for-granted definitions of that boundary and in particular to resist the translation of public wrongs into personal troubles; but it is equally important not to deny the people immediately affected their share of responsibility which constitutes their human dignity. The different European welfare systems, and the process of European integration itself, do have a bearing on the practice of social work. Social workers in turn represent and interpret these systems through their methods of intervention, and they constantly open up or narrow down the boundaries of social solidarity.

Chapter 2

Ideological positions and the origins of social work

Although social work practice is 'bounded' by the state and by social policies in their different European traditions, it is also the product of ideologies which were not necessarily expressed in official policies. They were transmitted mainly through social work training as the foundation of professional independence. The need for social work training in whatever form as a means of deliberating on the complex nature of the 'helping' role also expresses the need for a critical dialogue with society's dominant political interests. Social work training has always been more than 'on-the-job training'; educational programmes have to grapple with the dialectical tension between, on the one hand, preparing for very specific tasks and duties within given organisational parameters and, on the other hand, relativising and questioning these organisational constraints from the transcending positions of ethics and fundamental views on the nature of society and human behaviour. From the very start of social work education, competence was defined as something more than the ability to follow rules and directives, to assess people under fixed criteria and to get them to comply with official decisions, much as these considerations may have affected practice. But on the whole, the implementation of welfare procedures and regulations was the domain of other welfare personnel and social control agents, whereas social workers were needed to deal with the grey areas, with the mismatch between 'cases' and 'structures': delinquents unfit for straightforward punishment, children who had to be rescued as much from charitable institutions as from the dangers of their families or the street, and poor people who did not 'deserve' their unfortunate position.

Social work therefore represents values as much as it represents technical expertise, and although the history of social work education shows a gradual fading of distinct belief systems as frameworks for social work curricula and their replacement by scientifically inspired neutrality, the 'value question' remains acute. European social work can perhaps best face up to the actuality of value questions through a critical examination of its own historical roots and its 'received ideas' in the context of their various discourses (Rojek, Peacock and Collins 1988).

Social work education in Europe developed in the context of four broad ideological frameworks: Christianity, philanthropy, feminism and socialism. This differentiation is not to deny that many cross-currents exist between those traditions nor that, in examining the practice of social workers, one would usually find it hard to trace it back to the ideological flavour of their training. This interplay of training and practice will also feature in this chapter. A fifth tradition which warrants closer and separate examination, will be dealt with in Chapter 3; it concerns the deliberate creation of dis-welfare under the guise of welfare: National Socialism and Fascism have cast a dark shadow over social work and its grounding in values and have left a more fundamental legacy to be faced up to.

SOCIAL WORK TRAINING IN THE CHRISTIAN TRADITION

Schools of social work founded and managed by Christian churches can be found in all West European countries, with the exception of Ireland and the UK. This is a reflection of the churches' considerable impact on the development of welfare services in Europe and their established tradition in 'works of charity'. However, social work first appeared at a time in modern European history when secularisation was spreading to all aspects of society and when the traditional metaphysical consensus was finally giving way to private beliefs. 'Bourgeois triumph thus imbued the French Revolution with the agnostic or secular–moral ideology of the eighteenth-century enlightenment', comments Hobsbawm; this set the scene for the secularism characteristic of most working-class and socialist movements. 'However, the prevalent secularism of the new labour and socialist movements was based on the equally novel and more

fundamental fact of the prevalent religious indifference of the
new proletariat' (Hobsbawm 1977: 270–1).

The prominent role of churches in most of the original forms
of social work was a central part of their response to secularisation. The churches realised during the nineteenth century
that in order to keep a foothold in modernity their message had
to assume practical relevance for the new age, that they had to
reconstitute their legitimacy not in displays of privilege and
power, but in terms of service to people, and that they could
compete with the lure of socialism for the disaffected masses
more effectively by practical action than by preaching. The
regeneration of religious activities corresponded with the changing nature of spirituality. The impact of philosophical rationality
and the political reverberations of the French Revolution had
severely shaken the established churches; religion began to turn
'inward' to become a matter of personal feelings and experiences and 'outward' to express personal caring. This change in
the nature of religion, which echoes the sentiments of the
Romantic Movement, had a profound effect on the 'politics of
charity', which came to stress personal commitment and shared
experiences of suffering not as gestures external to religious
convictions, but as the very forms in which faith retained its
relevance. The plethora of 'inner-city missions' in the industrialised centres of Europe in the Protestant traditions arose out
of this renewal, just as Catholic religious orders began to
proliferate, to revive their social mandate and to found hospitals,
orphanages, schools and other social services.

In post-revolutionary France, Catholic orders and associations recovered from persecution under Napoleon and intens-
ified their social commitment, which was modelled on the
previous work of St Vincent de Paul (1581–1660) and his
'sisters of charity' (filles servantes des pauvres de la charité).
This religious movement broke with the pre-eminence of vows
and clerical regulations and many lay women became affiliated
with charitable projects, expressing through them a 'safe' form
of emancipation. Training and ethical commitments raised
activities in caring, nursing and teaching towards professional
standards, with some orders specialising, for example, in hos-
pital care (Bon Secours sisters), residential care (Soers de charité
du Bon Pasteur) or education (Ursuline sisters) (Wendt 1985:
72). These orders were all to play a leading role in providing a

non-governmental (i.e. non-colonial) infrastructure of care and education services in Ireland after the ban on the Catholic Church was lifted and religious orders could establish themselves as alternatives to state and Protestant services.

The equivalent Protestant religious orders, representing a new nineteenth-century movement, were inspired partly by these examples in neighbouring France and partly by the early Christian concept of *diakonia* (service). Their main aim was to facilitate access for women to a religious life of devotion through practical social service. The founder of the German female movement of *diakonia* orders was Amalie Sieveking (1794–1859), who described herself as a 'rationalistic mystic' but was highly influential in the Protestant charismatic revival movement (*Pietismus*). Her 'Female Society for the Care of the Poor and Sick' (1832), together with Johann Heinrich Wichern's *Rauhes Haus* (a rescue station for children in 'moral danger') and Theodor Fliedner's asylum for discharged female prisoners, established at Kaiserswerth in 1833, inspired the development of care services aspiring to professional standards. Sieveking's lecture tours to places like Reval, London and Copenhagen sparked off similar initiatives in those places (Sieveking 1992: 1747), just as the work of Elizabeth Fry, the English Quaker and campaigner for prison reform, and of the Scottish Presbyterian Thomas Chalmers, who had used 'deacons' as visitors to poor families in his Glasgow parish, had earlier inspired Wichern and Fliedner.

Within the Protestant religious orders the 'mother houses' of diakonial activities also became training centres for members. In 1836 Fliedner founded the first 'Educational Institution for Protestant [female] Carers' in Kaiserswerth (visited later by Florence Nightingale, among others), and the training programmes combined religious education with vocational training in nursing, pre-school and primary teaching and 'general care' (*Pflege*). Wichern's residential project in Hamburg used family-type group homes and was also backed by a training programme for the 'brothers' who staffed it. Later their role expanded to work with homeless and alcoholic people, family work in slum districts and care for the elderly (Wendt 1985: 77–79). The official church hierarchy recognised the urgency of keeping control of these developments and began to train their own workers to officially agreed standards for parish and institutional care activities. 'Deaconesses' and 'deacons', acting primarily not as preachers but as community and social workers, are still prevalent today in Dutch, German and Scandinavian Protestant parishes and new training courses commenced in 1992 in Italy and Hungary.

On the whole, however, church-managed schools of social work in the twentieth century only became viable once they also trained social workers for a variety of 'secular' settings; all sixteen German denominational schools of social work offer state-recognised qualifications in social work/social pedagogy in addition to the theologically-inspired *diakonia*. At some schools in Sweden and Italy students are taught theological studies and can gain a theological in addition to the social work qualification.

In almost all European countries the churches had a direct influence on the founding and development of social work training. Even in Ireland, which perhaps surprisingly has a completely secular, university-based approach to social work education, church influence (and signs of competition between the two main denominations) promoted the inception of social work training in the 1930s at the two Dublin colleges, one with a Protestant, the other with a Catholic tradition (Darling 1972: 34). In other countries the denominational composition of the population was broadly reflected in the orientation of schools of social work. Most schools in Italy were Catholic foundations, the overwhelming majority of them being small schools in the south, before Decree No. 162 of 1982 forced their affiliation with universities and thereby reduced the number of private schools drastically (Cavallone 1986: 366).

In Franco's Spain the majority of social work schools were also affiliated to the Catholic Church and some church involvement continues today, although the integration with universities is well under way. Spain's first school of social work was founded in Barcelona in 1932 as the 'School of Social Studies for Women' and had links with a Belgian Catholic School of Social Work, an indication of its international and gender-conscious traits which were quelled by the dictatorship and replaced with rigid conservative church influences (Rimbau Andreu and Rossell Poch 1986: 451).

All three social work schools in Portugal were private foundations of the Catholic Church dating back to before the revolution of 1974. In the aftermath of that revolution two of the schools broke their ties with the church and eventually set themselves up as cooperatives with state recognition. Interestingly, this change also implied a change in conceptual orientation away from the classical casework model, which had been dominant at the Catholic schools under American influence, and towards community action models. Links with schools in Brazil began to be forged, and the emancipatory pedagogy of Paulo Freire became a strong influence on the otherwise generic courses.

Two of the earliest French schools also had denominational affiliations, one Catholic and one Protestant, but although the majority of schools in France continue to have private status, the influence of the churches has receded. The loss of church influence on social work education in Germany, where most schools were founded under the tutelage of the churches during and after the First World War, was less pronounced; today, however, due to the rapid expansion of state institutions, they only manage a minority of schools (Brauns and Kramer 1988: 174). Church influence on social work education in Nordic countries is far less pronounced than it is in central and southern Europe. Only Norway and Sweden have one school each that is managed by a private church organisation and these were not the first schools of social work to be founded in those countries.

The Greek Orthodox Church sponsored one of the schools of social work that emerged in Greece after the Second World War, first as a graduate school for women theologians and later as a general non-graduate school. *Diakonia* had remained a strong tradition in that Church since the days of early Christianity and had been kept alive during the long period of Turkish occupation in the form of self-help initiatives in the parish. This tradition was overlaid by modern bureaucratic structures of welfare, and the school also passed into state control in 1983 when the three private schools of Athens merged under the state system of Technological Educational Institutions (Stathopoulos 1986: 258).

As far as formerly communist countries are concerned, a small but very active Protestant school was established in Potsdam under East German communism and survived all official hostilities, largely through the professionalism and reputation of its graduates. The school had steadfastly defended its autonomy, and its use of the title 'social worker', thereby signalling its determination to remain within the international professional discourse and not to yield to political pressure for 'incorporation'. Unfortunately the school did not survive German unification; it was taken over and later closed by a West German church school (Lorenz 1991c: 20). Since the end of communism other church schools came into existence in East Germany through the upgrading of schools for deaconesses and deacons. It remains to be seen whether the high profile shown by churches in welfare matters in other Central and East European countries after the political changes, particularly in Lithuania, Poland and parts of Hungary, will also result in the founding of church-managed schools of social work.

PHILANTHROPY AND SOCIAL WORK TRAINING

The influence of secular philanthropy on social work education has been far less pronounced than its influence on the development of welfare services, although it has to be borne in mind that the pragmatic secularism of the middle classes in the nineteenth century, as mentioned above, kept fluid the boundaries between organised religion and free, humanistic or romantic spirituality. Origins and objectives also merged: the fear of the bourgeoisie for its privileges faced with possible organised outrage by the mob was to be countered by strengthening social cohesion, bringing the disaffected into the fold of 'one nation' and appealing to their 'moral qualities'. In most European centres of industrialisation (and indeed in rural areas suffering the effects of agrarian capitalism) the religious life of the churches had become marginal to the lives of the working class (McLeod 1980: 192) so that alliances more broadly based than the denominations had to be mobilised against social disaffection. As with religious charity work, the rationale behind the involvement of philanthropy in the training of welfare workers was that the chaotic growth of charitable projects needed to be controlled by guiding principles and moulded into an organised, coordinated approach. This implied a rudimentary kind of social policy, more pronounced than in religious traditions, which rose above the individual case and yet individualised the intervention. Social work training in this tradition had to reconcile the task of preparing workers for 'effective' (ultimately cost-effective) individual attention to cases with that of imparting to them knowledge about macro-societal processes and an understanding of economic principles and the wider causes of poverty, destitution, child neglect or unemployment. With this step towards training, the philanthropic ideal necessarily transcends the boundaries of charity and enters the realm of social policy.

This became evident in the historical compromise between the Charity Organisation Society (COS) and the Fabian Society, which allowed COS training to find a home in 1912 within the London School of Economics (the bastion of Fabianism). Schools of social education had previously been linked with universities in Birmingham, Liverpool, Leeds, Manchester, Glasgow and Bristol (Bosanquet 1914: 404). Similarly, the first school in social work in the Netherlands (and probably in a professional sense the first in Europe), founded in Amsterdam in 1896, owes its existence to philanthropy, and a parallel development occurred in Sweden in 1921 with the founding of the Institute for Social, Political and Municipal Education and Research in Stockholm (Ricknell 1986: 484). The school in Amsterdam was associated more widely with the adult education movement in the form of *volkshuizen*, and was part of the international settlement movement (an early form of 'community development'), which manifested itself in France as *maisons sociales* and in Germany as *Volksheime* (Wendt 1985: 151). The training dimension was most pronounced within the settlement movement both for the recipients of philanthropic attention and for the middle-class participants in its activities, and settlements, with their emphasis on 'practical learning', had a lasting influence on the applied nature of social work training.

Overall, in contrast to the Christian tradition, the impetus of humanitarian philanthropy did not survive as an independent organisational and ideological basis for social work training. Most of the schools founded on its principles came under direct state control in line with the states' unequally phased acceptance of their public welfare responsibility.

SOCIAL WORK EDUCATION AND THE WOMEN'S MOVEMENT

The fact that social work is predominantly a female profession does not in itself mean that feminism as an ideological position played a major role in its history. Nor can it be assumed that feminism represents a consistent ideological position at all, as opposed to a collection of very different trends, actions and demands. Perhaps the aspect of the women's movement that had the greatest influence on social work training is its incomplete 'conscientisation': the women formed, to paraphrase Marx, a class *of* themselves, not *for* themselves. In line with much of its other ideological heritage, social work connected on the whole with the bourgeois sections of the women's movement which, in relation to society as a whole, reproduced rather than challenged dominant class interests. The actions, ideas, self-help initiatives and political demands of the proletarian and socialist women's movement, which found it hard enough to make itself heard within the European labour movement, do not form a part of the official history of social work and were certainly not reflected in the nature of social work schools and training programmes. The revolutionary ideas of a Rosa Luxemburg had no place for social work – their whole point was to render charity and liberal welfare obsolete.

Social work is one of a range of professions, together with nursing, teaching and other forms of caring, through which, initially, middle-class women were able to enter the public arena and create personally rewarding and socially desirable occupations for themselves; later it also became a means for working-class women to escape manual or domestic jobs and the competition for jobs with male labourers. To them the goal of public recognition through (unpaid or paid) work appeared more tangible than that of the universal franchise. For instance, the German women's movement dropped its revolutionary demands for voting rights, articulated in the revolutionary years around 1848, to replace them with demands for access to careers and education (Brinker-Gabler 1983: 56). Liberal feminists sought to build these careers around qualities and skills which they had been socialised into accepting as their female prerogative, liberating themselves from domestic restrictions yet leaving the unequal structures of society largely unchallenged. Social work often provided a personalised form of emancipation, just as it in turn offered personalised assistance and solutions. Octavia Hill, a leading figure in nineteenth-century British philanthropy, opposed universal suffrage, yet was able to conduct her 'politics' through personal influence on account of her position in society (Boyd 1982: 146). Women were at the forefront of philanthropy and of religious renewal, putting ideas and concepts into practice outside the traditional power structures and consequently also across national frontiers. The growth of voluntary organisations led by women was related to industrialisation and the division between private and public life in its wake, through which women had lost their positions of relative power. Their movement signalled the growing importance of a civil society without yet fully grasping its 'political' implications, which 'second-wave feminism' would follow through in the second half of the twentieth century.

> Middle and upper class women developed new kinds of alliances as they finally came to understanding the stripping process they had been through. By 1880 they were prepared to by-pass the nationalistic struggles of Europe and forge alternative structures for the solution of what they already perceived to be global, not national problems, of social justice and human welfare... The phenomenon of the women's NGOs stemmed in part from the inability of women to get men to give priority to decentralism and non- violence, and in part from the fact that men could not perceive women as individual human beings in their own right, let alone as partners in major public enterprises.
>
> (Boulding 1977, 213ff.)

Most schools of social work founded directly by the churches had a clearly defined 'mission' for women within the organisations' ideological and social purposes (defined mostly by men), as women were regarded as the natural and traditional embodiment of charity. However, other schools were founded independently by women themselves in an emancipatory spirit. Forerunners of these had been 'women's associations': for instance, in England the Ladies' Sanitary Association of 1857 and the Association for Promoting the Employment of Women, founded in 1859, both as branches of the Social Science Association (Bauer and Ritt 1979: 88); in Germany the umbrella organisation for women's associations *Allgemeiner Deutscher Frauenverein*, set up at a women's congress in 1865 (Wendt 1985: 158); and in France educational associations in Saint Simonite circles with whom Anna Wheeler, the Irish feminist pioneer, maintained contact (Pankhurst 1954: 134). These associations had several features in common: they sought to promote access for (middle-class) women to public employment; they underlined the important contribution women could make to strengthening, integrating, and improving society through their female qualities; and they advocated and initiated educational activities, both for participating women and for 'the masses' under the leadership of middle-class women. There was a whole world out there, and inside the women themselves, to be apprehended through knowledge of every kind as well as through personal experience. The movement was sustained by enthusiasm and the faith that learning (*Bildung* in the German tradition of the neo-classical revival) entailed change at both the personal and the societal level.

> Like the labour movement, the women's movement was in danger of becoming centred on the representation of self interests. . . But while firmly holding on to its demands for rights it has become something quite different. During the last decades it was less a rights than an education movement. The demands for rights and liberties were means towards gaining responsibility. All individualistic starting positions were superseded by social objectives.
>
> (Salomon 1919: 13)

What contributed to German social work on the whole 'inheriting' a less politicised form of feminism were two factors: first, a Prussian decree of 1850 (which remained valid until 1908) banned women from joining associations 'which discuss political subjects in assemblies' (Brinker-Gabler 1983: 53); this channelled at least the middle-class strand of feminism towards educational and career campaigns. Second, the working-class side, the German social-democratic party had adopted women's equal rights quite early on in its party programme, after they had been fought for energetically by the socialist feminist Clara Zetkin (Brinker-Gabler 1983: 69). With the achievement of the franchise in 1917 German feminists began to be absorbed in party politics (Hering and Kramer 1984: 146). Social work training on a broader scale in the 1920s was conducted by women who addressed their own and their clients' condition outside this political discourse.

One decisive impulse for the development of social work as a female profession in Germany had come from the 'Girls' and Women's groups for Social Assistance Work', first organised by Jeanette Schwerin in Berlin in 1893, whose aims were the training for and introduction to a variety of social institutions led by middle-class women (crèches, kindergartens, hospitals, soup kitchens, institutes for the blind, etc.). In the context of these training programmes, which were deliberately kept 'generic' in contrast to the rather narrow vocational training programmes for kindergarten staff or for deaconesses, the term *soziale Arbeit* (social work) was used for the first time in Germany, and in the American settlement movement. '*Soziale Arbeit*' originated in response to a demand for an activity bringing together helper and recipient and transcending the individual human being to promote societal as well as cultural–ethical renewal, to bring about concrete reforms without being tied to a particular ideology' (Wendt 1985: 165).

In 1908 these training activities became integrated into a *Soziale Frauenschule*, (social school for women), sponsored by the *Pestalozzi-Fröbel-Haus* and led by Alice Salomon. This energetic pioneer of German social work, whose qualifications were years of practical experience in welfare projects as well as a Ph.D. in economics, was also a member of the executive of the Confederation of German Women's Associations and had developed close contacts with members of the movement worldwide, among them Beatrice Webb, Mary Richmond and Jane Addams. Her educational programme addressed the knowledge, skills, character and social commitment of the worker simultaneously, and she was convinced that only women could create a culture of caring and allow welfare services to rise above a preoccupation with material concerns. Together with other equally 'generic' schools brought into being by churches, municipalities and educational trusts at about the same time, she resisted any moves towards becoming affiliated to or subsumed under university departments, which were mooted at the end of the First World War. Quite practically these women's schools had to avert the threat posed by men, who, during and immediately after the war, had begun to seize new career opportunities in social work, often as war invalids and frequently with the backing of local government officials who wanted to shift public welfare towards a bureaucratically tighter and more controlling line. By keeping schools reserved exclusively for women Alice Salomon wanted to avert a 'take-over' by men and preserve a 'women's agenda', with the transformation of 'natural abilities' into professional qualities. She quotes the complaints by a former student of her all-female school:

> Ever since social work has been taken over by public agencies, since I work in a department of the local authority, I am the subordinate of men who hold completely different views, the views of administrators. For them there is no difference between running the finance department or the water works and dealing with people in personal difficulties. They criticise me for not coping with piles of reports and formalities.
>
> (Salomon 1983: 214)

Furthermore the schools declined to have their academic status raised to equal that of the university, a decision motivated by the rejection of the male-dominated discourse prevalent at universities. In 1925 she instituted instead a 'German Academy for Social and Pedagogical Work by Women', an 'academy by women for women' which was to combine scientific stringency and enquiry with practice competence and provide a 'life-long post-qualifying training resource' (Wieler 1989: 7). This meant, however, that male university graduates in social science subject areas gained access to higher positions in public welfare services. The split between social work and social pedagogy, typical of German social professions, still contains elements of this gendered dichotomy, with the latter tradition having established a firmer base in the university.

Women wanting a 'meaningful' occupation remained one of the forces driving the development of social work education, and as an alternative to challenging the combination of economic and social constraints of the time directly they found the niche of 'social activities' relatively independently in several countries. For instance, the Norwegian national women's organisation, *Norske Kvinners Nasjonalråd* pioneered social work training in Norway with a school founded in 1920 (Hildeng 1986: 425). In Spain it was the work of the Female Committee on Social Improvement (under the aegis of the Catholic Church) which in 1932 brought about the *Escola d'Estudis Socials per la Dona* in Barcelona (Rimbau Andreu and Rossell Poch 1986: 451). A similar combination of Catholic Church interests and middle-class women seeking a new social role led to the foundation of the first Austrian school of social work in 1917.

By 1937 the international survey of schools of social work conducted by Alice Salomon on behalf of the International Committee of Schools for Social Work revealed that among the 179 schools that were then in existence in thirty-two countries worldwide there were eighty-three schools exclusively reserved for women (nine for men, the rest mixed). Most European countries had separate social work schools for women and in Austria, France, Hungary, Italy, Norway, Portugal, Romania and Switzerland these represented the only social work training institutions. Even in Britain two of the fourteen schools and colleges trained only women, but by far the largest number of women's schools existed in Germany (thirty-three out of forty-two, with six others for men) (Salomon 1937: 265). Segregated schools continued into the era after the Second World War, by which time the reference to 'motherly qualities' had been totally discredited by the misuse it had suffered at the hands of Fascism, and the newly promoted consensus over the case-work model centred on the 'personal relationship' as a non-gendered principle.

But despite the pronounced middle-class orientation of early female social work schools their brand of feminism had shared the conviction of second-wave feminism that 'the personal is political'. When the pioneers of German social work education sought to turn 'female and motherly qualities' into professional attributes it appeared to them as a means of transforming society, of overcoming the existing political structures and processes which had proved so utterly inadequate in preventing war and the political instability that ensued. By forging solidarity across social and political divisions and striving for the good of all beyond the sectional interests, as a mother 'naturally rises above self-interest when the welfare of her children is at stake' (Salomon 1919: 11) and also by maintaining international links through the women's and the peace movements, they had regarded their work as the anticipation of a 'renewal of society'. Social work for them was no longer the sum of individual expressions of goodwill, pity or emancipation from a paternalistic strait-jacket; it was striving to become very much a public affair, the cornerstone of the transformation of public culture and hence a corrective of existing social and political processes. 'Traditional' though the social work curricula of those women's schools might appear from today's perspective, with their emphasis on domestic science subjects, hygiene and other extensions of traditional female roles, they nevertheless dealt with issues of public welfare and were conceptualised as a contribution to social policy at the level of the civil society.

SOCIALIST EXPERIMENTS IN SOCIAL WORK TRAINING

Mainstream social work in Europe resulted from an ideological blend which, despite the links with the women's movement, kept its distance from more radical feminism and which in its commitment to social reform opposed socialism. An episode from the early period of Dutch social work training serves to illustrate these boundaries. As mentioned above, social work training in Amsterdam started in association with a 'People's educational centre' with a school originally entitled *Opleidings-inrichting voor Socialen Arbeid* ('training institute for social work'). But the title 'social' seemed to convey hints of 'social-ism', so it was soon changed to *School voor Maatschappelijk Werk* ('societal' work) which remains the Dutch equivalent for social work. In order to dispel any impression of feminist leanings, admission was also open to men (although none came forward; Wendt 1985: 167).

The ideological forces, illustrated in the above examples, which gave rise more immediately to the bulk of social work training in Europe were all broadly aligned with dominant government policies on social issues: for instance, either the liberalism of Britain, the Bismarckian paternalism of Germany and France or the corporatism of the Netherlands, which ulti-mately designated the private sphere as the 'proper' area of competence for the profession. Social work featured only in-directly in these governments' official social politics; it was vital as a means of smoothing out the imbalances and contradictions created but had to appear politically neutral.

Nevertheless, there were a few social work schools in Europe founded in the socialist tradition. A school in Belgium at the

College for Workers (*École Ouvrière Supérieure*) reflected the particular interests of the labour movement in keeping welfare initiatives in industry, which were particularly well developed in that country in the early 1930s, under the control of the trade unions after the Catholic Church had recognised industry as a priority for its welfare work (Salomon 1937: 84). But one of the most interesting 'experiments' was a school in Vienna established after the end of the First World War. The declared purpose of this school was to provide the socialist city government, which had gained power after the fall of the monarchy, with working-class social workers. The socialist city council of 'Red Vienna' confronted the catastrophic social conditions in the city – a legacy of war and gross social inequality – by means of a comprehensive social programme. This included a public housing programme (to which the functionally designed complex of the 'Karl-Marx-Hof' still bears witness today), a thorough school reform, which again became a model for 'compensatory education initiatives', and an integrated health and welfare programme. The council member responsible for the Department of Welfare, Youth and Health, which was set up in 1921, was Julius Tandler, a medical doctor by profession and an enthusiastic advocate of comprehensive, preventive and integrated health and welfare provisions 'from the cradle to the grave'. In his view spending on ante-natal care and health education, on compulsory infant and school medical examinations, on youth services and other forms of non-residential care was an 'investment in human capital'. Indeed, his programme achieved a remarkable reduction in general and infant mortality as well as in the incidence of tuberculosis (Seliger and Ucakar 1985: 1106–1112). His programme did not exclude private and voluntary services – on the contrary, he instigated 'district welfare committees' on which city officials, professionals and members of voluntary organisations were jointly represented and he founded welfare institutes which trained and deployed members of the wider community in health education functions. Welfare for him was a 'popular movement' spanning class divisions, and among the 5,440 volunteers of the institutes in 1924 he counted 13 per cent skilled workers, 25 per cent employees and almost 30 per cent traders (Tandler 1927: 350).

However, central to his scheme were professionally trained welfare workers (*Berufsfürsorgerinnen*), who would provide assessment, counselling and support according to an agreed philosophy. They had to carry a message to the population at large, not just to social work clients, a message about 'collective, mutual responsibility, duties and rights' (Sablik 1983: 207). Their training was provided in a specially instituted school of social work run by the city of Vienna in competition with the 'bourgeois' school already in existence in Vienna under Catholic management. Tandler's school educated only women, and only working-class women qualified for admission, including women who had been at the receiving end of welfare themselves. He expected them to 'be in touch with popular culture' (to have *Volkstümlichkeit*), and to be 'humanistic, ready to make sacrifices, inspired by idealism, believing in humanity' (Sablik 1983: 289). While their training was very much about knowledge of rights and entitlements, hygiene and needs of children, and about educational skills in making their preventative intentions effective, they were to base their work on the strength of their 'natural female abilities – a good heart, clear mind, adjustability and confidentiality' (ibid.).

The comparisons with the social work education ideals of the institutions founded in the tradition of the bourgeois women's movement are striking. Tandler realised that the socialist policies and their realisation through measures like new housing, health services and a reformed school system needed to be sustained by a new, non-patriarchal civil society, a new social contract between individual citizens and the city administration. But his approach, in line with the Austrian Socialist Party governing Vienna, was to bring 'culture' and 'civilisation' to the working class, rather than to recognise their inherent forms of solidarity.

> As a rule the party's cultural reformers denigrated the existing cultural forms and life styles found among the workers, characterizing them as barbaric and/or reactionary as a whole. They were determined to create a tight network of institutions aimed at producing a higher socialist workers' culture composed of transformed humans – the 'neue Menschen'.
>
> (Gruber 1984: 649)

Tandler resorted to ideals and appeals for the building of a 'culture of caring', ideals similar to those that had featured in religious and philanthropic programmes. The transmission of those ideals fell on teachers in mainstream and adult education, but also on medical and welfare staff like social workers, whose actions assume at once practical and symbolic significance. Neither did Tandler hesitate to build coercion and social control into the social workers' mandate: they had a duty to visit every newborn baby bringing the 'greetings of the city of Vienna' (and a parcel of baby clothes and baby-care items), but at the same time keeping a close watch on mothers, their child-care practice and their compliance with hygiene, standard diagnostic tests and inoculation requirements.

In a radio programme recorded in 1932 and published in a welfare journal, a social worker trained at Tandler's school gave a vivid account of her daily duties. Poverty is at the heart of most of her cases, mainly caused by unemployment, which she knows is beyond her control. But she makes sure that clients receive all their entitlements, advises them on the procedures concerning applications for discretionary benefits, counsels on the futility and potential harm of a mother wanting to place her children in care in financial desperation and checks on whether discretionary grants for children's shoes have resulted in more regular school attendance (Lichtenberg 1932). Her agenda is no different from that of social workers operating under any other system, nor are her methods different from those of middle-class colleagues – what sets her apart from her clients is her power and control over resources, not her own class background. Her clients remain objects of official policies and attention who have to be persuaded to comply with measures whose beneficial nature has been determined by experts. Elfriede Lichtenberg's practice only became 'socialist' by virtue of the political framework within which she practised and the rights and entitlements which that had brought, not through her training and methodology.

The radicalism of the alternative methods that were being developed in the same city of Vienna and during the same period hardly affected social work training at all. They originated in the field of pedagogy and psychology as applied in residential care and youth work settings, and corresponded more to a 'grass-roots movement'. The continental youth movement, with its ideals of building a new society on a radically new social-isation of young people, had started in Germany before the First World War and had also spread to Vienna. The *Kinderfreunde* (friends of the children) were an organisation at first geared towards non-denominational leisure activities, but in the light of the distress experienced by children as a result of the war and of widespread poverty they extended their activities to residential care, running for instance the palace of Schönbrunn as an 'alternative children's home' after the war. It operated on democratic principles, i.e. children had a say in the running of the home, and this self-generated learning was meant to equip them with the skills to play an active, competent part in adult society (Gulick 1948, II: 308).

The pedagogical principles developed by this movement stress the value of groups and communities and derive their theoretical foundations from the version of psychoanalysis which the Viennese psychiatrist Alfred Adler had already attempted to combine with the social theories of Karl Marx since 1907. As a socialist pedagogy movement it received further decisive conceptual impulses from Siegfried Bernfeld, who structured a Jewish orphanage according to principles derived from a 'sociological reading' of Freud, putting children collectively in charge of their daily lives (Bernfeld 1969: 113; Ekstein 1966: 420). Bernfeld's work for 'children's republics', and his Zionist activism, laid the ground for the Kibbutz movement. Social work as such took little notice of this radical movement, which aimed at reversing the existing hierarchies of (welfare) power and subverted the position of the 'expert'.

These latter observations indicate that the diverse ideological starting positions in social work education made surprisingly little difference to the actual delivery of social work services. Social work in all national contexts in Europe seems to have its place allocated by the prevailing social structures and political agendas. Questioning, resistance and emancipation were indeed a feature of various approaches to social work and of the forces giving rise to the development of social work training, but they seem to have become effective only in a purely personal context and above all in the biographies of the women seeking to express their own emancipation by gaining access to this new profession.

Social work's vulnerability to being subjected to serving the interests of the state, and the inadequacy of social work as a form of private emancipation and perhaps resistance, came to light most devastatingly in the rise to power of Fascism.

Chapter 3

Social work, Fascism and democratic reconstruction

Any attempt to map European social work within an historical and conceptual grid must include a hard and, at times, uncomfortable look at social work under Fascism. At no time was it easy for social work to maintain a balance between striving to develop professional skills and a body of scientifically derived knowledge universally applicable to all societies and yet having to address the particular social conditions, social policies and laws that prevail in each country. Finding this balance is an extremely difficult task fraught with compromises and distortions. As was argued above, systematic and professionally-oriented training gave social workers a degree of independence from the 'system' they were meant to represent, from class interests, the religious or ideological missions and the state's welfare agenda. They also forged international links so as to underline their ability to rise above narrow national concerns as an autonomous profession and to identify the universal features of their work.

This chapter will examine how the insistence on value neutrality failed to stop social work from falling prey to, or actively putting itself at the disposal of, ideological misuses. It will also show how attempts at 'purging' the defeated fascist countries of Europe of ideologies through a massive programme of 're-education', within which a social work model built on client self-determination was an important ingredient, represented a retreat to the 'neutrality position' and fell short of addressing the political dimension of social work.

These historical reflections are by no means intended to establish a higher moral ground from which to judge the *naïveté*, stupidity or depravity of colleagues of a bygone era and to reach for certainties which separate the present lastingly from those 'aberrations'. On the contrary, this chapter aims to highlight social work's vulnerability to political misuses at all times and to caution against all preconceived moral certainties – these always contain the seeds of final solutions (*Endlösungen*) which place the success of the method above all other considerations.

SOCIAL WORK IN THE 1920s

The motivation for forming an international association of social workers in the 1920s came from the internationalism that had been an important source of support for the women's movement and in which many social work pioneers had played leading roles. When the International Congress of Women met in Berlin in 1904 it provided a platform for women engaged in early forms of social work to meet and to exchange views. It was in conjunction with her travels through Northern America, as German delegate to the 1909 congress of the International Council of Women (held in Canada), that Alice Salomon, a pioneer of German social work and social work education, met Jane Addams and received decisive impulses from her work in Chicago. The friendship between the two women remained intact during the war years and was indeed strengthened by their mutual commitment to international pacifism. Jane Addams and Caroline Wood, a New York social worker, visited Germany and Austria immediately after the war on behalf of the Society of Friends to make arrangements for the distribution of humanitarian aid under the 'Hoover Plan'. They also visited Alice Salomon's school of social work in Berlin, and were determined to maintain their international links in the face of considerable opposition from 'patriotic' quarters of the bourgeois women's movement in Germany (Wieler 1987: 44). A network of similar international contacts between women helped to make the 1928 International Congress for Social Work in Paris a resounding success, attended by almost 5,000 participants. This conference, organised by the Belgian doctor and social reformer René Sand, gathered the existing international networks under the organisational umbrella of the 'International Conference of Social Work' (which in 1967 became the International Council on Social Welfare (ICSW); Blankenburg 1988: 81). The congress underlined the need for schools of social work to organise themselves cross-nationally and in the same year the International Committee for Schools of Social Work (later the International Association of Schools of Social Work (IASSW)) was founded, with Alice Salomon as its first chair. One of the earliest concerns of this committee was to achieve compatibility between course programmes and qualifications so as to facilitate the exchange of students between countries. But beyond those concerns internal to the profession the internationalism sought by social workers had a wider aim:

> War annihilates everything that social work tries to accomplish . . . this is the reason why social workers should be the first ones to facilitate and maintain peace-creating international relations.
>
> (A. Salomon, quoted in Wieler 1989: 19)

However, at the national level of Germany social structures, values and roles were in such a state of flux in the 'roaring twenties' that social work offered a real alternative to either sitting on the side lines of change or becoming embroiled in the bitter political controversies. Despite sporadic moves towards socialist political mobilisation among social workers at the end of the 1920s, when unemployment even among social workers was rampant, most social workers regarded their job as a way of holding on to the personal achievements of feminism and of making the most of the general economic circumstances. 'Those who like myself chose social work as a profession in the 20s knew that it wasn't out of career thinking. It was quite satisfying, not having to develop career ambitions. You could remain what you were and use your energy for the humane but purposeful care of those in need', reminisces one social worker who trained in the late 1920s (Hering and Kramer 1984: 66).

THE IMPACT OF NATIONAL SOCIALISM

However, with the sudden rise to power of Hitler's National Socialist Party in the elections of 1933 the ambivalence was tipped all one way: there was only a future for the profession if it presented itself in total conformity with the system, if it merged its vision of a better society with that of the Nazi state, and if it reverted to its original, pre-professional task of sifting deserving from undeserving cases.

The paradox was, as is revealed from a careful reading of the case reports and comments in the professional journals of the late 1920s and early 1930s, that social workers, therapists and residential care staff had often promoted highly innovatory forms of intervention and treatment, which had also been outlined in the youth welfare legislation of the Weimar Republic. But resource limitations prevented the full implementation of that law and the escalation of economic and social problems weighed heavily on the 'front line' of welfare staff, who were squeezed between growing problems and dwindling resources. Welfare benefits were being cut while unemployment reached on average over 30 per cent in 1932 (Kramer 1983: 173). Nevertheless, experiments with 'reform pedagogy' – in residential care, for instance – led to democratically run group homes where troublesome youngsters could learn to take responsibility for their actions in a non-punitive environment. But frequently those places were overburdened with young people too disruptive and socially damaged at the stage of admission to benefit from this approach (Harvey 1989: 205). Equally, intensive work with parents with learning disabilities was being developed which reduced the need for institutional care, but often these families' large number of children, as well as their material hardship limited the effectiveness of the programmes. Ideas and pleas arising from such dilemmas were articulated in the pages of professional journals well before 1933. Authors speculate that if social workers were given greater statutory powers to intervene earlier or to detain the most disruptive youngsters in secure places, and if the state were to introduce compulsory sterilisation to limit family size and to halt the 'cycle of hereditary disease', then the more progressive methods would stand a better chance of succeeding. Under the impact of ever harsher financial constraints and a paralysing political polarisation the distinction between educable and ineducable youngsters – between 'valuable' and 'inferior' persons – was beginning to enter the language and practice of welfare staff in Germany during the 1920s, in striking parallel to the demarcation between deserving and undeserving cases that had characterised the nineteenth-century responses to poverty. The fixation on technical solutions obscured the social rights perspective, which had not developed in social work training and was inadequately secured in social policies. National Socialism offered these technical solutions (and their 'scientific' legitimation in Neo-Darwinism) a pervasive ideological framework, and supplied the legal and political power to implement them ruthlessly (Harvey 1989: 220).

Racism and welfare under National Socialism fed off each other: welfare needed racism to justify its denial of human rights; racism presented itself as welfare by declaring that the well-being of the nation as a whole depended on the fitness and well-being of the strongest members of society, which demanded 'sacrifices' from the weaker members in the national interest.

It is still difficult today to form a comprehensive picture of the role of social work under the National Socialist regime. The evaluation of this grim chapter of social work history is divided between those who regard social workers as the largely innocent victims of the new ideology and those who attribute more than mere naïveté to them. It is a fact that the welfare machinery of Nazi Germany, by 'doing its duty' willingly or reluctantly, delivered thousands of people into the hands of the henchmen of the regime, caused untold anguish and suffering, deepened divisions at all levels of society and discredited its own humanitarian ideals. The murder of millions of Jewish citizens of Germany and its occupied countries, by which the regime is most vividly remembered, was not an isolated case of extremism disconnected from other 'achievements': it is the epitome of its politics, including its welfare politics. Its true horror and significance is not captured by portraying these mass murders as the products of pathological minds, but by realising that this final solution was contained in the logic of a state which claimed an absolute, unrestrained power to grant or deny human rights at will, a logic towards which all activities of that state, carried out by myriads of officials and volunteers, were potentially directed.

Once the granting of human rights became conditional on economic factors (residential institutions and asylums had their financial support cut immediately in 1933), backed by ideological criteria, the logic of discrimination, segregation and exclusion established itself as an unimpeded force in everday professional discourse and could eventually not stop short of extending the line to extermination. The insufficient attention to rights in social work concepts and practice was revealed at the second conference of the International Council on Social Welfare, held in Frankfurt in 1932 on the topic of 'Family and Welfare'. The contributions demonstrated a broad international consensus on the importance of 'organic links' between family and community, the building of community through family support and on the moral, cultural and 'educative' role of social work in maintaining people's dignity through fostering self-help (Blankenburg 1988: 112). Formally the Nazi rhetoric of the 'people's community' (it is difficult to translate the racist overtones implied in the term *Volksgemeinschaft*, which implies an ethnic definition as to who can claim to belong to 'the people' (*Volk*)) fitted the bill perfectly, with its emphasis on the family as the building block of community and on altruism, voluntary efforts and sacrifice, and with its rejection of the liberal *laissez faire* role of the state (Hilgenfeldt 1937: 26). Indeed, Nazi propaganda fully exploited the third international ICSW conference in 1936, held in London and bearing the motto 'Social Work and Community'. It could advertise the dramatic reduction in the rate of unemployment as proof of its concept of 'social integration' and of the mutuality between the state's concern for individual well-being in return for the individual's 'idealistic', selfless commitment for 'the community' (Althaus 1936: 6–8). The new system was committed to the prevention of social problems through the development of social services at all levels by means of youth work, residential care, voluntary work programmes and rehabilitation, etc. But running through all these measures was the distinction between 'the healthy' and 'the parasites' and 'anti-social elements' – those who had to be cast out of the legitimate ambit of welfare since welfare measures were wasted on them. Only then could welfare efforts show their true benefits and reach their full educative, rehabilitative and integrative potential. The legitimation of that dividing line was its basis in objective, scientific criteria, medical knowledge, sociological research and economic calculations, which placed it beyond ethical questioning. Welfare, social work in particular, had to be freed from its 'sentimentality', its misplaced leanings towards the weak which had after all hampered its professional development (Althaus, ibid.).

Segregation advanced very quickly. On 14 July 1933, as one of the earliest 'social policy' measures, the Nazi government enacted laws allowing for the sterilisation of certain categories of people (congenital 'feeble-mindedness', schizophrenia, manic-depressive illness, hereditary epilepsy and St. Vitus's dance, hereditary blindness and deafness, severe hereditary physical malformations and alcoholism) as an instrument of 'public welfare and racial hygiene'. The professional literature had raised the topic and discussed its 'benefits' well before Hitler's rise to power, and had pointed out how much more medical science could contribute to the care of the 'strong, healthy' part of the population if resources were no longer to be 'wasted on incurables' (Klee 1985a: 31). Indeed other countries, including Britain, had seen 'eugenic societies' being founded or had brought in similar legislation (for example, Denmark and Switzerland), and at the International Congress for Prisons and Penal Laws in 1935 experts from many countries basically agreed on sterilisation as a legitimate medical means of improving the future state of health of whole populations (Harmsen 1935: 1210–19). What National Socialism added were the powers, backed by an overtly racist state ideology, for such measures to be carried out against the will of those concerned. During the Nazi period approximately 300,000 such operations were performed, two-thirds of them for alleged 'mental debility' (Knüppel-Dähne and Mitrovic 1989: 189).

Under the law the duty to report cases extended to dentists, parish nurses, midwives, physiotherapists, directors of residential institutions and medical officials of health departments. But the actual legitimation of the procedure depended essentially on experts such as doctors and social workers making the 'right diagnosis', i.e. to give it the appearance of a therapeutic intervention when lack of consent had to be compensated for by the diagnosis of 'diminished responsibility'. It therefore depended on close cooperation between medical and welfare staff, particularly since the 'medical' evidence was so spurious. 'Social assessment reports' assumed more direct political significance. A medical official of the city of Frankfurt spelt out the importance of close collaboration between medical and social welfare departments in ensuring a healthy 'stock of population' as early as September 1933. In order to reverse the falling birth rate the government had started to provide loans to newly-married couples subject to a public 'health' check with the following implications:

The examination of hereditary biological factors requires extensive investigations in order to establish a clear picture of the marriage partners and their families in hereditary biological terms. The Division for Hereditary–Biological Assessment of the health department of the city of Frankfurt/Main draws on reports of the child care service, the services for alcoholics, the welfare section of services for people suffering from tuberculosis, the psychiatric services, on the files of the social welfare department, on the register of criminal records as well as numerous other sources of material which round off the hereditary picture'.

(Fischer-Defoy 1933: 242)

The noose of social control, exercised often unwittingly, began to tighten.

The same article goes on to link these 'medical–hygienic' purposes with the general policy of 'combating alien domination' (*Bekämpfung der Überfremdung*) of the German people, i.e. the racist policies immediately enacted in July 1933 allowing only 'Aryans' to enter public service and prohibiting public employees from marrying 'non-Aryans'. And continuing its line of (un-)reasoning it speculates on the inevitable necessity for the state to tackle the 'extermination of unworthy life' of 'imbeciles', whose existence as 'parasites' is medically and economically unjustified (ibid., 243). These ideas, openly circulated in the social welfare literature, refute any notion that the eventual organised mass murders in the concentration camps were the result of German fanaticism during the war – they were part of the racist design right from the beginning, and sterilisation and incarceration were early substitutes for 'euthanasia' (Klee 1985a: 95). The financial crisis brought about by the preparation for and the outbreak of war only provided the 'justification' when directors of asylums were confronted with the choice of reducing their food rations to starvation levels or to single out untreatable cases (Klee 1985a: 62).

Where sterilisation was considered to be too long-term a measure to take effect, internment and incarceration were increasingly ordered in the same spirit of 'protecting' the 'healthy part' of the population and of concentrating welfare resources on the 'deserving', i.e. those willing to work, adjust and to support National Socialism. An immediate target were beggars and vagrants, who were deported to concentration camps as early as September 1933 after a concerted campaign between police and the SS. 'The streets appear swept clean of them' (Klee 1985a: 39); the diagnoses of mental illness, vagrancy and social depravity merged slowly into one, as did detention and murder through forced labour, starvation or execution. This apparent 'medicalisation' of (ideologically defined) social problems soon extended to homosexuals, those convicted for sexual offences, drug addicts, prostitutes, the 'work-shy' and political dissidents. The dominance of economic dictates over welfare criteria became established at every level, and citizenship became conditional on economic usefulness. In many cities receipt of welfare and unemployment benefit was linked to the willingness to work in communal projects of public works; workhouses became operational again, borstals emphasised the work ethic, and inmates of concentration camps were ruthlessly put to work in slave labour. The gates of Auschwitz bore the legend, *Arbeit macht frei* (work liberates).

In all these developments, the welfare organisations were expected to play a supportive role. Pogroms against beggars were reported beforehand to the voluntary agencies working with the homeless in order to secure their support. Public dismay was countered with the argument that the sentimentality of charities had only exacerbated the problem and that the new welfare policy of firmness was now proving its worth.

Superficially the duties of social workers under the Third Reich showed a great deal of continuity with welfare functions carried over from previous times, such as the assessment of benefits, and advice and support in difficult social situations (Kramer 1983: 211). The skills were 'transferable', which seems to indicate the weak connection between methods and values in social work.

1 Assessment. The report writing, and thereby the tangible link with the bureaucracy, which had become an increasing burden to social workers in the late 1920s now became much more systematic, feeding directly into the discriminatory purposes of Nazi welfare measures. It would be unfair to say that all social workers conformed willingly with the ideological impositions; indeed there was widespread resistance as social workers realised the potential implications their reports had and the power that was vested in them through assessment.

But since assessment and diagnosis had become such a distinguishing skill of social work, a refusal to assess would almost have meant giving up one's profession altogether, and many workers believed that the 'objectivity' of their observations would win through.

2 The task of counselling in relation to the sinister purposes of the regime could take the more indirect form of helping victims and their relatives to come to terms emotionally with measures to which they had been subjected (crisis counselling, as it would be termed today), i.e. institutionalisation, sterilisation or deportation. Alternatively, their skills would be used often more directly to persuade victims and their relatives to comply with these measures voluntarily, an approach very much in the interests of a regime wanting to present a benign image.

Most social workers not employed by the party's 'voluntary' welfare agency, the NSV (*NS -Volkswohlfahrt*), were only rarely direct representatives of the state with a statutory mandate, although the lines of command were tightened in that their actions were to have an 'exemplary', educational character (Kramer 1983: 209). But on the whole they represented themselves and their own way of coming to terms with what they saw (and refused to see) going on in society. Yet society was looking over every social worker's shoulder, quite literally, thereby destroying every possibility of trust being established within the 'normal' work context. Any trust and autonomy social workers did show (and the history of that resistance has yet to be written and evaluated) became very much a matter of secrecy, if not subversion, and therefore highly dangerous. As at all times, social workers learnt ways of bending rules, of 'interpreting' directives and stepping outside their mandate (for instance to collect food for Jewish families in hiding; Hering and Kramer 1984: 103).

Segregation along racist principles affected every aspect of welfare, including the welfare agencies themselves. Immediately on gaining power the regime closed down two of the seven leading welfare organisations which would not have fitted into its plans: the welfare organisation of the labour movement (*Arbeiterwohlfahrt*) and the welfare association of Christian workers. The Jewish welfare association was not officially closed, but was excluded from all consultations and cooperation. At the same time the NS party promoted its own welfare agency, the

NSV as the ideological leader of all private welfare associations. In contrast to them, however, this organ of the state party devoted itself entirely to the support of the 'hereditarily healthy' sectors of society, mainly the (employable) unemployed and 'mother and child' (*Hilfswerk Mutter und Kind*) to advertise the social-mindedness of the state. The dominant and well-resourced position of the NSV made the 'punitive' effects of resource shortages imposed on the work with 'outsiders', left to other voluntary agencies, stand out in even starker contrast. In addition, the bulk of assessment work (both in terms of decisions on welfare benefits and for racist-'eugenic' purposes) became concentrated on public services whose reputation therefore plummetted as their functions became identified exclusively with social control.

Fascism and National Socialism saw social work and welfare as far too important an instrument to be eliminated from the political landscape, although they could easily have replaced it entirely with medical, educational, administrative and law enforcement services. The origins of social work and social work education in Italy actually fell in the early period of Fascism. A 'Higher Fascist School for Social Assistance in Industry' (*Scuola superiore fascista per assistenti sociali di fabbrica*) was set up in 1928 in Rome jointly by the confederation of industrialists and the women's movement of the National Fascist Party (Canevini 1991: 142). Similarly, Franco's right-wing regime in Spain promoted welfare work through Catholic welfare associations and set up its own social work training schools, having first closed down the school that existed in Barcelona. In all instances discriminatory practices such as the distinction between 'deserving' and 'undeserving' cases were the key to social work's use for extreme right-wing regimes. The 'case-by-case approach' suited the NS ideology ideally, as it sought to negate all social causation and reduce problems to individual pathology (Knüppel-Dähne and Mitrovic 1989: 195). This was constructed as either genetic and hence untreatable, or attitudinal and hence to be 'corrected', and social work had a useful part both in making the distinction and in the 'pedagogy' of adjustment. Whether a more secure and self-confident tradition of professional autonomy would have made a difference is questionable in the light of the 'adjusted' picture presented by the medical profession in the Nazi period.

SOCIAL WORKERS AS REFUGEES

The onslaught on the social work profession and on its ethics, professional autonomy and identity wrought by the National Socialist regime was completed by direct threats to its members and particularly to its teachers. A large proportion of social workers, estimated at more than 50 per cent of those working in and around Berlin, were Jewish or had close Jewish connections (Wieler 1987: 74), and were therefore immediately excluded from public posts. Many others were attacked and persecuted for their social-democratic leanings. SA mobs or newly appointed party officials forced them to give up their positions and eventually to flee the country or perish in the camps. Never before had a professional group so directly experienced the suffering characteristic of the situation of so many of their clients: discrimination, persecution, poverty, existence as refugees, isolation and imprisonment. And never before had as much social work experience, knowledge and competence been transferred to other countries as through this enforced wave of emigration.

The professional resettlement in another country was far from easy. Organisationally the participation of emigrant European social workers in US public services was hampered by the strict nationality rules. In addition, American social work education was in the process of establishing itself at university level and qualifications obtained at European schools were treated as inferior and as requiring 'academic upgrading' (Wieler 1987: 299, quoting A. Salomon).

Conceptually, however, there was considerable scope for understanding and collaboration. Alice Salomon, for instance, completed a busy lecture tour of the USA in her retirement (although this did not lead to much personal recognition). While case work had been developed much more elaborately and explicitly in the USA, its original principles had had some influence on German social work – not least through the works of Alice Salomon and Siddy Wronsky, another woman pioneer of German social work education who, in enforced exile, founded the social work school in Jerusalem. There was much gratification in social workers on both sides of the Atlantic continuing to speak the same language.

And that language had become enriched quite considerably by

the advancement of methods parallel to case work, namely social group work and community development. With regard to the former method, it is mainly the figure of Gisela Konopka who forged the link between European and American traditions. She had just qualified as a pedagogue when the Nazi terror was unleashed of which she, as a woman closely connected with the socialist labour movement, was to become a victim, once in a German concentration camp and once in prison in Austria. Yet she also managed to flee to the USA and by integrating various intellectual strands (from Dewey's philosophy to Kurt Lewin's psychology, quite apart from her grounding in the works of Kant and Freud) to fully develop her group work approach.

> 'Social group work' . . . for me was a very important concept. Back in Germany the discussion had always been how to solve the following dilemma: to subdue the individual for the sake of the community or emphasise the individual regardless of the community. I was quite simply thrilled to discover that a way of integrating both had been found here in America, and this was social group work. This strengthened the individual through group interaction while he was given the opportunity to contribute to the whole group.
>
> (Konopka 1982: 233–4)

With regard to community development another German pioneer in enforced exile, Hertha Kraus, made an impact on American social work scholarship and practice. In her capacity as director of the welfare department of the city of Cologne she had promoted neighbourhood centres, modelled on settlements, as focal points for self-help and educational activities. In the US she became professor at the Graduate School of Social Work of Bryn Mawr College, Philadelphia, professional consultant to major social policy committees of the era and a driving force in projects for refugees initiated by the Society of Friends. In all these capacities she sought to establish the primacy of the communal nature of tasks and processes in everyday life over an individualistic perspective and the importance of the social context in action, from which she derived the criteria for a more conscious, professional use of these human social abilities in the form of community action (Müller 1988: 100).

These biographical sketches indicate that European social workers were indeed party to the formation of what were to

become the 'three methods of social work' – case work, group
work and community work – in the period after the Second
World War. The image of these methods as 'American exports'
is misleading and hides the fact that they contain a variety of
European sources and that European social workers in exile
contributed to their transfer to Europe, often in the belief that
they were thereby picking up original threads of methodological
traditions which had been cut by the evil of Nazism. That this
historical memory, this sense of continuity could have got lost
until very recently in German and European social work is
perhaps a further indication of the intellectual devastation
wreaked by that evil.

Cross-fertilisation was facilitated by the shift in US social
politics through Roosevelt's New Deal in 1933, which had given
social workers a wider and clearer role in public welfare
agencies. The experience of German social workers with the
consolidation of public welfare and the coordinated relationship between voluntary and statutory agencies during the
Weimar Republic was invaluable in that regard. This realisation
motivated the University of Chicago to engage Walter Fried-
länder as lecturer on its social work programme. He had been
trained as a lawyer, and his work as a judge and a city councillor
of Berlin decisively influenced the development and implementation of public youth and family services. He had lectured on
social work courses in Berlin, including those at Alice Salomon's
school, where he firmly established social policy as a key subject
area. His outspoken support for socialist principles in matters of
welfare and his role in the welfare organisation of the German
labour movement (the *Arbeiterwohlfahrt* founded by Marie
Juchacz, who also had to flee to the USA) made him an
immediate target of Nazi persecution. From Chicago he took up
a chair at the University of California in 1943 and through his
academic work and world-wide consultancies shaped the development of personal social services internationally after the
Second World War. His book *Introduction to Social Welfare*
(Friedlander 1955), with its comprehensive review of all fields
and methods of social work, became, though written specifically
against the American background, probably the most widely
used textbook on social work courses world-wide and appears,
in translation, on almost all the reading lists of European social
work courses.

But the experience and threat of the Nazi dictatorship is not just reflected in the personal biographies of these refugees. It reverberates in the new directness with which concepts of social work address the profession's political mandate. This is often overlooked in critiques of the casework model as the dominant method in the late 1930s and 1940s. In fact the concern for the dignity of the individual and for basic democratic processes at the 'micro-level' of personal interactions between worker and client shows the outlines of a political concept, insufficient though that principle might be in itself. The importance of this model in the post-war discourse was a reaction against the violations of human dignity perpetrated by welfare services under Fascism.

SOCIAL WORK AND DEMOCRATIC RECONSTRUCTION

The renewed and powerful 'internationalisation' of social work after the Second World War, promoted by the USA and the UN through their various programmes, took place in a context of world politics driven by three major agendas:

1 the defeat of Fascism as a political system in Europe;
2 the confrontation between capitalism as the symbol of individual enterprise and communism as collectivised egalitarianism;
3 the independence movements in developing countries and the growing realisation of poverty in those countries.

The development of social work internationally was closely related to all of these three factors, whose common denominator, from the perspective of the Western, developed, democratic countries, is the importance and the dignity of the individual and of individual choices as the legitimation of all social measures (including welfare and development measures). A 1955 survey by the US Department of Health, Education, and Welfare of responses by social workers from all over the world who had taken part in training courses in the United States under schemes such as the US Foreign Operations Administration and the United Nations Fellowship and Scholarship Programs states:

The democratic concepts of the worth of the individual, his right to share and participate in the common efforts and his

responsibility for the common welfare of all people, which is basic to the organization of social welfare programs in the United States, made a marked impression on some of the trainees and undoubtedly influenced their total experience in the U.S.
(U.S. Department of Health, Education, and Welfare 1955: 5)

and concludes: 'Perhaps the most important gain is the deepened understanding on the part of many of the way democracy works and the attitudes toward people' (ibid.: 27)

The epitome of this belief in the value of the individual and of the importance of participation of individuals in the solving of their social problems is undoubtedly the case-work method. This method was 'exportable' because it fitted the agenda of 'the Western World' as it was shaping itself in the political world scenario after the Second World War, and because it does contain a political message. A former visitor to the US from the Netherlands wrote in the above-mentioned survey,

The greatest impression was the fact that casework and casework attitudes were accepted nearly everywhere. Casework attitude and method is being more accepted in the Netherlands and this is certainly due to the fact that so many of us had an opportunity to see casework in practice in the United States. Besides ... students can observe the democratic way in which conferences are managed and the acceptance of the other persons with a different point of view.
(ibid.: 9)

The same 'democratic principles' were identified as the core of the other two main methodological planks of social work practice – group work and community work (or rather community development, as it was then called almost universally) – so that the entire magic triangle of modern social work methods pointed towards the aims enshrined in case work (Hollis and Taylor 1951: 251). The 'collective' methods (group and community work) were frequently treated as means towards the promotion of case work, as interim measures prevalent while a country, particularly a developing country, does not yet possess the resources for individualised services. A training consultant working with foreign social workers in the US during the period writes:

In general the students have responded somewhat more to group activities than to casework activities. In part this is due, it is believed, to the fact that group activities have been less subject to the limitations imposed by the lack of facilitating services available to meet the problems presented by individuals. Also, the difficulties of providing service outside of an organized agency structure have been greater with respect to the casework practice than with respect to group work.

(Altmeyer 1955: 69–70)

Social work as a central coordinating discipline in welfare programmes had high priority within the foreign aid programmes of the US and the UN in the period after the Second World War. The programmes devised for Europe were part of the world-wide agenda of dealing with the social disruption and personal devastation caused by the war. They had both practical and 'exemplary' significance in preparing for a new democratic world order in which welfare measures function as a source of legitimation. Social work had an important part to play in the 'rebuilding' of the European societies by imparting self-help skills and replacing fascist authoritarianism with egalitarian practices. Democratic methods geared towards fostering individual initiative also soon became an anti-communist, anti-collectivist propaganda tool in the rapidly escalating Cold War.

Practically, the task that lay ahead defies description as a 'welfare problem': death on a scale of some 40 million in Europe alone, 12 million Germans absent from their families as prisoners of war, and 9.5 million people fleeing or expelled from Eastern Europe, on the move towards western Germany where 41.2 per cent of the housing stock had been totally destroyed, the infrastructure lay in ruins and no semblance of normal economic activity was possible. Most of the immediate, improvised welfare activities were initiated by anti-fascist survivors who had been engaged in social work before National Socialism deprived them of their positions, but the task they faced was way beyond their means (Müller 1988: 17).

The cliché of the colonisation of Europe through American social work methods fails to do justice to the complexity of the post-war situation and the role of social work within it. In many ways the situation resembled the task faced by social planners, social educators and politicians in Central and East European countries in the 1990s: a task of rebuilding civil society at three levels, through the support and improvement of tangible material conditions of living (housing, health, social security); through the setting up of professional personal social services within a network of state and non-governmental organisations; and through the 'pedagogical values' implicit in the social work process as non-authoritarian 'help towards self-help', supporting in particular the 'unofficial' voluntary welfare organisations that had not been too closely associated with the system. Although the military wing of the occupying powers maintained a strong role in early post-war German politics, the conviction prevailed even in those circles that ideological re-orientation and 'de-Nazification' could not be achieved by coercion but was better promoted through the use of liberal educational principles.

One of the leading figures of the US Area Division for Occupied Areas, Eugene Anderson, explicitly based his approach on the ideas of John Dewey – that is, that democracy can only be transmitted through giving people the opportunity of experiencing it in action and of practising it themselves. This led to the approval of an extensive programme of the so-called Smith–Mundt Act of 1948 for the sponsoring of educators, social workers, journalists, doctors, trade unionists and community leaders for observational and training periods in the USA where they would see 'democracy in action' (Müller 1988: 38). Re-education in democracy paved the way for the relaxation of occupational military control and the gradual transfer of social, educational and political responsibilities to the German population, and the notion of 'social science' in its American version was central to this: 'Social sciences should contribute perhaps the major share to the development of democratic citizenship' (Tent 1982: 117).

Similar measures were extended to other countries of Europe and indeed the developing world, and while social workers formed only a small minority of the professionals trained under these schemes, the ensuing internationalisation of ideas affected social work in a very special way as the profession found itself at a crucial stage of its development. It was with the aid of these exchange programmes that many European teachers of social work from practically all countries – Scandinavian, Mediterranean and Central European – came into contact with American social work education, obtained American textbooks in translation and prepared themselves for key positions in the new schools of social work which were being founded all across Europe. This programme was backed up by deploying US experts on training and lecture tours to Europe.

Among the 'visiting experts' singled out by the American administration to work with educators and 'multipliers' in the new Germany were also some of the former refugees: Annemarie Schindler, Hertha Kraus and Gisela Konopka. The latter two, in particular, not only brought with them the results of their American research and the work on the development of social work methods, but a strong sense of continuity with the concepts and traditions that had begun to blossom on the European Continent in pre-Nazi times. Gisela Konopka inspired numerous budding social workers on the European side of the Atlantic by the combination of her sensitivity for the personal guilt and incomprehension that had burdened many of them on realising the full implications of their functions under the dictatorship, and her enthusiastic macro perspective on social work's potential: 'I was impressed when I went on overseas assignments, with how wide the application of social work principles is when we get out of the narrow confines of vocational settings from which our profession sprang' (Konopka 1953: 279).

Her own professional principles ruled out a straight transplant of American social work methods. Instead she encouraged the fostering of indigenous approaches rooted in the specific historical and social situation of the country and related closely to the priorities expressed by users. She gave her own summary of her assignment in Germany in 1951 as follows:

Social work has developed some basic principles of help such as:
1. One must understand where the person or the group one wants to help starts.
2. One must accept them as they are and only then help toward change.
3. The helper can only be an enabler; the individual or the group must finally solve his own problems.
4. People resent being helped (at least there is ambivalence about it). The helper must be able to accept hostility.
5. In helping groups we must understand about subgrouping, about scapegoat formation and isolation.

6. In helping a group the helper must slowly move away from the central role and let the group find its own strength.

Those principles can be and must be used in our dealings with those nations which are helped by us.

The only reward of the helper should be the fact that the one who was helped can stand on his own feet.

(Konopka 1953: 280)

Leading figures in the British re-education programme for the defeated Nazi Germany had cooperated earlier and more closely with a group of German emigrants and formed the German Education Reconstruction (GER) as early as 1943 under the presidency of Eleanor Rathbone. The group included the pedagogues Minna Specht, Fritz Boronski and Werner Burmeister, the social pedagogues Magda Kelber and Erich Hirsch and the sociologists Karl Mannheim and Curt Bondy, and it organised training and youth exchange programmes well into the 1950s (Anderson 1978: 262). This enabled the British government in Germany perhaps to come closer to Konopka's principles and to foster a number of educational initiatives in the widest sense, including the re-establishment of the youth work organisations of the churches and of the Social-Democratic and the Communist parties, as well as adult education in close partnership with the trade unions (Burmeister 1978: 241). This approach preserved the 'pedagogical', youth work-oriented methodological and conceptual strand of German social work, which therefore continued to represent a development parallel to the social work tradition promoted by American influences.

Among those British initiatives were (re-)training centres like the *Jugendhof Votho* and the *Haus Schwalbach*, the latter originally an American foundation but led by Magda Kelber of the GER circle, who turned it into a seminal centre for training in social group work (Müller 1988: 53). The educational style of that house included role-play, awareness training and sociodrama as well as the use of audio-visual aids long before these established themselves more widely on social work courses. But behind the practical question of whether to offer German social work the opportunity of making a completely new start or to emphasise and build on continuities with the pedagogical reform concepts of the 1920s lay the political question of whether those German ideas of pedagogy had not been completely discredited through their (albeit distorted) use in National Socialist 'welfare' services. The 'democratic component' of all methods became the touchstone of their acceptability.

On the wider European horizon the assimilation of American methods in social work education had to do partly with the availability of American social work literature translated into several European languages, and partly with the convergence of the political agenda as it developed in Western Europe and the USA during the Cold War period and its concomitant economic determinants. Most countries made a determined effort to establish, or at least move towards, a welfare state in that period as a compromise between diverging class interests. Within these social policy moves towards welfare as an entitlement, the case-work model offered the chance of raising social work to a professional level by ridding it of its traditional stigma as a tool for sorting 'deserving' from 'undeserving' cases. The promise of social policies which potentially lifted the threat of poverty from all social work clients left the profession free to concentrate on its educational and therapeutic roles. However, the organisation of social services on the Continent left social workers with responsibilities for welfare benefit assessments, so that their definition of case work tended to be broader, as the following French definition from the 1950s indicates: 'Casework is not, as some would say, psychological help destined to resolve psychological problems (which they contrast with or differentiate from material help), it is a comprehensive form of help (*aide totale*) which, in every case without exception, takes account of psychological factors in order to assure the effectiveness of whatever help is indicated: material, financial, health, moral support' (quoted in *Training for Social Work* 1958: 41). For British social workers, freed from such obligations, it was easier to bracket out the political agenda from their awareness – at least until the 're-discovery of poverty' in the 1960s brought about a new questioning of the political context and the political implications of social work.

It would be tempting to discount ideological influences on social work as a matter of the distant past from which the profession has managed to emancipate itself. The experience of the very overt ideological interference of National Socialism, as well as the more covert impact of 'free world' politics on social work after the Second World War, contain uncomfortable lessons: 'scientific neutrality' served more as a disguise than a defence, as did the recourse to 'professional values'. Gunar Myrdal expressed this in his evaluation of the UN social reconstruction programmes as a critique of its technological and scientific orientation:

> The main value premise which I have introduced, and one which is relatively rarely made explicit, is that a *sine qua non* for considering change as an improvement for society is that it increases and does not decrease human dignity or, more particularly, the opportunity for active participation of the population itself or, in one word, democracy.
>
> (Myrdal 1955: 24)

As the political consensus over the welfare state and its collective solidarity is under threat in the 1990s, social work could easily become once more the unwitting instrument of a political programme. The democratic ideals of case work established the approach which needs to be followed through, with the insistence on social rights as the only viable basis for a non-oppressive form of social work.

Chapter 4

Social work and academic discourses

The previous two chapters gave an outline of the various ideological influences on European social work to the point where a consensus seemed to emerge after the end of the Second World War that gave priority to the role of theory over ideology. This inaugurated a search for the 'definitive' method, at first in rival 'gladiatorial' battles (Rojek 1986: 66) for the commanding position and later as a 'unitary' view that made room for various approaches under a systemic umbrella.

Today's post-modern climate seems to be settling for 'discourses': the parameters within which language, terminology, concepts, ideas, values and actions move freely and without dominance in the humanities so that the quest for distinct intellectual traditions seems obsolete. The following overview is not intended to isolate these traditions from their historical and political context, but simply to identify some of the intellectual sources that the various forms of social work practice in Europe feed upon, incorporating and indeed transforming their material for purposes derived from daily practice (Philp 1979: 92). As social work education is becoming more and more firmly established in the university sector in Ireland, Italy, Spain, and of course now in the UK, educators might register with dismay that social work appears to be homeless in academia and at the mercy of other disciplines. Historical reflections might help to place this in a different light.

SOCIAL WORK AND THE SOCIAL SCIENCE PARADIGM

Although usually located in social science departments from the start, social work in Britain has always had an uneasy relation-

ship with its host. 'Social work bears witness to the idio-
syncrasies of human nature, while social theory reminds social
workers of the extent to which human nature is socially determined' (Pinker 1990: 12). Social theory, particularly as norma-
tive theory (or 'practical doctrine', in Durkheim's phrase),
perhaps contains the message that social work practice misses
the point, is useless or even counter-productive.

It is important to acknowledge that bringing social work
under the social science umbrella in the first place was a useful
corrective of the moralistic preoccupation with individual character deficiencies which had been the hallmark of the philanthropic origins of social work. The Fabian opposition to charity,
even organised and systematic charity in the form of the COS,
had rightly highlighted not only the paternalism and ethical
ambiguity of the philanthropic enterprise but above all its
ineffectiveness in tackling the problems it claimed to address.
Social science through scientific surveys showed that persistent
poverty in society was not primarily the result of personal
failings but of systematic structural inequality. If social work
was to become an academically respectable and honest profession it had to take cognizance of these empirical findings. But
reformers and philanthropists compromised and in 1903 a
School of Sociology was founded at the instigation of the COS
which in 1912 transferred to the London School of Economics,
the bastion of Fabianism (Pinker 1990: 81).

As was noted above in relation to the founding of social work
schools within a particular range of 'value positions', social
work also aligned itself with a particular paradigm of sociology
that was pragmatic, apolitical and disinclined to challenge
existing social structures. In his seminal analysis of sociological
textbooks, written in 1943, C. Wright Mills criticises their low
level of abstraction and their preoccupation with 'social pathology' (Mills 1943: 166). The focus on 'practical problems' in his
view arose from a direct polemic against the 'philosophy of
history' approach to sociology brought into America by sociologists trained in Germany. He comments on the usefulness of
this 'situational approach' to social problems for social workers
as follows:

In M.E. Richmond's influential *Social Diagnosis* (1917) we
gain a clue as to why pathologists tend to slip past structure to

focus on isolated situations, why there is a tendency for problems to be considered as problems of individuals, and why sequences of situations were not seen as linked into structures.

(ibid.: 170)

And he goes on to quote Richmond:

Social diagnosis . . . may be described as the attempt to make as exact a definition as possible of the situation and personality of a human being in some social need, – of his situation and personality, that is, in relation to the other human beings upon whom he in any way depends and who depend upon him, and in relation to the social institutions of his community.

(ibid.)

This 'fit' between social work's institutional single case orientation and a particular type of social theory accounts in Mills' eyes for a tendency in social workers for their 'occupationally trained incapacity to rise above series of "cases"' (ibid.: 171).

Social science as a vehicle for social reform only had a marginal influence on social work on the European continent. This is not to say that there was no social reform movement broadly parallel to that of the Fabian Society in Britain; indeed, the equivalent of what in Britain is social administration and social policy was an academic discipline at German universities from about 1850, producing its own discourse within the Historical School of National Economy, which in turn led to the founding of the Association for Social Policy in 1873.

The strong practical reform agenda of this group of academics came in not only for political criticism but also for scientific opposition in the course of the development of sociology as an academic discipline. Max Weber, who has had a lasting influence on the course of German sociology, left the Association for Social Policy in a highly publicised gesture to found the German Society for Sociology and to promote sociological research on a 'value-free' basis, albeit not in the positivist–scientific tradition but in the hermeneutic tradition. Despite his own (private) political commitment Weber insisted on the 'detachment' of social science and social policy research. But while his sociological research elaborated on the social and economic processes which produce modern society and on its bureaucracy, separate spheres and contradictions, it did not influence in any way directly the translation of these findings into social policy strategies or social action, let alone the training of social workers.

The only early foothold social work training in Germany had in university social science was through the work of Christian Jasper Klumker, an academic trained in theology, history, 'national economics' and statistics, who took over the Institute for Welfare (*Institut für Gemeinwohl*) in Frankfurt in 1897. From 1914 he held the first Chair for Social Welfare at Frankfurt university which in 1920 became the chair for Welfare and Social Pedagogy. Besides his practical work in child care and homelessness he conducted extensive research into poverty and proposed a 'Theory of Poverty' in 1911. This, and other works by Klumker, were intended to refute the liberal myth which attributes poverty to moral character deficits. He argued that, on the contrary, material deprivation and social marginalisation leads to demoralisation, and social work needs to give high priority to the material circumstances of clients. Nevertheless, Klumker was 'realistic' enough not to expect social changes to result from the actions of social workers, although his own campaigning made a decisive contribution to the shaping of the child and youth welfare legislation of the Weimar Republic. Klumker's practical orientation led him to believe that the non-university sector was a more appropriate level for social work training, as the university could not provide a practical component (Neises 1968).

It is somewhat ironic that although German sociology in Weber's tradition focused so much on human action and on developing concepts of understanding (*verstehen*) its causes and meaning, it influenced social work only indirectly. The positivist version of sociology, prevalent in France and other continental countries, concerned itself more with empirical data and 'social forces' and thus provided social work with 'maps of deviant behaviour' on which it could locate its fields of action.

The popularity of the 'system theory' approach in social work training in the 1970s was a sign of the continued attraction of functionalist social science for social work. Pincus and Minahan appeared on most reading lists on social work theory classes in Europe, probably as an escape from the dilemmas caused by the widespread criticism of the ineffectiveness of the case-work model. The 'unitary approach' does not force social workers to adopt a position on the nature of society, nor does it relate action causally to social analysis, and it seems that the model has exhausted itself as a result of its broad generality.

By contrast, the application of Marxist social theory to social work which began in the early 1970s represented a concerted critique of social work's traditional 'neutrality' and exposed the (often unintended) oppressive effects of the preoccupation with individual pathology. It is perhaps a unique feature of British 'radical social work' models that they sought to transform mainstream social work practice. The equivalent Marxist challenges being voiced in other European contexts usually concentrated on community work, or on work in specialised 'alternative' settings such as psychiatry, as the only viable settings for such transformation. Community action also received vital impulses from the encounter with literature from the liberation movements of the Third World. The impetus of the 'radical' challenge lives on sporadically in projects to combat poverty and in other initiatives arising from social movements. Intellectually the Critical School of Sociology associated with Jürgen Habermas in Frankfurt is now beginning to provide practice paradigms for social work in a broader sense on the strength of its analysis of communication processes.

PSYCHOLOGICAL PARADIGMS

The minimal impact of social science paradigms, and especially of structural concepts, on social work reflects the general dynamics of theory formation in this field, which run from existing forms of practice to theory. Practice remained focused on individuals, generating the need for theories that primarily explained interpersonal processes. In this regard social work's first textbook, Mary Richmond's *Social Diagnosis* (1917), highlighted, more than remedied, the deficit. It drew on social science concepts for making the assessment task of social workers more systematic and 'scientific', but had little to offer in terms of interventive strategies. In Germany, Alice Salomon wrote her own textbook under the same title (with conscious reference to Mary Richmond) in 1926 and criticised 'commonsense' approaches to social work which tend to reduce social problems to a matter of individual failings (Salomon 1926: 17).

But again she did not utilise a scientific system for intervention, although she emphasised the emotional involvement of the worker in the helping process. The lifeline thrown to a profession adrift at this point was Freud's psychoanalytic theory, which began to disseminate among US social work educators after his visit to Clark University in 1912. However, the gradual adoption of these theories in the USA and also on British social work courses from the 1920s failed to provide social work with a viable intellectual home. It did not satisfy the core criterion set by Flexner in his famous address to the National Conference of Charities and Correction in 1915 as the benchmark of full professionalism, the development of a coherent scientific base to social work practice:

> The usefulness of Freudian theory for fulfilling one of the requirements of the Flexner myth is reflected in the rapid adoption of Freudian principles as a fundamental component in social work curricula. This took place in spite of the fact that no form of social work practice used the specific techniques of psychoanalytic treatment, and that only a very small proportion of social work practice in the field was, in any way, directly based on the systematic application of the developmental theories of Freud.
>
> (Austin 1983: 370)

While there is good evidence that 'psychodynamic case work' by no means dominated American social work practice in the 1930s despite the myth of a 'psychiatric deluge' (Field 1980: 498), Freudian concepts were certainly widely used in US social work training. The two dominant theoretical schools – the diagnostic and the problem-solving – both relied on psychodynamic concepts like 'ego-strength' and 'unconscious processes' and all the classical texts by Garrett, Hamilton, Hollis and Perlman acknowledge the Freudian influence approvingly (Alexander 1972: 519). European practitioners and trainers visiting the USA in the early years after the Second World War experienced the psychodynamic model at the apex of its influence, but missed the subsequent wave of criticism (Olk and Otto 1989: XVI).

Ultimately the plurality of methods, the merging of their boundaries and the tendency towards legitimating 'eclectic' uses of theory were brought about by statutory and voluntary services dealing with much more diverse client groups, coordinated as in France, Italy, Greece and Germany as 'territorial units', and the differentiation of the models themselves (Dal Pra Ponticelli 1985: 48). The immediacy of the encounter with distressed individuals continues to call for skills and insights which allow the worker not to get overwhelmed and to turn frustration, anxiety or anger into constructive action. Knowledge about transference can be a safeguard against social workers slipping back into the moralising, punitive attitudes of pre-professional days, and the 'liberating' aspects of Freudian concepts are still being treated as relevant in modern welfare settings, for instance in the prevention-oriented health and social services of Catalonia (Rossell 1987).

The fundamental dilemma of social workers' infatuation with Freudian psychology was that the more closely they followed its concepts, the more indistinguishable they became from psychotherapists and the more they adapted and modified them for social work purposes, the less status they were seen to have. It remained a 'borrowed' theory.

SOCIAL WORK AND SOCIAL PEDAGOGY

The most powerful and influential alternative to the case work paradigm is that of pedagogy and the derivation of social pedagogy. About half the German social workers hold a qualification in social pedagogy and there are more professionals working in social occupations in France and Italy with a qualification in 'animation' or as 'educators' than there are qualified social workers. In English the term 'education' inevitably evokes associations with the school system, with formal qualifications and with the hierarchy of teacher over learner. Pedagogy has a wider and more radical meaning, best known perhaps in the English-speaking world through Paulo Freire's 'pedagogy of the oppressed' (1972). Pedagogy in this sense refers to self-directed learning processes. Some educational reformers were sceptical about the child-oriented implications of pedagogy (*pais* in Greek means child) and introduced the alternative term 'andragogy' to stress the adult or life-long aspect of learning (Knowles 1985: 9; Humphries 1988: 5–6), but this term is equally prone to misunderstandings (*andros* = man). Unfortunately the Dutch usage of 'agogic' for all self-initiated educational and developmental action (including 'community work') again has not found general acceptance and the following historical overview will therefore use 'pedagogy' in a universal sense.

This is not to say that the term pedagogy itself is unambiguous. Just as social work contains elements of social control *and* of social advocacy and liberation, so a particular form of pedagogy may treat the learner as an empty vessel, as the sometimes compliant, sometimes recalcitrant object of educational efforts, or it may bring to light the educational potential that lies dormant in every individual. Politically there are therefore no inherent advantages in having the social professions grounded in the pedagogical tradition as against conceptualising them as applied social science or as a derivative of psychology. The advantage of pedagogy as a conceptual framework might be, however, that it already 'contains' social work as one of several equally important fields of social work practice, instead of social work being a 'borrowed' set of concepts.

Pedagogical science also has a well established place in the university structure of most European countries; in France, Germany or Italy, for instance, this subject area already gives social work access to the university sector. In the Czech and Slovakian Republics and in Poland social work training has the opportunity of linking up with pre-existing intellectual traditions at university level, despite the hiatus created by communism. The modern European history of pedagogy has generated ideas which are of relevance both for the school system and for the development of personal social services. It has also conceptualised conflicts and tensions which are exactly parallel to those analysed within other social work theories.

EDUCATION AND MODERN SOCIETY

It is worth remembering that in early modern times educational initiatives had an intrinsic social (and spiritual) dimension, as is evident in the intentions of the humanist movement and the various mendicant religious orders devoted to the 'education of the poor' (Tuggener 1986: 10). 'Formation' (in contrast to the much more instrumental 'education') is at once a mystical concern, steering the soul to reach its salvation, and a social programme as it aims at the transmission and the improvement of appropriate forms of social life. The growing complexity of knowledge and of social relations in the age of modernity on the one hand make educational efforts more urgent, and on the other make them infinitely more complex and contentious. The 'discovery of childhood' (Ariés 1962) is really a crisis in the transmission of social and cultural values: society needs to take on the task of reproducing its heritage consciously and deliberately and thereby to reflect on its values, on its methods of transmission and on human nature as presented by children in its as yet 'un(in)formed' state. Through education society reflects upon itself, grounds itself and reproduces itself.

In this sense, Jean-Jaques Rousseau's (1712–1778) ideas on education became programmatic: with the confidence characteristic of the French Enlightenment he seeks to restore education as a natural process which keeps the influence of civilisation at a distance until the innate abilities of the young person are sufficiently developed. In his educational novel *Emile*, the role of the educator is restricted to providing the young person with 'educational opportunities', while the educational momentum is provided by the nature of the young person. Pedagogy concentrates on non-repressive learning *processes*, not on the imparting of distinct contents, and Rousseau formulates the pedagogical aim free from theological and economic interests: to enable people to live according to their human nature (Tophoven 1992: 54). Rousseau's ideas foreshadow Jean Piaget's psychological work on the stages of cognitive development in their insistence on the didactic importance of objects and of 'learning by doing' in early childhood as the precondition for abstract intellectual development, a sequence which is also constitutive in the method of the Italian educationalist Maria Montessori (1870–1952). The practical legacy of those educationalists, which continued to characterise the French 'educational sciences' in contrast to the philosophical leanings of German pedagogy (Schriewer 1983: 369) consists mainly of specific teaching methods and therefore of an individualised, not a social, pedagogy. Nevertheless, Rousseau's more general tenets concerning the autonomy of the learner still reverberate today in the familiar case-work values of 'self-direction' and 'non-coerciveness'.

Rousseau stands accused of abstract speculation. The testing of his ideas in practice and their translation into programmes of social pedagogy owes much to the initiatives of religiously inspired pioneers. Pastor Johann Friedrick Oberlin (1740–1826) for instance, operated a kind of prototype pre-school in the Alsace village of Steintal (Ban de la Roche) by employing and training women as *conductrices d'enfants*. Oberlin regarded pre-school education as an essential contribution to the spiritual and economic renewal of the village, in which he also organised public construction projects and agricultural credit unions and to which he attracted 'enlightened' industrialists. His design directly inspired Robert Owen to give his cooperatives in England an educational dimension, from where Theodor Flied-ner, the German pioneer of the *Diakonie* movement, in turn derived the notion of training pre-school teachers at his philan-thropic institution of Kaiserswerth in Germany in 1836 (Janssen 1959: 1275). In such experiments in different parts of Europe, which anticipate community development concepts, education was seen as the midwife of true human nature and of a new society.

The most decisive impulse for the development of a *social* pedagogy came from Oberlin's contemporary, the Swiss re-former Johann Heinrich Pestalozzi (1746–1827), who had been strongly influenced by Rousseau and Voltaire but whose own principles were developed out of the often painfully futile practical experiments he instigated. He, too, regards civilisation as evil but proposes a return not to nature, but to the simplicity of social bonds in family and village life. All his projects – a model rural farming community, an orphanage, and a resi-dential school – have a crucial social dimension: the fulfilment of material human needs is linked to a sense of belonging, acceptance and love. The behaviour of traumatised children does not change under coercion, but as a result of loving acceptance expressed through the satisfaction of material and emotional needs simultaneously (Rusk 1965: 213). Pestalozzi's pedagogy contains the nucleus of a comprehensive social pro-gramme and of a paradigm for all interventions which refuse to be split into therapy and social action, individualism and collectivism, technical expertise and common sense.

The name of yet another practical educational reformer be-longs in this European panorama. Friedrich Fröbel (1782–1852) is best remembered for giving pre-school education, the kinder-garten, a professional profile and a key social function, especially with advancing industrialisation, but this initiative was but one aspect of his comprehensive educational ideas. Education is the unfolding of innate abilities, as the growing consciousness begins to grasp freedom, and therefore has to be 'passive, following (only guarding and protecting), not prescriptive, categorical, interfering' (Fröbel 1910: 7). Exploratory play epitomises the fundamental value of self-directed learning and is, far beyond its developmental significance, a social act of freedom which puts the child in charge. The political consequences of his programme did not fail to get noticed – kindergartens were prohibited by the Prussian government after the failed revolution of 1848 (Bluhm 1971: 104).

THEORIES OF EDUCATION

The systematic elaboration of pedagogy and the first decisive steps towards making it an academic discipline were undertaken by the two German philosophers Johann Friedrich Herbart and Friedrich Schleiermacher. For Herbart (1776–1841) the task of pedagogy is to facilitate the moral self-determination of the individual person by engaging the 'moral willing' of the student without bending or forcing it in a pre-determined direction. The self-generated interests of the individual form a guide leading to experience and insight (action and reflection); however, this occurs only under the skillful guidance of an educator who can deepen the experiences by challenging and questioning, thus making the learner more aware. The skills of the educator therefore combine psychology and ethics, and the ultimate test of these pedagogical processes is the ability to act, not simply to know (Rusk 1965: 240). This leads the learning process continuously beyond the confines of 'lessons' and into concrete social situations, into 'praxis' (Tophoven 1992: 59). The 'transfer of learning into practice' is not an additional educational problem, it *is* the pedagogical question.

Schleiermacher (1768–1834), a philosopher and theologian from Silesia who was much influenced by the Enlightenment, goes beyond the pedagogical principles of 'natural self-development' to embrace an 'education for community', (*Gemeinschaft*). How can sociability come about without coercion, without distorting the personal manifestations of the will? One of his theories is that individual intentions are already directed (by their very nature as human intentions) towards sociability, towards universal social goals. The other is that only democracy allows the individual will to form. Public life needs to correspond to and reflect what is pedagogically, psychologically necessary for the healthy growth of the individual. The conditions for good education are those of a sound democracy; pedagogical and political processes condition each other.

These philosophical considerations laid the foundations for both school pedagogy and *social* pedagogy, a term which came into use in Germany around the middle of the nineteenth century. As far as documentary evidence is concerned it was first used in 1844 by the educationalist Karl Mager, who explored the societal aspects of education more specifically (Kronen 1978: 222). 'Pedagogy is the theory of the acquisition of culture' he states (quoted in Kronen 1978: 223), referring right back to the function of pedagogy in ancient Greece. He explicitly criticises the 'newer pedagogy of Locke, Rousseau, the philanthropists, Pestalozzi, Herbart, Benecke etc.' (ibid.) for their preoccupation with the individual. Social pedagogy signifies a concept which pays attention to the formation of society as a whole within which formal educational institutions play only a limited part.

This very comprehensive, universal view of social pedagogy was again narrowed down to, albeit quite liberal, proposals for the reform of the primary school system. F.A.W. Diesterweg (1790–1866), a Prussian pedagogue in the tradition of Pestalozzi, recognised the potential the school system had in reversing the pauperisation and demoralisation of the proletariat if schools could be wrenched from the influence of church and politics. In a manual for teacher education he draws attention to the responsibilities of the teaching profession in relation to what was termed in the bourgeois political debate of the time the 'social question', i.e. the appearance of large-scale social problems associated with industrialisation which threatened the stability of society (Hämäläinen 1989: 117; Rohde 1989: 7). Diesterweg sees in those social problems the result of faulty socialisation, and attributes to teachers the responsibility for fostering the social abilities of pupils and thereby reforming society not with church exhortations or fear and discipline but with pedagogical means. Diesterweg's liberal ideas define education as a means of emancipation and thereby anticipate the concepts of community and adult education of the late twentieth century mediated by Freire's pedagogy, yet he confined his political efforts to the reform of the school system. Unlike the philanthropic programme of tackling social issues at the fringes of the state, this challenged the state to make education a central part of social policy.

Within the paternalism of the German states in the nineteenth century this also meant that social pedagogy could serve the state as a new form of social engineering. Already in the version of the Neo-Kantian philosopher and pedagogue Paul Natorp (1854–1924) social pedagogy becomes education which directs the individual will towards the higher level of a communal will; social pedagogy is for him the 'concretisation of pedagogy *per se*' (Rohde 1989: 7). This approach gives society, as the embodiment of what is rational, priority over the needs and interests of individuals, and social pedagogy becomes a programme for bringing about better social adjustment.

The polarisation visible in this early debate is of lasting relevance for social work and social pedagogy: is social pedagogy essentially the embodiment of dominant societal interests which regard all educational projects, schools, kindergarten or adult education, as a way of taking its values to all sections of the population and of exercising more effective social control; or is social pedagogy the critical conscience of pedagogy, the thorn in the flesh of the official agenda, an emancipatory programme for self-directed learning processes inside and outside the education system geared towards the transformation of society? The tension between the institutional and the emancipatory, anti-authoritarian version of social pedagogy continues today and reproduces itself in all new conceptual paradigms, including the pedagogy of Paulo Freire, as Taylor's detailed analysis of Freire's texts and their conceptual origins has shown (Taylor 1993: 70).

INSTITUTIONALISED SOCIAL PEDAGOGY IN GERMANY

In Germany the first political opportunity for putting social pedagogy into practice occurred with the social-democratic reforms of the Weimar Republic. Their social service aspects were strongly influenced by the work of the philosopher and pedagogue Herman Nohl (1879–1960). For him social pedagogy is the third area, besides the family and the school, which requires a supportive social policy framework in its own right and consequently needs appropriately trained staff. The use of the term 'social pedagogy' means that such diverse areas of practice as work in créches and nurseries, day-care centres, youth clubs, work with offenders and probationers, vocational training of unemployed people and denominational parish work can be united under one conceptual and professional umbrella. For Nohl this underlying unity is of great importance as it raises all these activities above the level of sectional, political interests to address the material and spiritual well-being of the nation as a collective body (Nohl 1926a: 21) – an idealisation which a short decade later would be usurped by Nazi propaganda. Taking up the high-spirited ideals of the youth movement of the pre-war era, Nohl considers the 'experience of life itself', and the values contained in friendship and personal solidarity across all social divisions, to be the pedagogical material and the pedagogical impetus for a fundamental social reconstruction. His pedagogy also seeks to integrate the ideas and energies contained in other initiatives 'from the basis' like the women's or the labour movements, and he specifically refers to the value of Freud's and Adler's psychology for personalising pedagogical practice (Nohl 1926b: 152). Gertrud Bäumer, one of the pioneers of German social work and social work education and later assistant secretary at the Ministry of the Interior of the Weimar Republic, defines social pedagogy more concretely as an instrument of social policy. In the opening chapter of a 1929 textbook on social pedagogy, edited by Nohl and Pallat, she acknowledges that social work originally served to fill gaps in poor law provisions and to dispense charity (Bäumer 1929: 3ff.). But just as school-based education has now come to be recognised as a primary and no longer a residual provision (with compulsory aspects), so public personal social services now need to assert their universal function positively. For Bäumer the 'social' in social pedagogy implies a public mandate to aid the educational socialisation (*Erziehungsfürsorge*) of children according to their developmental needs and regardless of the material and attitudinal disposition of their parents.

In one of the earliest policy programmes for personal social services in Europe she identifies three strands of social pedagogical intervention: (i) monitoring, correcting and if necessary substituting the child care practices of families and contributing therefore 'to a new distribution of tasks and responsibilities between family, society and state'; (ii) identifying and remedying the structural, economic causes of social problems as they affect families and individuals in their 'educational functions'; and (iii) providing remedial help for children whose difficulties stem from learning and developmental disabilities (Bäumer 1929:5).

Tragically, the comprehensive social-pedagogical programme of the Weimar Republic, enshrined in the Children's Act of 1922 (*Reichsjugendhilfegesetz*) foundered on the shortage of public finances and the political paralysis of the government. But as mentioned above, some elements of social pedagogy both as a method and as the ideal of a democratic society featured in the Anglo-American efforts at re-starting youth and social work services in Germany after the Second World War. The work of training centres like *Jugendhof Votho* and *Haus Schwalbach* focused on small group interaction as the training ground for democratic processes. The American programme for purging Germany of Nazi ideology, particularly in its early phase, was indeed planned on educational lines. '"Re-education" became the conquerors' catchword to describe their efforts to democratize Germany' (Trent 1982: 1). But the ideological misuse of education had also left the occupying powers with doubts about the usefulness of 'social peda-gogy' and caused them to support 'social work' initiatives as the ideologically 'neutral' and scientifically based alternative (Oelschlägel 1992: 2047).

To some observers this influence was responsible for a narrow-ing of the original universal perspective of social pedagogy to the level of individual crisis work (Kronen 1978: 225). It became a metaphor for individualised interventions under the policy heading 'educational measures in exceptional circum-stances', confined to particular institutional settings (pre-school and remedial education, residential work, and youth projects) where 'deficits' in the socialisation of young people had to be redressed.

This was to change gradually with the reorganisation and expansion of German social work/social pedagogy training in the 1970s. The applied, vocational tradition of social work training was raised to the level of *Fachhochschulen*, i.e. post-secondary level colleges where courses in social work and social pedagogy became parallel streams. The original difference – that social work training prepared students more specifically for positions in public social services, which in Germany include welfare benefit functions, while social pedagogy was geared towards creative and therapeutic services – became less pronounced, and many courses now lead to a combined award. Simultaneously, courses in social pedagogy commenced at several universities within departments of educational sciences where it constituted one area of specialisation parallel to those of 'school pedagogy', 'special pedagogy', adult education and industrial education (Rauschenbach 1991: 6). Through this development conceptual and historical links with the older pedagogical tradition became possible and continue to provide reference points for the contemporary theoretical discourse. For instance, the pedagogical emphasis on socialisation into a community articulated by Pestalozzi, Schleiermacher or Natorp informed theories of social intervention promoting social skills and 'integration'. On the other hand, the radical critique of 'total institutions' diverted pedagogical activities away from traditional settings (schools, homes, the family) and towards the complexity of everyday situations. Social learning and change can only occur through open communication and with full participation of the 'client' or 'learner', not under 'artificial' conditions controlled by the social worker or the agency. Thiersch, in advocating this critical stance, has even elevated the 'everyday situation' to the rank of *the actual* pedagogical situation (the *Alltagswende* of German pedagogy, Thiersch 1986: 186), an approach which faintly echoes the ideas of Nohl.

The tension between social work and social pedagogy indicates the counterflow of theory formation characteristic of this profession, the flow from a central idea to the differentiated application in various specialised fields and the coming together of common conceptual elements and the consequent professional unification of fields of practice which had grown out of various practice contexts. Social pedagogy defines the task and the process of all 'social activity' from theoretical positions beyond any distinct institutional setting and instrumental interest, and thereby safeguards the autonomy of the profession and appeals to the reflective and communicative abilities of the worker as the key to competence. Social work, by contrast, tends to take the diversity of social services and agency settings as the starting point for the search for appropriate theories, a search which used to be guided by the desire to find a general, unifying theory of social work but has since given way to the more pragmatic and often eclectic use of theory elements from neighbouring disciplines (Tophoven 1992: 62). This dichotomy itself has probably been overtaken by developments in the last decades of this century. The critique of professional elitism represented by self-help initiatives and social movements, as well as the post-modern intellectual critique of all 'grand theories' and 'received ideas', have taken the initiative away from academia and are once more giving recognition to 'praxis' as the place where specific theories and actions materialise together.

THE PROFESSION OF SOCIAL EDUCATORS IN EUROPE

A perceived lack of 'academic respectability' has been familiar to a group of practitioners in the 'caring field' who mostly develop their concepts out of and around their practice setting. 'Social educators' – as residential and day-care staff, youth workers or nursery nurses – practise and develop their skills very much by 'living with people' in everyday situations. Indeed 'living with others as a profession', as the sub-title of the major overview of this field in Europe puts it (Courtioux et al.: 1986), has been chosen by exponents of this professional group as the unifying criterion of their diverse professional titles and specialisations.

'Living with people' – young people, for instance – has its own pedagogical tradition, exemplified most vividly perhaps by the Polish medical doctor Janusz Korczak (born Hersh or Henryk Goldszmit) whose style of pedagogy at his Jewish orphanage in Warsaw in the 1920s and 1930s became an international reference point. His 'theoretical position' is hard to categorise as he combined idealism and realism (Waaldijk 1985), and set up democratic structures with the children but built in safeguards for his own ultimate responsibility. He regarded the orphanage as a 'children's republic' which had its own 'children's court' to underline the fact that children have rights and obligations as citizens (Lifton 1988: 136). He was critical of social and political experiments which use children to demonstrate ideo-logical positions, yet felt strongly that the transformation of society has to begin with a new way of interacting with children. His pedagogy took its lead from the children and Korczak was prepared to enter into the ambiguities of everyday conflicts with an open mind and negotiate rather than impose solutions (Wolins 1967). His 'living with' led to the ultimate consequence of 'dying with', as he refused to save himself from the Nazi pogrom against the Warsaw ghetto and was prepared to go to his death in the gas chambers of Treblinka along with all his children.

Because of their complexity and immediacy, such experiences and the methods contained in them are notoriously difficult to classify and to subsume under general headings. Traditionally the titles in use for 'care workers' in different countries refer to the setting in which or the age group with whom the work takes place: for example child-care workers in Ireland, *Bornehave-paedagog* in Denmark, *jardinière d'enfants* in France, *inrichtings-werker* in the Netherlands, *Kindergärtnerin* in Germany. Some titles actually affirm the 'living with' as a central characteristic (*leefsituatie werker* in Dutch, translated as 'life space worker', or *lähikasvattaja* in Finland, from *lähi* = close and *kasvattaja* = pedagogue; Kalcher 1986: 51). But increasingly some version of 'educator' is taking their place, often with the attribute 'special' to distinguish them from teachers (*éducateur/trice spécialisé/e*; *educador especializado, Erzieher/in*); '. . . despite these national differences due to distinctive history, ideology and culture it is not difficult to identify this group of professional workers who help other people by sharing substantially in their daily living' (Davies Jones 1986: 74). The process of European integration and the networking through ERASMUS programmes has led to a very active search for cross-national compatibility of competences and also for a unifying professional title (Marcon 1988). It remains to be seen whether the notion of a 'special educator' or 'social educator' will become universally acceptable or whether 'pedagogy' will continue to form the invisible subterranean stream which erupts at different times and under different names as the source of new ideas.

ANIMATION AS A SOCIAL MOVEMENT AND AS A PROFESSION

Educational initiatives outside the school system and within the broad domain of social work have certainly experienced a revival since the late 1960s, in line with other social movements.

For these the term 'animation' has come into use in France and French-speaking parts of Belgium and Switzerland, in Italy and in Spain, revealing the curious interdependence between Latin-based languages and this concept. What gave rise to the concept of 'animation' in France was first of all the re-discovery of the importance of 'popular education' as a possible answer to the alarming withering away of social life in urban and equally in rural communities. The threatened death of social life was to be remedied through an injection of life, to effect its re-animation ('animer, c'est-à-dire donner vie'; Ion and Tricart 1984: 41). The need for this renewal became accentuated by the increased availability of free time to the working population and the subsequent 'discovery' of leisure as a mass phenomenon by sociologists.

The other root of 'animation' in France is to be found in the social unrest and critical questioning of society exemplified by the May 1968 events which led to a renewed interest in social action, democratic processes and client participation. Animation combined both agendas, renewal and democratisation, if only for the pragmatic reason that leisure, including the 'involuntary' leisure imposed by prolonged unemployment, can turn into a source of conflict if access to meaningful activities is distributed too one-sidedly. The big challenge was to target the needs of particular sectors of the population seen as lacking in social stimulation, in opportunities to participate in public life and in the resources to develop their interests and potential while still keeping the newly emerging profession focused on the universal social goal, the creation of a participatory society, responsive to the needs of all sectors of the population. It seems apparent at the beginning of the 1990s that notwithstanding the social commitment of small groups of *animateurs* (and indeed of members of all sectors of social work in France) towards the transformation of society along these democratic ideals, the profession of 'animation' has chosen the pragmatic road of 'providing services' to particular interests and interest groups, often on a commercial basis (Astier 1985: 136).

This is apparent in the wide range of activities now loosely linked under the title 'animation' and its two main branches, *animation socio-éducative* and *animation socio-culturelle*. Taking the adage that learning is a life-long task to its full conclusion, pedagogy/animation has now begun professionally to address the educational potential of leisure activities for all ages, at museums, nature parks, archaeological sites, clubs for the elderly, on educational tours, adventure holidays and ecological projects (Placier 1989: 89). It also addresses the need for social skills in everyday situations, for instance of marginalised groups of young people or of migrants, where the social agenda of 'insertion' into society has become a political priority, albeit often under the guise of 'cultural adjustment'. And last but still not least animation in France envisages the potential for political change arising from community groups learning to handle issues that affect them directly. With this agenda animation has established itself very clearly as an independent profession in France, allied to other social professions (which in that country tend to be particularly numerous) but with its own distinct methods (Cannan, Berry and Lyons 1992: 103).

In other countries the opportunities for the creation of separate professional identities have not been equally fortuitous. Yet without clear organisational frameworks, training and career structures the emancipatory potential of the pedagogical ideal must assert itself perhaps all the more energetically. At certain critical historical moments the 'revolutionary' potential of the project of 'education' undertaken in the spirit of modernity seems to get retrieved from its institutional ossification in schools, residential homes and other institutional regimes. Animation in Italy started very much as a movement in the revolutionary spirit of 1968. It attempted to move the focus of education from the school to the locality, from young people to the entire life-cycle, from the imparting of technical knowledge to the development of the whole person, from fixed notions of normality to the areas labeled subnormal and deviant, from a traditional code of 'cultural heritage' to cultural pluralism, and from hierarchical domination to creative participation. At its most fundamental level, animation is geared towards everyday situations, towards realising their potential, their 'future content' which raises them above 'ordinariness' into which they are locked.

Each activity gets seen as a 'utopian cell', as something that already contains a meaning which is offered as a gift to the subject who lives this moment. This meaning, albeit as a seed, is already there. Animation has the purpose of giving life to this hidden meaning as against treating it as "everyday" in a concrete sense. It sets out to liberate the everyday activity from its treatment as banal, mechanical or a matter of habit. In other words, it proposes to live experience and activity as 'actions'.

(Floris and Pollo 1992: 33)

The movement found its first concrete expressions and applications in areas like community theatre and festivals, aided by the parallel interest of the public services in making themselves more 'community-oriented' and open to the wider interests of the community. The 1980s brought a greater methodological clarification and professional diversification around a core definition of animation: 'A form of social practice oriented towards the conscientisation [*presa di coscienza*] and development of the repressed, deprived or latent potential of individuals, small groups and communities' (Contessa, quoted in Maurizio 1991: 30). The strands of animation in which these pedagogical ideas concretised themselves were first of all creative–expressive activities, using theatre and play as a means of self-expression with community groups, children and people with learning difficulties. The second could be called 'socio-cultural animation' and has links with the adult and community education movement as it relates to communities and aims at 'promoting the development of abilities of people and groups to participate in and to manage the social and political reality in which they live. It is education as liberation which makes use of community action as well as of psycho-social methods to advance the expressive capacities of people' (Pollo 1991: 12).

The third strand of 'cultural animation' really represents more an educational–didactive approach applicable to school and after-school activities and sees education mainly as socialisation. Finally there is a growing field of 'leisure-time animation', itself differentiated between initiatives relating to pre-school and school children, such as adventure playgrounds, toy libraries, outdoor activity centres, play in hospitals and in treatment centres, and organised sports activities, in which field the commercial sector is also very strongly represented with outdoor pursuit centres and activity holidays.

The latter development, in particular, indicates how far the concept might have moved away from its original political intentions, or rather, how even this very radical approach can be put to use for commercial purposes. Participation and empowerment become mediated by money, depend on the capacity to pay, and become divorced from the context of oppression in which those terms can only retain their emancipatory meaning (Ward and Mullender 1991a: 22).

But quite apart from the particular colonisation of 'leisure pedagogy' by the tourist industry, animation always steers a precarious course between on the one hand the political aims of creating non-discriminatory, non-stigmatising projects which do not single out social problems and individual deficits for public attention but offer educational opportunities for all those interested in them, and on the other hand concentrating on uncontentious fields of social activity while leaving the 'heavy end' of non-voluntary, less creative and crisis-oriented work to other professionals. Some educationalists, like Paolo Marcon in Italy, therefore oppose the creation of animation as a separate professional identity as this would leave 'special educators', dealing with 'problematic' people and situations marginalised and stigmatised together with their service users. What is at stake is whether animation will get reduced to a 'set of techniques' which become the exclusive property of a separate profession intent on furthering its own career opportunities or whether it describes a total 'way of being and operating' (serving the growth potential of every person), in which case it represents what is good educational practice anyway (Marcon 1991: 189). This vantage point of abstraction merges not only the aims of animation and education but also those of education and social work.

The concept of animation is also beginning to be explored in the social work field in German-speaking countries. In 1989 an Austrian social work school (*Akademie für Sozialarbeit der Stadt Wien*) started post-qualifying training in *Sozio-Animation* for social workers in statutory social work positions. This was a deliberate attempt to introduce a methodology which stimulates creativity, openness and partnership in statutory work and to inhibit the development of a split between case-work methods as implying social control and animation as reserved for the field of leisure activities. A follow-up study of the participants revealed that about half of them had managed to 're-interpret' the tasks and principles of their agencies with the methods of animation, although again there was a general tendency to reserve such methods for users and situations beyond a traditional 'core'. The study found that the more effective use of these methods would require a marked re-orientation of services towards prevention (Karlusch and Rössler 1992: 311–13).

Animation has some affinity with the activities and the philosophy of 'community education' which emerged in English-speaking countries. It has roots partly in the 'village colleges' promoted by Henry Morris in England in the 1920s, and partly in community development in former colonies (Fletcher 1987: 6). On the whole community education is about the extension of formal mainstream education in the form of Midwinter's primary schools in Education Priority Areas, of comprehensive schools which often became centres for adult and continuing education initiatives, particularly in Scotland (Pilley 1990), or of the opening of third-level education for 'the community' as pioneered by Magee College in Northern Ireland (Lovett 1987: 145). It also influenced community work in an attempt to lead it out of the 'social pathology trap': instead of highlighting the deficits of a neighbourhood, a community education initiative can demonstrate the resourcefulness of oppressed people. Taken to its full conclusion, community education challenges both the concept of community and of education:

> A basic premise in community education is that social reality will never be completely free of pain or injustice; that prior to and beyond any curriculum, any educational activity, or discussion, there is a concrete and often oppressive and evil reality; and that the purpose of education is not to ignore, conceal, or distort this reality, but to transform it.
>
> (Fasheh 1990: 35)

In this sense the term community education has also come into use in other European countries (Friesenhahn 1988: 158; Poster and Krüger 1990) to denote the common, intercultural concern of all 'social work' education; the European Centre for Community Education, for instance, is a network of over twenty colleges in the social work/social pedagogy/youth and community work fields across the majority of European countries.

Despite the unifying potential at the conceptual level, the professional development of social pedagogy remains divided, fixed within traditional structures of institutions and work practices. Professional groupings such as nursery nurses, logo-therapists, residential workers, and literacy teachers, to name but a few at random, have developed their own professional boundaries and are part of a hierarchical system which manifests itself not least in the differential pay scales they can command. The divided field of social, caring and educating occupations feeds on a multiplicity of conceptual sources. Nevertheless, it is gratifying to note that in this diversity certain constant themes recur which allow practitioners in different settings and countries to understand each other. The ideas expressed through the pedagogical language proclaim that becoming a member of society and becoming an individual is a life-long process, mediated through groups, families, teachers, social workers and myriads of other official and unofficial 'helpers'. This mediation has its own complex dynamics which psychology and social sciences help to elucidate but whose mastery ultimately derives from 'doing it'. Social work's conceptual fuzziness, though often used as an excuse for intellectual short cuts, may be a safeguard against the profession becoming defined by its agency settings and by instrumental targets ('to bring down the crime rate', 'to prevent child abuse occurring'). Social workers are first and foremost learners themselves, learners with a conscience and with an unashamedly utopian streak. The inner eye for what is 'not yet realised' in the present has at all times been the motivating force of educators.

Chapter 5

Social work and social movements in late twentieth-century Europe

It appears from the observations of the previous chapter that the renewed uncertainties over the nature and identity of social work can no longer be resolved by having recourse to strong theoretical positions. Yet the danger is that this identity deficit could get filled by more stringent organisational and legal regulations defining the task and making social workers conform to the objectives of agency systems. This chapter argues that these uncertainties reflect wider social processes and that the critique of traditional professionalism offers social work the opportunity of aligning itself more closely with user groups and self-help initiatives.

Giddens notes that in the last decades of the twentieth century everyday life has become much more fragmented and social relations have developed in an ever more complex way, forcing people to adopt constantly changing identities depending on the nature of these relationships. As a result we have become 'displaced' from familiar, stable contexts (Giddens 1991: 141). More and more importance is attributed to 'individual life styles', yet the choices often turn out to be products of external manipulation. The whole process of European cultural and political integration has accentuated this development often for reasons of poorly concealed commercial expediency. The quest for a possible European identity is polarised between the acceptance of a multicultural blend of tastes and styles within which national reference points are merely quaint remnants of a bygone age, and the – often nationalistic – insistence on national traditions as inalienable possessions which have to be reproduced or re-designed at European level in terms of a 'Cradle of Civilisation' or 'Christian Europe' construct.

There is a sense that impersonal, powerful systems dictate the contents of private lives, that the dream of modernity, of bourgeois society gaining the freedom to create its own private sphere is receding. The system, in the analysis of Habermas, has differentiated itself into an ever greater number of sub-systems, each carrying its own legalistic and bureaucratic regulations into areas which had so far been left unregulated. Leisure, for instance, has become an industry, a vital part of the economy, bringing with it the need to regulate access to nature, safety of users, insurance liabilities, etc. Habermas called this process the 'colonisation of the life-world' which reaches even the consciousness of individuals (Habermas 1987, II: 363).

Welfare is one such sub-system where the sheer volume of new legislation indicates the systematic public scrutiny to which private lives are now being subjected, and this largely for the better protection of vulnerable people. Children and their safety have become a direct concern of the state and the boundaries between the rights and responsibilities of the family and those of the state have been redrawn. Several countries in Europe (Denmark, Germany, Greece, Ireland and the UK) passed new child-care legislation or at least brought child protection under closer public scrutiny during the late 1980s (Armstrong and Hollows 1991: 154; Lorenz 1991a). While these moves are supported by a generally high level of public consensus, it means in practice that more people experience the presence of officials of the state, such as social workers, in their private lives and resentment is building up, leading to a desire to 'get them off our backs'. And with regard to welfare benefits:

> The financial redistribution it [i.e. the welfare state] operates comes to be viewed as almost entirely divorced from the social relations which are supposed to be its sphere of concern. The interface serves to blur the realm of the social. Actual social assistance is rendered by anonymous, impersonal mechanisms to such a degree that it is no longer perceived as social assistance as such . . . Relations of mutual support between people assume the form of reified relations between individuals and 'the system'.
>
> (Rosanvallon 1988: 210)

These developments in the relationship between the private and the public sphere have accentuated the 'crisis of the welfare state' precipitated at the fiscal level. This has variously been identified as the widening discrepancy between the increasing obligations of the state, caused by expectations of an ever more comprehensive safety net of public social security, and decreasing returns caused by economic crises and by monetarist responses to them. The budgetary difficulties are, however, mere symptoms of problems of legitimation and solidarity which become thereby visible in all types of European welfare states (Offe 1984: 144).

The crisis and the political uncertainties associated with it focused attention on the mediating structures modern societies possess between individuals and state in the realm of 'civil society' (Keane 1988: 7). This stratum of society, the aggregate of activities carried out by private citizens, brought about the modern nation state in the first place through the establishment of democratic processes which regulate the separation of state and civil society. And it is at the level of civil society that important new developments have begun to manifest themselves lately, movements which try to re-assert the autonomy of civil society. The crisis in traditional politics and the mistrust of established political parties shows the 'exhaustion of the traditional image of collective action' (Melucci 1988: 245).

Among these developments the emergence of 'new social movements' in all parts of Europe is of special significance for political life in general and also for the future shape of welfare and of personal social services. The protest movements of the 1960s, which had been generated by particular sectors of society (students, workers) and which had pursued very broad political objectives gave way to movements which address either localised or personal issues directly or global issues through specific, often personalised issue targets. Examples of this are actions by the peace movement or the ecology movement which focus on very immediate events and installations (Greenham Common in the UK, Wackersdorf in Germany, Pershing missile stations in Italy) in a very loosely coordinated manner which gave credibility to the spontaneity of much of the action (although the events were often hijacked by political interest groups).

On the economic front, workers' cooperatives, which had long been a means of self-defence, self-help and solidarity among poor rural people in Greece, Ireland and Italy, gained new momentum in response to growing unemployment (Kelleher and Kennedy 1988: 5). On health issues there had also been forerunners to the new self-help initiatives, manifesting themselves in stunning diversity. Alcoholics Anonymous had pioneered the concept of mutual support among people with substance abuse and dependency problems. Now 'patient collectives' sprang up, often in association with the women's health movement, and in the context of a general questioning of institutional and technology-oriented care. The best-known movement was perhaps *psichiatria democratica* in Northern Italy which, despite having been initiated by professionals, championed client participation and self-direction as both a therapeutic and a political goal (Trenchina and Serra 1983: 16).

SOCIAL WORK AND THE WOMEN'S MOVEMENT

The social movement that had the most profound impact on social work was the women's movement. It posed a challenge to some cherished traditional principles such as 'value neutrality' and the aspirations of the profession to leave behind the 'typically female characteristics of caring'. It also brought hope that social work's traditional concern with personal issues might have a liberating potential: 'By breaking down the false dualism between the private and the public, feminism has, quite literally, publicised the hidden areas of women's oppression' (Hudson 1985: 645).

Women's groups sprang up spontaneously in all industrialised countries in the 1960s. Their main characteristic was the multiplicity of issues they dealt with (reflecting the diverse forms that women's oppression took), all of which, however, could be traced back to systematic and structurally endemic forms of discrimination. They developed characteristic 'strategies' for change whereby the process and the personal involvement of the participants was as important as the objective of the action. The forms and means of discrimination and oppression experienced by women in different countries varied, but the effects were strikingly similar: biological differences became reified, justifying social, economic and political subordination. In the light of this universal experience cross-national links formed very quickly. The overall effect of women's campaigns was to bring new, personalised and hitherto taboo issues into the public arena and to have them treated as political issues (Hernes 1984: 34).

For instance, women in Italy in 1968 began to challenge the concepts of the left and to replace Marxist rationalism, which had dominated the political debate, with deliberate references to characteristics traditionally ascribed to women, such as emotions and caring (Birnbaum 1986: 83). Groups were forming inside and outside the parties, as local 'collectives', sometimes specifically related to campaign goals like legal abortion or autonomous health clinics. This new form of political action by women was remarkably effective in improving welfare areas as defined by women. A divorce law was 'suddenly' passed in 1970, and nursery school legislation followed in 1971 together with protective legislation for working mothers and a repeal of the law prohibiting birth control information. Feminists took up the issue of sexual violence as early as 1976, with simultaneous demonstrations throughout Italy under the banner 'Let's reclaim the night' (Bono and Kemp 1991: 386).

The legalisation of abortion in 1978 was unexpected in a country steeped in Catholicism. Demands for legalised abortion had been formulated by the *Movimento di liberazione della donna* in 1971. Italy shows an interesting interplay of power and legitimating processes between parliamentary democracy (wrestling with unstable coalition governments) and the recourse to referenda where non-party groupings and social movements can exert their influence more directly. For instance, the divorce and abortion legislation was passed by parliament, but soon afterwards challenged by conservative circles calling for referenda. However, both attempts at repeal were defeated in the referenda (Birnbaum 1986:103).

Feminists in Italy cut across all organisational structures and displayed a distrust of organised power. Nevertheless they became a political force in the mid-1980s also within established structures like the Communist Party (then the PCI). Within circles of the Catholic Church inspired by Vatican II and liberation theology, feminist nuns and theologians gained prominence (for example, Roberta Fossati, Lidia Menapace, Rossana Rossanda and Adriana Zarri). However, the late 1980s brought a marked reduction in public activities by feminist groups, either because action had become institutionalised in 'services' through the rise in general voluntary 'welfare' activities, or because of a further fragmentation of society in the wake of the growing affluence of the middle class. The impact of feminism on social work training in Italy seems to have been marginal.

By contrast, feminism in Spain, which developed later, was less effective politically and in its influence on welfare developments. The new constitution introduced in 1978 after the end of the Franco regime prohibits in article 14 any sex discrimination and affirms the equality of husband and wife (articles 32 and 39), but these constitutional changes had a slow and uneven impact on the actual position of women in Spanish society (Duran and Gallego 1986: 202). The numerous women's groups that did emerge during the 1970s had a small though vociferous and radical following, mainly of professional and middle-class women. On the whole women did not penetrate effectively into political or trade union organisations, which left the traditional economic division of labour largely untouched. Women felt let down by the newly formed democratic parties and organisations.

> Nobody at that time had any experience of normal political practice. For the groups of women that had struggled for democracy in their political parties and trade unions, with no lessening of their feminist convictions, it was logical to assume that these organizations would take up, as part of their responsibility, the rights and claims of women'.
>
> (ibid.: 209)

In Ireland the country's constitution still ties women to domestic and family duties. Article 41.2.1 states:

> 1. In particular, the State recognises that by her life within the home, woman gives to the State a support without which the common good cannot be achieved.

> 2. The State shall, therefore, endeavour to ensure that mothers shall not be obliged by economic necessity to engage in labour to the neglect of their duties in the home.

'In practice, the State ensured that women did not work outside the home not by removing "economic necessity" but by active prevention' (Beale 1986: 7). The constitution also prohibits divorce and abortion. Nevertheless, legislation on equal pay and employment equality was introduced in 1974 and 1977 respectively, partly as a result of EC directives, partly as a response to the demands of women's groups that did form in Ireland. As in other countries women set up Rape Crisis Centres, refuges for women fleeing violent relationships, and family planning centres, against initially vigorous resistance by the establishment. But it is perhaps a distinguishing feature of the women's movement in Ireland that working-class women in urban areas have become very active on poverty issues, organise education and advice centres and take a lead on welfare rights issues, further encouraged by the election of Mary Robinson, a leading civil rights lawyer, to the office of president of the country.

Although the Catholic Church officially maintains its familiar repressive stance against women, many nuns express practical solidarity with the women's movement by organising women's hostels and living in private houses on housing estates which become meeting places for women's groups and centres for community action. The issue of abortion, more than any other issue, brought to light the hypocrisy of 'total prohibitions' which compel some women to find their own private and secret solutions, often by availing themselves of abortion services in Britain. Women's advice groups, as well as social workers generally, constantly risk breaking the law by practising good social work in encouraging women to make their own choices on the basis of open information.

The observation that women in all the West European countries resorted to broadly similar forms of action with converging goals such as women's refuges, alternative health centres, neighbourhood pre-school projects and adult education schemes, as well as leading civil rights campaigns in countries with quite differing political structures and cultural traditions, is a sign of women creating their own forms of politics, outside and beyond the politics of the nation state. As Rose (1986: 82) states: 'In "Three Guineas" Virginia Woolf wrote that women "have no country". In the sense that women have not been political subjects and thus created any country, it is perhaps easier for feminists to respond to the inner connections for women within the present crisis.' This also suggests that feminist politics are essentially about welfare, but welfare in a revised form: feminist analysis of welfare is international and cuts across the 'masculinist and nationalistic construction of the welfare state debate' (ibid).

The example of the women's movement illustrates some of the general features of new social movements and their general relevance to social work. Firstly, they 'don't fit' conventional categories and structures of political organisations, class interests and public action. They eschew hierarchies and role specialisation, although they sometimes mesh with established structures. They appear fragmented yet form networks, they focus on tangible concerns and yet demonstrate their global implications, they are inspired by high principles yet relativise all dogma. Secondly, they acknowledge and value self-actualisation, process and group relationships as essential aspects of action and social change leading to autonomy and identity (Offe 1985: 829). Thirdly, 'whereas prior social movements fought to secure political and economic rights from the state and other institutional actors, new social movements target their activities away from the state' (D'Anieri, Ernst and Kier 1990: 446).

These characteristics have an affinity with social work's traditional way of operating, its emphasis on personal relationships, its reluctance to become absorbed in official structures and its complex, uncertain class structure. The re-emergence of feminism also helped social work to examine its own gender composition anew: only in the Netherlands are male students almost equally strongly represented on social work courses, in Germany and the UK their proportion is only one-third and in France, Greece, Italy, Portugal and Spain they amount to ten per cent or less of the student body (Brauns and Kramer 1991: 89). Why redress this seeming 'imbalance' when it offers the potential of articulating social concerns in a manner appropriate to the political dynamics of the present time?

THE RISE IN VOLUNTARY INITIATIVES

Social movement also challenge social work to re-examine its relationships with volunteers and self-help initiatives, relationships which are so uneasy because they are reminders of social work's pre-professional past and professional insecurity. Social movements are not merely an attempt to fill gaps in the provisions of services, they also provide alternative modes of realising social solidarity which the state is no longer credited with. All European countries experienced the international surge in voluntary organisations which began in the 1970s (Adams 1990: 24). In the UK the number of registered charities doubled between 1970 and 1986 to reach a total of 158,000 (Evandrou, Falkingham and Glennerster 1991: 256). In Italy almost 60 per cent of associations that existed in 1989 had been founded since after 1970 (CENSIS 1989: 61). Most national self-help organisations in the Netherlands started to form and organise in the mid-1970s and have taken off very rapidly, articulating concerns and interests in all areas of 'welfare' (Bakker and Karel 1983: 161). Even in France, a country with a heavy reliance on state services instead of a strong tradition of charity and voluntarism, the number of new associations in the social and cultural field escalated by over 20 per cent annually since 1981 to amount to more than half a million (Ferrand-Bechmann and Murswieck 1987: 57).

There are indications that the commitment to voluntary and self-help activities does not represent a return to 'Victorian values' and is not intended to replace but to supplement public services.

In a representative survey of German households it was found: (1) that only 3.2 per cent of the population have experienced self-help groups; (2) that most of those in favour of self-help are middle-class; (3) that most of the people who use self-help groups do not see them as an alternative, but as an important *addition* to the public services; and (4) that in spite of all the talk about excesses and misuse of the social and health services, three-quarters of all social and health complaints are met by primary helpers – e.g. 80 per cent of the bedridden are cared for in the family homes; only 5 per cent of whom use additional out-patient nursing services.

(Grunow 1986:200)

In the mid-1980s the growing number of self-help groups in Germany was estimated to have reached about 40,000 involving up to 600,000 people. The proportion of groups forming around different issues is probably representative of other European countries. Cooperatives topped the list with over 10,000 projects, followed by groups addressing mental and physical health issues (the majority dealing with alcoholism), Third World initiatives, and youth and unemployment centres. About 1,000 women's projects were counted and an equal number of peace groups. A far lower number had elderly and homeless people among their projects, an indication of how the concept by its very nature tends to benefit the already better-off in society and fragments participants according to their categories of need

(Nowak 1988: 99–100). Nevertheless, in Grunow's survey a much larger proportion of the population (about one-third) expressed interest in becoming involved in self-help groups, largely with the aim of expressing their concern to do something useful for society, but also in order to 'limit bureaucratic and professional inflexibility and arrogance which is seen as endemic in the welfare system' (Grunow 1986: 202).

Also important is the trend towards local 'contact and information centres for self-help initiatives' being instigated all over Germany (about 120 in 1990; Deimer 1992: 1194), and often run in conjunction with the big non-governmental welfare associations. Some, like the centre in Berlin, see themselves having a community development role with the intention of engaging wider sectors of the population than the traditional middle-class volunteers. The Berlin example sparked off a similar development in the Flemish part of Belgium and gave self-help initiatives there a high public profile (Branckaerts 1983: 151). Through their coordinating function the boundaries between volunteers, self-help groups, neighbourhood initiatives and established charities dissolve, although the centres themselves have to fight against incorporation into the politics of public cuts and private self-interests.

Local employment creation projects, combining economic, cultural and social functions, are springing into life in poor and rich European countries alike. In Lioni, a small town near Naples in Italy, a local development cooperative launched the *Museo Vivo* project which created employment at a museum of local culture (ERGO 1990: 3). In Allihies, a remote village in the West of Ireland, a crafts and folklore project specialising in local history is making a small contribution to stemming the tide of emigration which left the area demoralised and to strengthening the cultural roots of the population. In Norberg, a small town in Sweden hit by the closure of steel mills, a theatre festival gave rise to local mobilisation against the closures and to alternative employment projects (Nilsson and Wadeskog 1988: 48).

As far as government policies are concerned, the re-emergence of volunteers and spontaneous welfare initiatives provides a welcome boost to their restrictive fiscal policies. It was found that in Germany 'the self-help movement is increasingly used as a legitimation for the cutbacks in welfare benefits . . . The main prong of the "attack" is directed at the heart of the recent developments of the welfare state: the personal (professional) services' (Grunow 1986: 200). Even in Scandinavian countries, where a dismantling of the basic welfare state structure is not (yet?) on the agenda, emphasis is placed on voluntary efforts and an appeal to the responsibility of individuals, families and voluntary groups. The government's long-term plan for 1986–1989 in Norway stated the following:

> The goal must be a society where not only the public sector, but also individuals, neighbourhoods, and voluntary groups to a greater degree feel responsibility for providing contact, care and support. The important contribution to community well-being which is today realized by voluntary groups and individuals must be further stimulated. Emphasis must be given to programs which can mobilize volunteers and preventive activity in neighbourhood environments. The tendency to exaggerate professional and institutional care within the health and social welfare sector must be countered by favoring simple, locally based projects with a multi-professional approach.
>
> (quoted in Hildeng 1991: 176f.)

The emergence of new social movements, and especially of self-help initiatives, contains a complex message for social work spelling at once danger and new opportunities. The danger lies in the political exploitation of people's willingness to step into the breach of inadequate public provisions with voluntary efforts. There are indications that the critique implied in social movements is being transformed into compliance with conservative policies through manipulative funding policies (Offe 1985: 818), for instance in the allocation of state lottery money to voluntary groups in Ireland. The need for resource shortages to be bridged by voluntary fund-raising brings an erosion of rights and entitlements and a further bias in favour of middle-class initiatives (Finch 1984: 17) on top of accentuated inequalities between people representing different categories of need. 'Empowerment' can become a facade hiding self-interest 'unless it is accompanied by the commitment to challenging and combatting injustice and oppression' (Ward and Mullender 1991a: 22).

But a realisation of the pervasive nature of oppression has caused self-help initiatives to feel solidarity with other oppressed groups and among themselves. 'Our aim is full participation or equality for all disabled people . . . disabled people are the only people who can translate this aim into reality' states the Derby-shire Coalition of Disabled People (quoted in Collins and Stein 1989: 92). Self-help groups begin to form among people who were traditionally characterised as 'dependent on services', like the 'Grey Panthers', who constitute a very vociferous lobby of elderly people in Germany in the fight against cuts in services and benefits (Deneke 1983: 140).

Women, above all, have experienced this political cross-current engulfing social movements: 'mobilisation from below', if it wants to effect structural change, needs at some stage to involve itself with the centres of power, but as the effectiveness of autonomous groups grows so does the danger of 'incor-poration from above', as Hernes demonstrated in her European study on the role of women in voluntary associations and organisations (Hernes 1984). She found differences between European countries in the proportion to which women enter official politics after having been part of the women's move-ment, but this is an unreliable measure of their political effec-tiveness: their refusal to become incorporated might bear witness to their political astuteness and the transformation of politics brought about by women (Hernes 1984: 28).

COMMUNITY DEVELOPMENT OR COMMUNITY ACTION?

Social work encountered the dynamics affecting social move-ments perhaps most immediately in the area of community work. In the Netherlands community work had a prominent part in social reconstruction after the Second World War, initially totally 'incorporated' into the government policy of rapid industrialisation and improved social planning. By the start of the 1960s all cities and communes over 75,000 in-habitants had a neighbourhood-based form of community work primarily to coordinate the influence of established interest groupings (of the churches, trade unions and other civil organ-isations, (see above, Chapter 1). Since the start of the 1970s community work, in the light of the profound social critique of the late 1960s, began to meet the need for stronger local participation and for mediation between state and population (Ellemers 1984: 142).

Community work was very much promoted by the government through all three periods, since 1965 through the Department for Culture, Leisure and Social work which initiated the founding of the Dutch Institute for Society-building (*Nederlands institut voor maatschappelijke opbouw* – NIMO). Community work became an answer to the social crisis precipitated by the unrest of the 1960s. Community work gave the illusion of participation while in fact engaging only 'community activists', 'leaders' of the residential areas. Their view of community defined as residential neighbourhood produced recreational improvements and better services but omitted the politically contentious matters of employment and poverty (Sielert 1985: 187). The final irony was that by 1990 barely 700 community workers were still in post when there had been over 3,000 in the 1970s (McConnell 1991: 106), and 'incorporation' certainly was not rewarded by the system.

A similar dilemma affected community workers in Greece, a country with a political culture totally different from the Netherlands. Most (largely EC-funded) community development programmes in the late 1980s 'are focused around specific services rather than questions of social rights and advocacy, as there is no legitimate criterion for such roles by community workers. This domain is claimed by political parties, social movements and labour organisations.' (Stathopoulos 1991: 126). The pressure on professionals is to provide services; turning to rights issues can cause resistance and competition with political movements who claim this as their prerogative.

This was also the experience of many community workers involved in the British Community Development Projects and later in various phases of the EC Combat Poverty Programme. Their task, to investigate and address the local causes of poverty, had inevitable political overtones and those projects that tried to challenge the vested political and economic interests did not as a rule survive the transfer to national public funding. Projects in the crisis areas selected (rural areas in Greece, Ireland, the south of Italy, Portugal and Spain and inner urban areas in the more prosperous regions) eventually had to settle for job and skills training in response to unemployment, and for promoting more sensitive public services as an 'answer' to discrimination (Room 1989: 6–7). The third EC programme on poverty, launched in 1989, stresses 'integration of the economically and socially less privileged groups in society' through partnership with public bodies, voluntary organisations, employers and trade unions. It remains to be seen whether this apparent success of 'mobilisation from below' in terms of bringing the issue of poverty from the margins to the structural centres of power will be swallowed up by 'incorporation from above'. The UK experience with community work does not augur well: 'Community work never became a real social movement' (Marilyn Taylor in Miller and Bryant 1990: 322). Perhaps the movement will start at a cross-national level as networking across Europe has added to that growing sense of confidence in oppressed groups refusing to accept the blame for their disadvantaged position.

CIVIL SOCIETY IN CENTRAL AND EASTERN EUROPE

The dramatic political changes in the formerly communist countries in Central and Eastern Europe demonstrated dramatically the power of social movements against unresponsive, unaccountable systems that had sought to extinguish civil society by total incorporation. What is at stake in the development and reorganisation of welfare services under changed political conditions is whether they will further or hinder the development of a civil society, reproduce dependency or enhance welfare on the basis of solidarity and rights.

The rebuilding of social services and social work in Poland, for instance, needs to take account of the strange relationship between the state services and volunteers that had developed during the last twenty-five years of communist rule. Social welfare centres staffed by psychologists, sociologists, lawyers and social workers were introduced in 1964. The tasks of the full-time workers consisted mainly of the administration of welfare benefits and the organisation and coordination of voluntary associations. Most of the face-to-face social work was carried out by volunteers (some 44,000 in 1983, as against 9,500 social workers) who worked under the direction of the social workers (of whom only about 30 per cent were professionally trained) (Ksiezopolski and Sienko 1988: 300). The hierarchical organisation of the system, reflecting the nature of the communist state and its monopoly of power, limited the initiative of workers and volunteers alike. 'They do mainly what the state has commissioned them to do' (Ksiezopolski and Sienko 1988: 302) and a survey in the early 1980s noted a dwindling of volunteers accompanied by 'doubts about the sense of collective voluntary activity in its present institutional form' (ibid.: 309). There are exceptions, however. In Poland, as in many West European societies, parents of children with learning difficulties and other congenital illnesses organised themselves in an effort to over-come the notorious lack of state services.

Another initiative that also gained some new momentum was *Monar* (Youth movement for counteracting drug habits), founded in 1981 but one year later already incorporated into the public health care system. Nevertheless this movement inspired many young people to participate and managed to raise public awareness on drug dependency.

Caritas, the welfare organisation of the Catholic Church, had operated independently from the state in the immediate post-war years, but in 1950 it was nationalised under the title 'Catholic Union Caritas' and remained under the supervision of the Polish communist state, posing acute moral dilemmas for its members. The organisation had a reputation for providing some of the best care and treatment institutions in the country, but more significantly, perhaps, many voluntary initiatives flourished at the parish level, many of them in a semi-clandestine manner and their full scope only became known after the fall of the regime when Caritas began to resume its former tasks as the main rallying point for voluntary and professional care work (Constable and Przybylska, forthcoming).

Sociologists disagree over whether the emergence of the trade union movement Solidarity in 1980 signalled a rebirth of civil society in Poland or of 'political society' (Pelczynski 1988: 369) defined purely from its opposition to the communist state. But despite its concentration on workers' rights and political changes, self-help initiatives in welfare matters also developed under its umbrella which often merged with those of the Catholic Church.

The rebuilding of social services after the end of communism in the Czech and Slovakian Republics had to take cognizance of the fact that the old regime had attempted to annihilate civil society completely. This accentuated the predicament for plan-ners – how to distinguish legitimate social policy functions of the state from, on the one hand, the ideological misuse they had suffered previously and, on the other, from a narrow economism with its 'nihilistic approach to social needs' which absolves the state from all responsibility (Castle-Kanerova 1992: 105). This dilemma centres on the question of how the transition to 'autonomous citizenship' is to be mediated. The events of 1968 have left the former Czechoslovakia with a sense of the power of citizens taking action themselves that now needs to be applied to the new tasks.

> The two seemingly contradictory views, one of the minimal state with the maximum of 'active democratic' participation by the individuals themselves, and the other with the state as a dominant institution in the economic lives of the people, are resolved in the light of the ultimate goal, which is a 'legal state', not the arbitrary administrative system of the past.
>
> (Castle-Kanerova 1992: 105)

But it is as yet unclear whether the state in former communist countries will be capable of acquiring this role and legitimacy. Criticism of the excessive power of the state can rapidly turn into calls for a stronger state in the absence of intermediary structures which, when decreed by the state, reproduce similar dilemmas: participation by command from above cancels itself out. Referring to the situation in Poland at the start of the 1990s, Kolarska-Bobinska comments:

> The state of anomy favours social disintegration and is an essential barrier to social participation and to the undertaking of self-organizing actions starting from the grass roots. The question arises whether civil society can develop in a situation of anomy.
>
> (Kolarska-Bobinska 1992: 186)

In this precarious situation it becomes essential that social projects see themselves as part of a new civil society and not as servants of the state. This is the arena in which the 'anti-political politics' (Havel 1988: 396) of the former dissidents need to form and grow again. There are indications, however, that many campaigns have a decidedly conservative outlook in an attempt to link up with a 'lost past' and to imitate the consumerist preoccupation of Western societies (Tausz 1990: 306). It is interesting to note that the Protestant Church of the GDR had much greater direct influence over its social services, which operated often in opposition to communism, than it did after German unification. The host of laws and regulations operating in the Federal Republic of Germany, which aim at 'incorporating' the non-statutory sector into the totality of its welfare provisions, have a restricting effect. Activities have to be tailored to the limits set by these laws and regulations (Willenberg 1992: 59).

For this reason the formulation of social work methods in Central and East European countries had to take place with an eye towards the rebuilding of civil society. To hide behind the psychologically legitimated individualism characteristic of Western social work traditions would add to the disenfranchisement of social service users, accentuate their deprivation and delay the development of a new civil society. This means being prepared for conflicts perhaps becoming more visible rather than being smothered by welfare measures.

> If the social sphere were to become more visible and capable of recognizing itself this would encourage the establishment of more genuine relations of mutual assistance, even if the procedures governing them would be more conflict-prone . . . The acceptance of conflict lies at the heart of the process of the self-production of the social. Far from denying or ignoring conflict under the guise of an improbable 'consensus', the democratic ideal makes such conflict productive and constructive.
>
> (Rosanvallon 1988: 211)

COMMUNITY CARE, PURCHASERS AND PROVIDERS

Developments in social services in former communist countries therefore have perhaps direct relevance to the restructuring of social services in West European countries like the UK where profound changes were instigated at the start of the 1990s.

'Community care' became a central concept in the British debate, and is a term which seems to endorse both the professional criticism of an over-reliance on residential and institutional care and the philosophy of self-help movements. Two official reports had noted, unsurprisingly, the enormous contribution that informal care continues to make to overall welfare services despite the growth of the welfare state. The Wolfendon Committee (1978) recognised that family members and other informal carers will have to shoulder the bulk of care in a society in which demographic changes alone necessitate more care, much like the Griffiths Report ten years later which affirmed:

> Families, friends, neighbours and other local people provide the majority of care in response to needs which they are uniquely well placed to identify and respond to. This will continue to be the primary means by which people are enabled to live normal lives in community settings.
>
> (Griffiths Report 1988: 5)

But the political programme for the restructuring of health and social services in the UK continued a 'top down' approach of decentralisation and diversification 'by decree' or rather 'by market incentive', rather than by recognising what participation by users and carers actually means. In Northern Ireland, where social and health services were already merged in 1985 to form joint boards directly under the DHSS, four community units under these boards applied for trust status in 1992. For the first time in the UK a community-based social work service was set up completely outside the local authorities' control. 'There is no obligation to include service users in their decision-making structure', John Park, chair of BASW in Northern Ireland, is quoted as saying (Neate 1992: 14).

Some argue that the introduction of the 'purchaser/provider' scenario will have a stifling effect on the 'culture of volunteerism' and in particular on its critical and radical dynamics out of which self-help and other new social movements could develop. Judged by criteria of cost-efficiency, voluntary agencies have to present their proposals in 'acceptable terms' for purchase by the statutory sector and also 'need to appear "respectable" to a range of institutional funders and individual donors' (Mullender and Cox 1992: 19). Grass-roots voluntary organisations 'are concerned they will lose their traditional role as innovators, as advocates of the interests of services users and as campaigners against the authorities who are now set to become their managers' (Langen 1990: 67). The British approach amounts to a colonisation of civil society by political interests, as is evident from the enforced adaptation to the principles of the market economy, i.e. cost-effectiveness, in social services. This is an ideological imposition equivalent to that of communist ideology 'suspending' the autonomy of civil society. Despite the lip service being paid to 'citizenship', conservative policies have eroded the democratic powers of local authorities and consistently use democratic procedures to sharpen social divisions (Johnson 1990: 216).

Surveys in Sweden in the 1970s and in Germany in 1978 and 1980 have confirmed that the 'market' is an inadequate means of distributing services and resources and leads to a mismatch between demand and supply: resources tend not to reach persons for whom they are intended, because these groups cannot articulate their needs strongly enough to trigger the market mechanisms, and resources get absorbed by groups whose needs are not of the highest priority (Oppl 1992b: 153). Germany's system of subsidiarity has produced a relatively small commercial sector. Across all welfare services in Germany (hospitals, youth support, family support, services for the elderly and for people with disabilities and people with special needs) the major nongovernmental welfare associations are responsible for 70 per cent of all services (which includes 5 per cent provided by self-help organisations), with public services responsible for 20 per cent, and commercial profit-oriented organisations for 10 per cent (Oppl 1992b: 153). Self-help organisations have to be affiliated to the big welfare associations in order to be able to claim public grants. Whether the negotiations over the resources for an agreed standard of service always result in greater user participation and autonomy is an open question in Germany.

A cornerstone of the Swedish approach to community care remains the right of all citizens to a 'reasonable level of living' contained in the Social Services Act passed in 1981:

> Public social services are to be established on a basis of democracy and solidarity, with a view to promoting economic and social security, equality of living conditions, and active participation in the life of the community. With due consideration for the responsibility of the individual for his own social situation and that of others, social services are to be aimed at liberating and developing the innate resources of individuals and groups. Social service activities are to be based on respect for the self-determination and privacy of the individual.
>
> (SFS 1980/620: Section 1)

In Swedish practice these responsibilities are delegated to the municipalities, each of which has to set up a social welfare

committee with responsibilities for comprehensive social planning and social services including personal social services. Since
the late 1980s tight financial controls have affected social
services and departments and units have had to manage their
own budgets and prioritise tasks within them. But the legal
rights of users set limits on these restrictions and it seems
unlikely that a provider/purchaser split would occur. The role of
the voluntary sector has been marginal so far, and it remains to
be seen whether the framework of social rights will be seized
upon by autonomous movements in the welfare field.

The imposed restructuring of social services also puts social
workers personally under a lot of stress. A Norwegian study of
the dilemmas faced by social workers in services whose tasks
and priorities were unclear found that this adversely affected
these workers' emotional well-being. It suggested that the only
way to overcome this was to transform agencies so that they can
be controlled by social workers in coalition with clients, in other
words that the institutionalised antagonism between workers
and clients be overturned radically, as is already the case in
'alternative' social work agencies such as hostels for abused
women and different forms of cooperatively run counselling
centres (Stjerno and Seltzer 1991: 252).

TOWARDS A RECONSTITUTED CIVIL SOCIETY

The wider European horizon in the 1990s shows that the
transformation of community care in the UK is part of a general
restructuring of the relationship between welfare state and
citizens. All welfare systems are strained under the impact of
demographic changes and rising unemployment. All have taken
steps to counter this pressure, mainly by extolling the virtues of
community care as provided by informal and voluntary carers.
At the same time, new social movements have manifested
themselves equally universally and there are signs that their
appearance represents a fundamental revision of civil society
and a crisis in the political systems. Despite the attempts by
these systems to manage, control and otherwise utilise these
movements for their own political ends the emancipatory
potential of grass-roots movements has clearly been demonstrated by the momentous changes they precipitated in parts of
Central and Eastern Europe. The fundamental controversy is

not so much about the level of social services, nor is it about whether state services are better or worse than private ones; it is about how solidarity, the 'social' in society, can be substantiated.

> Reducing the state intervention requirement and promoting sociability therefore go hand in hand. The alternative to the welfare state is not primarily institutional, but societal. The task is to bring into being a civil society of greater density and to develop its scope for exchange and mutual support, instead of 'externalising' these needs and abandoning their satisfaction to the twin poles of market or state.
>
> (Rosanvallon 1988: 204)

Solidarity can only come about through participation, through people having a material and symbolic stake in their society and being able to scrutinise the legitimacy of their representatives in authority. This scrutiny takes its reference points increasingly from cross-European comparisons and contacts. One of the overriding characteristics of social movements has always been their internationalism. New social movements especially network extensively within and across national boundaries, a process very much encouraged by the EC itself.

The formula that we are heading for a 'welfare mix' (Evers and Wintersberger, 1988: 17) or a 'mixed economy of (private and public, voluntary and statutory) welfare' is not in itself an answer to the crisis of the welfare state but begs the question what kind of principles and values should govern these mixed arrangements. Extending his analysis of Italian changes in the welfare state to all of Europe, Donati proposes that

> *we should pass over from the delegating centralistic solidarity of the Beveridgian Welfare State to new intermediate and primary solidarities.* The first ones are those existing between categories and social strata (occupational), between territorial groups and, finally, between generations (youth, adults, old people): they concern macro-problems of vertical and horizontal redistribution. The second ones are those of the familiar, amical, neighbourhood networks, networks of smaller or bigger local communities. The first ones *do not substitute* the second ones.
>
> (Donati 1987: 38)

In other words, the essential changes need to take place and are taking place in the 'life world' (*mondo vitale*), more so than at the level of 'the system'. Greater pluralism can mean more cooperation ('synergy'), if the value of solidarity, contained in all human relations, is not externally constrained. Signs of this 'bottom up' process are the importance attributed to human relationships in campaigns of protest and resistance today, the way in which they challenge rules from a position of values, and their emphasis on holistic approaches as opposed to technocratic solutions (Donati 1988: 209).

However, what structure and form relationships, participation and legitimation will take, what kind of civil society will emerge from this crisis and what kind of welfare states will replace the old ones is hard to predict. In trying to find its bearings within the profoundly changing welfare landscape of Europe in the 1990s, social work has to become more politically discerning than ever. The issue is not whether to fall in line with the growth of voluntarism and self-help initiatives or to take a stand against them as a threat to professional standards, but whether it will be possible for social work to realise and integrate into its practice the new form of politics contained in social movements. This will require opposition to the neo-conservative programme, which tries to incorporate the voluntary sector into its politics and to restore civil society to a non-political sphere which is easy to control. In this sense, social work neither belongs on the side of the system nor is it a totally private activity. It has a role to play in the transformation of civil society and possibly in the formation of a European civil society.

> In order to emancipate itself from the state, civil society itself – its institutions of work, production, distribution, family relations, relations with nature, its very standards of rationality and progress – must be politicized through practices that belong to an intermediate sphere between 'private' pursuits and concerns, on the one side, and institutional, state-sanctioned modes of politics, on the other.
>
> (Offe 1985: 820)

In a sense, new social movements in Europe confront social work anew with very basic principles and themes from its own history:

- They call for limits to professionalism by pitting the experienced volunteer, the user, the person 'who has been through it' against the power and elitism of certified experts.
- They value process and participation rather than technical efficiency and success as the key to self-directed learning and change.
- They search for identity, personally and collectively by way of questioning the oppressive use of labels and attributes.

Exposing itself fully to these challenges may plunge social work even deeper into crisis than restrictive government policies have done so far. Or it may lead social work back to principles which have always been the essence of good social work practice and which are recognisable within the complex texture of social movements.

Chapter 6

Social work in a multicultural society

The two sides of diversity and pluralism which feature in the encounter between social movements and the nation state are also at issue in the process of European integration. Much of the initial enthusiasm for and popularity of this process stemmed from the desire to gain access to the rich diversity of cultural traditions to be found in different parts of Europe. This diversity is now in danger of being incorporated into political and commercial interests which allow it to unfold only within tightly controlled limits, the limits set by the doctrines of 'fortress Europe'. As will be made clear, social work is implicated very directly in these processes.

At the start of the 1990s Europe was situated at the cross-roads between two migration routes, each growing in significance: one from south to north as the impoverishment of the Third World becomes more pronounced and its people are no longer prepared to wait until called in as 'guests' when European industry experiences labour shortages, and one from east to west where the removal of physical and political barriers and growing economic uncertainties in Eastern Europe have created similar migratory pressures. Europe found itself also ideologically at the cross-roads between an agenda of efficiency, profit maximisation and self-interest set by the principles of a market economy and an agenda of liberal democracy, humanitarian concern and solidarity in the tradition of the European Enlightenment.

As far as the economic agenda was concerned, the incipient movement of people was precipitated within the EC by the process of European economic and political integration. This has as its main planks the free mobility of labour between EC countries (and since 1992 also between EC and EFTA countries) and the unhindered functioning of market forces for the purpose of forming a highly prosperous and economically attractive core at the centre of Europe. The economic concentration caused acute general labour shortages in the 1960s and early 1970s and continues to show a demand for skilled, highly trained labour. As a result, the status of skilled and unskilled workers became even more polarised; unskilled work meant undesirable working conditions for which industry needed a pool of cheap, available labour only to be found in the 'periphery'. These economic trends were exacerbated by demographic changes in the most highly industrialised countries of Europe, which heralded an ageing population whose retirement payments and health costs would place increasing commitments on a dwindling labour force.

By the year 2030, according to new projections based on current demographic trends, there will be 20 million fewer Germans alive than there are today. The Institute of the German Economy (IW) has calculated that the number of young people below the age of 15 will drop from 13.7 million in 1990 to 10 million in 2010 . . . The IW findings designed to support a sober case for controlled immigration at a time of heightened political debate over asylum-seekers, suggest that Germany will need at least 300,000 immigrants annually just to fill the gap in its labour market. Its employed labour force has risen in the past six years of sustained growth by 3 million, largely by the influx of foreigners, east Germans and east Europeans of German origin that marked the late 1980s.

(*Guardian*, 4 February 1992: 6)

The actual mobility of workers between European countries during the late 1980s was relatively modest. About 1.8 million employees emigrated, the flow concentrating mostly on France, Germany and the UK, and in total 4.8 million EC nationals of all the 346 million moved to another EC country. This internal mobility was far outweighed by the number of non-European nationals entering the EC – estimated to be about 7.8 million – who had taken up residence in the EC by 1990 (Eurostat 1990: 212), and there is likely to be a high number of unregistered illegal immigrants. Of these millions, refugees represented a small minority of about 1.1 million in 1988 (European Parliament 1991: 121). 'Less than 2 per cent of the world's refugees today appear as asylum-seekers in Europe annually' (Loescher 1989: 618). By far the largest number of asylum applications were lodged in Germany reaching nearly 500,000 per year in 1992 (as against under 5,000 in the UK; *Guardian* 6/11/1992:24).

The fall of the Iron Curtain and later the war in former Yugoslavia and other widespread outbreaks of violence against ethnic minorities in other former communist states brought, for the first time since the end of the Second World War, considerable numbers of refugees from neighbouring countries into the everyday lives of Europeans where before they had become accustomed to associating 'the refugee problem' with far-away places. 'This influx will create a massive challenge to western liberalism and solidarity and could endanger the stability of the welfare institutions and the economy of the different [European] countries' (Ronge 1991: 49).

Europe's humanitarian agenda, enshrined in the European Convention on Human Rights ratified in 1954, was born out of the experience of the refugee problem of the Second World War. Several countries, Austria, Germany, the Netherlands and Sweden foremost among them, had formulated liberal policies in relation to refugees and asylum-seekers that express an understanding for the suffering caused by political systems. Other countries had responded openly to particular crises – for example, Britain's admission of Asians expelled from Uganda in the 1970s. This high moral ground helped to conclude the Conference on Security and Co-operation in Europe (CSCE) with the signing of the Helsinki Accords in 1975. These were originally intended as a human rights lever against communist countries restricting the rights of ethnic minorities, but after the end of the Cold War they began to involve Western Europe in unanticipated commitments towards migrants from the East.

By the start of the 1990s the authority and value of the humanitarian agenda, which had masked and to some extent counter-balanced the economic agenda, began to wane, ceding supremacy to more blatant economic arguments. The image of 'fortress Europe' needing strong defences in order to maintain its economic and ideological dominance in the face of world competition and against the 'onslaught' of migrating masses began to replace the 'cradle of democracy' slogan. Europe's humanitarianism was further eroded by the rise in nationalism and neo-Fascism all across Europe which seized on perceived threats to national identity and exposed the weakness of mainstream parties in not having put forward 'inclusive', nonsegregational political initiatives for which the end of the Cold War would have offered new opportunities.

REFUGEES AND ASYLUM-SEEKERS

This changing scenario and its divergent underlying dynamics of political and economic interests impacted on the treatment of refugees and asylum-seekers in Europe. The Geneva Refugee Convention of 1951 defines refugees as persons who cannot return to their home for fear of persecution for reasons of race, nationality or religious or political beliefs. The European Convention on Human Rights of 1950 and the UN International Convention on Civil and Political Rights of 1966 do not as such formulate a right to asylum, but set up 'a standard of protection of human rights which necessarily does include the right of asylum as an individual right of the asylum seeker' (Weh 1987: 84). This makes protection and granting of asylum a matter independent of the economic status of the applicant. However, the practice of most European countries by the beginning of the 1990s had begun to play on the distinction between 'economic' refugees, who 'simply want a better life' and 'genuine political refugees'.

During the years immediately after the fall of the Berlin Wall it became clear that resultant changes were affecting the stability of the whole of Europe, economically and politically, and that they could not be controlled by police and military measures alone. The humanitarian image depends very much on the right mix between charity and control, on the 'case-by-case' approach so familiar to social work from the days of the Poor Law to make sure that no 'deserving cases' were being treated harshly. Welfare can easily become a substitute for rights and volunteers and professionals alike need to assess very carefully the political context in which their work is placed.

This poses acute dilemmas for social workers. In Graz, for instance, a regional centre in the south-eastern corner of Austria, the city administration had adopted relatively liberal and constructive policies towards foreign nationals arriving in ever greater numbers as migrants, refugees and asylum-seekers. Since 1990 it has operated an advice centre for refugees in conjunction with the churches and private associations, staffed by volunteers and professional and student social workers. Their range of projects have, as a shared priority, initiatives to reduce the isolation of refugees. Language and orientation courses and social and vocational skills training are offered to the immigrant groups as the most important means of integration, backed up by counselling and individual advice on how to deal with bureaucracies or search for housing and jobs. In order not to let integration become a one-sided task they also hold events and meetings with the indigenous communities, creating points of contact aimed at reducing prejudice and hostility. For school children after-school activities in mixed language groups provide opportunities for socialisation and mutual integration, although it is difficult to persuade the German-speaking youngsters to come along (Tschmelak 1992: 71).

This experience raises debates within the projects as to whether they actually contribute to the formation of ghettos, whether they deprive the children of foreign nationals of the chance to form distinct identities, and whether their assumptions about multicultural integration do not open the door to cultural domination. Ultimately their objectives are determined by hard and fast legal reference points like the requirement that children have to be proficient in the German language in order to qualify for admission as regular pupils, the national employment limits that allow a maximum of 10 per cent foreign nationals being employed, or the asylum law which will effect the eventual deportation of most of the refugees anyway. Inevitably therefore, the grass-roots work of these projects can only make sense if it includes representation and campaigning at the political level for statutory changes, although this in turn might jeopardise the project's chances of future funding (Reithofer 1992: 3).

The work of such projects quite literally operates on the (internal and international) boundaries of the welfare state and has to confront the racist assumptions of the policies which determine such boundaries.

The implications . . . of the anti-racist critique of welfare policy lead directly to the need to raise the level of policy analysis from the nation state to transnational agencies and global inequalities of welfare . . . Within Europe an emerging issue of some importance is the welfare, employment and citizenship rights of migrant workers and ethnic minorities. This in turn raises issues concerning the differential entitlements to welfare within and without fortress Europe.

(Deacon 1991: 77)

NATIONAL SOLIDARITY THROUGH WELFARE

Migrating people, vagrants and beggars traditionally pose a challenge for society as they question the principles of solidarity upon which a society is founded. Early manifestations of this challenge are the Elizabethan Vagrancy Acts, which regulated the treatment of vagrants in the self-interests of settled communities (and their emerging economic functions) and were typical of vagrancy control measure across Europe.

> There seems to be little question that the Catholic and Protestant community showed an almost equally strong tendency to transform the wandering penniless stranger into the fearful and repulsive figure of the vagrant . . . Far more than that, he was (or became in the Italy of Borromeo and Sixtus V, in France a century later) a blasphemer, a heathen, a disturber of churches, contemptuous of the sacraments of marriage and baptism: indeed, a rebel against God, and one who transgressed the solemn commandment 'Thou shalt eat thy bread in the sweat of thy brow' and shrugged off his share in the penalties of original sin.
>
> (Pullan 1976: 17)

These Acts set the scene for a kind of division of labour: on the one side, state (welfare) agencies' competence centred on establishing who can lay claim to support from the community (parish) and on what terms; private charities, on the other side, concerned themselves with the 'tidying up' of grey areas and the mitigation of hardship caused by the harsh application of state rules. Many charities trace their origins to the fact that migration for the purposes of pilgrimage or trade apprenticeship was regarded as legitimate and these migrants needed hostels for shelter, hospices for the care of the sick and dying, protection and safe passage in hostile surroundings. Sociology postulates that the primary unit of solidarity of the pre-modern era was the community, defined not necessarily just by a geographical entity such as the town or village, but also by membership of religious orders or by a common trade or language that was geographically dispersed. Only with the emergence of the European nation states did the need arise to enshrine solidarity in such abstract entities as the state, to make it conditional on the notion of 'citizenship' as a privilege. But the alien or homeless always served as a marker for the boundaries of that solidarity. 'As late as 1894, universalization of the suffrage in Belgium explicitly excluded "les mendicants et vagabonds internés dans une maison de refuge . . . par décision des juges de paix"' (Pierson 1991: 109).

Simultaneously with the forming of nation states, internal migration and indeed emigration increased as a result of accelerating industrialisation, posing a threat to newly designed national identities as well as to the personal identity of those affected by the changes. And as the traditional Poor Law structure proved inadequate to contain the new instability the task fell upon philanthropic and other personalised welfare services to constantly redefine and thereby maintain the boundaries of solidarity and to recreate a semblance of community.

> Modernity makes all being contingent, and thus a 'problem', a 'project', a 'task'. Lifting identity to the level of awareness, making it into a task – an objective of self-reflexive activity, an object of, simultaneously, individual concern and specialized institutional service – is one of the most prominent characteristics of modern times.
>
> (Baumann 1992: 680)

Welfare in its broadest sense can be regarded as the most tangible peacetime manifestation of solidarity, and of the boundaries of that solidarity. Under modern political conditions, welfare has to be organised, structured, manufactured and brought in line with the project of the nation state as an essential means of national integration.

NATIONAL SOLIDARITY THROUGH EXCLUSION

The other mechanism for the maintenance of solidarity is of an ideological nature and operates by exclusion, by drawing boundaries around an identity whose homogeneity is variously derived from language, culture, religion or ethnicity. This is not the place to go into a detailed examination of psychological theories that speculate on the necessity of an 'enemy' in the formation of personal identity, but historically there is sufficient evidence that the construction of national identity in Europe relied excessively on the identification of an enemy, on military action to secure borders and on repression and discrimination against those declared alien within those boundaries. The systematic persecution of Jews as a group of people who allegedly do not belong to any of the European states is perhaps the epitome of this process of exclusion, elimination and extermination of what is presumed to be alien and threatening. But the process was and still is repeated in the discriminatory treatment of other groups whose reputation as being nomadic, hard to pin down and hence lawless serves to justify their stigmatisation. Groups such as Romanies and Sinti across Europe (Lucassen 1991: 89), travellers in Ireland (Noonan: 1992: 19), and to some extent the Sami people in Nordic countries (Svensson 1976: 126) have been discriminated against and excluded from the protection through equal rights, social solidarity and communitarian welfare. By extension these practices can be applied to other 'new arrivals', groups of refugees, migrant workers, or simply to minority groups finding themselves 'on the wrong side of the border' in the arbitrary drawing of European boundaries (Gstettner 1988: 20).

It is precisely because of the crass ideological, racist nature of the second mechanism and its negative character that it often relies on the support of substantive, legitimating welfare measures. Rejection masquerades as caring. Differences on account of cultural traditions, structural inequalities or features which are stereotypical prejudices projected onto a group (laziness, alcoholism, etc.) get interpreted as individual failings requiring remedial attention (Dominelli 1988: 51). This distracts from the political nature of discrimination and legitimates the distance created. Welfare and thereby social work have always been dragged into this political game and it is simply impossible for social workers to presume a position of neutrality and political innocence. Together with the education system, personal social services are therefore the arenas where the sleight of hand between inclusive and exclusive solidarity can most easily occur, where an agenda of caring can become subverted most inconspicuously by an agenda of racism and discrimination.

Welfare is closely allied to the project of 'nationhood', as Bismarck's strategy showed in founding the united German Reich upon international war and internal social policy. These mechanisms are again being invoked in the creation of European nationhood in the 1990s. This underlines more vividly than at any time since the 1930s (when the social work profession failed to grasp this point) how susceptible social work could be to being hitched to the nationalist wagon. 'Altruistic passion is sluiced into the reservoirs of nationalism' so that 'patriotism transmutes individual unselfishness into national egoism' observes Niebuhr in reflecting on the experience of Fascism (Niebuhr 1948: 91).

In order to forestall this danger, social work practice in its entirety needs to be geared towards anti-racist and anti-discriminatory practice. Practice experience from different corners of Europe also makes it clear that nationalism as racism uses different 'markers' to create exclusive boundaries which need not be skin colour but may just as well be language, creed, poverty, lack of education, etc. Social workers deal with people who potentially do not belong: homeless people, people excluded from mainstream life because of their poverty, their physical or mental difficulties in coping with social demands, people who have become victims of power inequalities within the family and therefore find themselves at odds with the social postulate of the primary solidarity of the family. Essentially, the work that they do with asylum-seekers, illegal immigrants and refugees is of the same nature and draws them into comparable conflicts because national boundaries and the limits of solidarity they symbolise are ideological constructs of the same nature and serve the same purpose as discriminatory ideologies within countries.

SOCIAL WORK AND INTEGRATION

However, it appears that the pervasiveness of the racism implied in 'European integration' and its implications for social work are only gradually being realised. Looking across Europe as a whole, the tasks social workers are carrying out in relation to migrant populations, refugees, and ethnic minorities can be distinguished into different levels, which are ultimately inter-related.

At a very basic level the securing of basic necessities – shelter, food and basic income – is of immediate relevance to people newly arrived in a country. In Italy, for instance, much of the work with refugees and illegal immigrants is carried out by voluntary organisations, principally Caritas, the Catholic welfare organisation. It operates frontline advice services which coordinate the other voluntary or even statutory forms of assistance that are available. In Rome the work of the Caritas centre has snowballed in the wake of the Yugoslavian wars, the crises in Albania and of the arrival of migrants from Africa in search of work. The work of that centre is supported by governmental funds and cooperation with state services is close; nevertheless, the centre prides itself on its autonomy and in fact refers most of its callers to local parishes where volunteers organise hospitality, temporary accommodation and further assistance (CNEL 1990: 167).

An organisation of the Protestant Church in Eastern Germany started a similar service in relation to the central reception camp for 'resettlers' from Eastern Europe in Peitz near Cottbus. To pre-empt any tensions between the inhabitants of the town (approximately 5,000) and the 800 people housed in a separate part of the town (who in time will be redistributed around the whole country to make room for new arrivals), church members organise social meetings and church services as well as advice sessions alongside the information and counselling service provided by a social worker visiting the camp once a week from Berlin. Eventually the model is to be extended to all other regional camps with similar involvement by churches and volunteers (Köhler 1992). The overall objective is 'integration': assimilation into the local communities, which in the German case derives from the migrants' understanding of themselves as being of German origin, although the presenting cultural differences are profound.

In other work with refugees and migrants the threshold between 'spontaneous assistance' and regular support is most precarious, particularly with regard to accommodation where shortages exist generally in those areas most sought after by migrants, and voluntary services soon come up against their limits. Yet being able to show that one has somehow obtained satisfactory accommodation is a crucial factor for the authorities in Germany and France in allowing family members to immigrate and join the migrant workforce (Lloyd and Waters 1991: 58). This not only makes housing an immediate priority for social work projects dealing with migrant workers but inevitably involves them in housing policies and in the need to develop a strategic systematic approach.

At a second level the question of information about human and legal rights arises, since these often determine the level and duration of material support and assistance citizens of foreign countries can claim. This requires more direct contact with state agencies, either at their initiative or through advocacy and lobbying. For instance, in northern areas of Italy, such as the Emilia-Romagna area around Bologna, governmental services play an active and direct role in offering assistance to migrants through emergency hostels, an AIDS advice centre and a counselling service for victims of torture (CNEL 1990: 101). This greater readiness by the administration to show concern might be connected with the fact that in that region seasonal and other unskilled workers are an essential section of the labour force and their numbers have so far been easily 'absorbed' and 'assimilated', and also with the fact that most of those migrant workers, though originating from Africa, would have worked their way up through Italy and have thus become socialised to a degree into Italian customs (CNEL 1990: 190).

Milan has gone so far as to rely heavily on a structure of representation from among the migrant groups themselves at the *Centro Stranieri*, with the acknowledged aim of thereby diffusing political conflicts. This policy also facilitates the translation of 'needs' into responses that can be processed by administrative and bureaucratic structures. Participation is designed as an educational process and thereby as part of the 'climatisation' migrant groups are expected to undergo. The aim is also to foster, especially among young people, an understanding of 'the authorities' and of democratic processes which they might not have experienced in their country of origin (CNEL 1990: 89; 102).

In Germany and other Central European countries with an 'established' migrant population this approach developed into 'pedagogical methods' – with a fifteen-year time lag after the first children of migrant workers started attending German schools (Hamburger 1992: 1027). Teachers and youth workers were being trained how to 'deal with problems of integration', an approach which in fact problematised the pupil rather than the school system. These approaches imply that 'integration' is the unquestionable objective, that it is the alien who has to make the efforts to adjust and that assistance primarily needs to address the deficits the ethnic group has in relation to the indigenous society. A programme of integration invariably remains fixated on such deficits and thereby reproduces the existing power structure and cultural hegemony.

SOCIAL WORK AND INTERCULTURAL EDUCATION

Would it be possible instead to aim for cultural diversity and co-existence instead of 'integration'? Switzerland is frequently cited as an example of successful multiculturalism. Why has ethnic integration in the multicultural Swiss state worked, at least as far as the integration of the three 'native' dominant cultures associated with the German, French and Italian language are concerned? One suggested factor is that the state is organised on a strict territorial basis. Citizens are incorporated into the state by virtue of their being members of local communities and cantons, which politically form the Swiss confederation and have a considerable degree of political autonomy, not by virtue of their membership of ethnic groupings. This, by contrast with the Belgian, the former Yugoslavian, and particularly the German model, de-emphasises the political significance of ethnicity and emphasises instead the equality of individuals before the law (Schmid 1981: 152). In addition, the relatively equal distribution of economic opportunities across all three linguistic communities, proportionality in public appointments and the civil service and a political culture favouring compromise stabilise the political and educational success of Swiss multiculturalism and secure the political credibility of the concept of pluralism. 'Despite its heterogeneity, Switzerland has been able to establish a common "civil culture" that transcends cultural and ethnic boundaries' (ibid.).

The Swiss experience and other examples of multilingual societies, turned into a framework for intervention, gave rise in the 1980s to a model of 'intercultural pedagogy'. It proposes a basic programme with three steps. The starting point is fostering tolerance towards what appears strange, linked to a critical questioning of one's own position. It moves on to providing opportunities for joint activities, projects or campaigns in which solidarity can be expressed. Finally, these two steps should lead to the recognition and formulation of values which are common to different cultural positions (Boos-Nünning in Hamburger 1991: 96). This approach is of great relevance within the school system, and particularly at the pre-school and primary school level where intercultural pedagogy can contribute both to a reduction of prejudices during crucial years of child development and to opportunities for children of parents born abroad to identify more easily with their culture and language and thereby prepare children for a life in a multicultural society (Filtzinger and Johann 1992: 16–17). The approach certainly goes much further than 'integration' in accepting the legitimacy of different value positions and therefore of the continued fundamental diversity in every community. This ties in with other 'radical' models of education such as community education as a means of articulating the variety of traditions and interests in neighbourhoods with high cultural diversity along the lines of Freire's Pedagogy of the Oppressed (Friesenhahn 1988: 156).

Critical observers of the intercultural approach in Germany note that it had its main constituency among 'alternative groups' and the Green movement, groups who saw themselves at odds with the 'dominant culture' of society and who might have an interest in projecting their longing for and belonging to a 'new age' onto 'exotic' cultural traditions, often ignoring the conflicts and contradictions inherent in those traditions and turning a blind eye to aspects that do not fit into the idealised programme, like the treatment of women in certain religious traditions. The most contentious aspect of the approach is its tendency to objectify the notion of culture. It presupposes culture as something original, a quality inherent in people's behaviour and outside the self-reflectiveness of modernity, an understanding of culture which is ironically akin to the very nationalism it is trying to dismantle (Hamburger 1991: 96).

Politically these also seem to be the limitations of the Swiss concept of multiculturalism. It has produced stability and toleration in relation to the accepted range of 'cultures' of its own nationals, but there is still much insecurity, and hostility is often felt towards migrant workers and asylum-seekers. Foreign nationals (still termed 'guest workers' in contrast to, for instance, Sweden, where they were at least always recognised as immigrants) since the 1970s have been permitted to stay for longer periods but are still largely confined to lower-paid jobs. The absence of an immigration policy reinforces their uncertain status, with residence permits only being considered on the basis of a federal investigation and after a stay of at least ten years (Schmid 1981: 143). All these differences do not feature in the 'cultural toleration' discourse. During the 1980s Switzerland also drastically restricted access to asylum-seekers. Whereas before 1980 about 80 per cent of the about 1,000 asylum-seekers per year would be recognised as refugees, in 1989 only 197 out of 12,708 applicants were granted asylum (Meyer 1991: 100). It is difficult under these circumstances for workers in 'multicultural projects' to avoid being drawn into the political mechanisms of discrimination. Cultural differences, which such projects seek to highlight, might well be used by populist politicians to justify discriminatory practices.

The crucial issues a multicultural approach must confront are whether the acceptance shown to certain groups and certain 'differences' is not in itself again excluding others, and related to that whether the acceptance of cultural diversity is backed by equal access to material resources and equal legal rights. A study among German teachers of their attitudes to multicultural education found a majority of them in favour of this approach. But most also underestimated the actual national and ethnic diversity among their pupils and seemed to be aware only of the largest minority groups. Most grouped the minorities by their nationality as a substitute for ethnicity, disregarding other differences within national groups (Diehm 1992: 107). 'The primary emphasis in multiculturalist analysis is on ethnicity, such that economic and sexual differentiations within the minority communities, for example, continue to be ignored' (Rattansi 1992: 38–9).

It makes a crucial difference whether 'ethnicity' is being ascribed to a group by members of the dominant 'host' society or whether migrants, minorities and refugees are given the means to define the nature and scope of their own identity. Welfare and education can easily become substitutes for democratic rights and justice in social policy, and social workers have to beware of promoting solidarity without critically addressing the rules under which it is to come about. Identifying and celebrating cultural differences through community festivals or features in the media is no substitute for exposing the social and political processes whereby cultural differences get constructed and made to serve distinct power interests, both between and within ethnic groups. This is not to deny the validity of the intercultural approach; but in order to give it validity and legitimacy, in order to differentiate it from ideological misuses of culture and ethnicity, in order finally to make it practicable and effective, it needs to be placed in the context of a critique of discrimination and racism as a feature of all European societies.

Chapter 7

Social work and anti-racist practice

In developing an anti-racist and anti-discriminatory orientation of practice, social work has to remain conscious that inclusive or exclusive practices against groups like travelling people, foreigners or asylum-seekers are not primarily a matter of individual likes and dislikes, of personal attitudes, but the product of systematic policies which frame social work interventions. This is not to say that values, and above all the value of tolerance, do not have a place in social work and social work training, but as the impact of Fascism on welfare showed, they are easily subverted and need to be anchored in organisational and legal structures. Josephine Kwhali's comments on social work in the UK apply to social work practice across Europe:

> Social workers operate at the interface between those with influence and power and those who are relatively powerless. The power and authority invested in the social worker's role means that she or he can be instrumental in curtailing the freedoms and liberties of individuals and families and imposing definitions of normality on those whose own definitions are seldom heard and acknowledged as having validity ... Issues of control, containment, inequality and oppression are central not simply to the social worker's daily tasks, responsibilities and dilemmas but to the wider organizational and societal context within which social work is located.
>
> (Kwhali 1991: 41)

EUROPEAN ASYLUM POLICY

Racism in Europe has to be seen in the context of the prevailing political climate in the 1990s and the way in which policies construct ethnicity and nationalist identity. For instance, a small country like Austria, placed on the border with the Iron Curtain and with a population of 7.6 million, experienced the arrival of over 2 million foreign people from 1950 to 1991, many of them refugees, of whom 650,00 remained and settled in the country. Its asylum law until 1992 had been 'liberal' and it recognised, together with Switzerland and Sweden, the highest number of refugees per head of population in Europe (Weh 1987: 51). After the 1956 uprising 300,000 Hungarians sought refuge in Austria alone and after the Soviet repression of the Prague Spring in 1968 162,000 people from Czechoslovakia fled there (Münz 1992: 37).

The reception and eventual integration of refugees from communist countries served to enhance internal solidarity, in Austria as well as in Germany, by focusing on external boundaries. The Berlin Wall and the Iron Curtain symbolised this dual function of the boundary, and those who managed to cross it or were brought to the West on account of various exchange agreements enjoyed the immediate protection of Western countries and especially of German citizenship. Indeed, the threatening mass emigration of East Germans in 1989 precipitated the eventual overthrow of the system there and in neighbouring countries. These refugees fitted into the ideological constructs of the West as martyrs and heroes and therefore 'deserved' protection and solidarity (notwithstanding their often miserly actual treatment). After the fall of the Iron Curtain and the removal of barbed wire, minefields and watchtowers on the eastern borders of Central Europe the political status of migrants changed radically. Now they began to be portrayed as a drain on resources, a threat to social stability; police and armed forces in Germany and Austria began to patrol the borders, replacing the barbed wire. In the face of the civil war in former Yugoslavia, EC countries and countries seeking EC membership began tightening their asylum practices in a way that gives scant regard to the spirit of human rights conventions and in fact places insurmountable practical obstacles in the way of refugees (the requirement, for instance, to apply for visas before entering the country or carrying documentary proof of identity). The common core of these policies is the externalisation and individualisation of conflict. Migrants and refugees themselves are portrayed as 'the problem'.

Europe was moving towards a joint policy on immigration and refugees from 1977 when the Council of Europe set up its Ad Hoc Committee of Experts on the Legal Aspects of Territorial Asylum, Refugees and Stateless Persons (CAHAR). There were considerable tensions between the interests of 'transit countries' like Italy and Austria and 'destination countries', mainly Germany and the Scandinavian countries, as it was proposed to place the responsibility for examining asylum applications with the country of first entry (Loescher 1989: 628). It is highly significant that the EC line of policies more specifically developed out of the work of the TREVI group, instituted in 1975 in Rome as a standing conference of ministers with security briefs. TREVI ('Terrorism, Radicalism, Extremism, Violence, International') grouped the asylum question together with terrorism and criminality, and the processing of refugees under the heading of 'security' became a feature of the 'Schengen Group' of countries (originally Belgium, France, Germany, Luxembourg and the Netherlands, which had been joined by Denmark, Italy, Spain and Portugal by 1991; Paul 1991: 62) who agreed in 1985 to harmonise their security policies and to transfer all controls from internal to external borders (EEC 85/C 210/02). The meetings of the security committees are not publicised and do not come under the authority of the EC Commission (Bunyan 1991: 22). The Dublin Agreement of 15 June 1990 formed the basis of a uniform EC-wide asylum policy, whose central points are that applications for asylum should be dealt with by the country which has first granted a visa or temporary residence to the refugee and that an application can only be made in one EC country. All this requires shared information systems covering asylum-seekers along with other 'security risks' such as terrorists and drug smugglers. The simplified assessment procedures are designed to reduce the waiting time and the associated high costs. They will also give governments a greater margin of discretion on the admission of certain categories of applicants.

MIGRANT WORKERS

A similar fundamental ambivalence attaches to migrant workers and their acceptance and protection. An expansionist European economy during the 1960s recruited millions of workers from the Caribbean, the Indian subcontinent, North Africa and South-

East Asia for European countries with former colonies in those parts of the world and from Mediterranean countries for Germany, Austria and Switzerland. During those years many illegal workers were tolerated as vital to particular sectors of the economy although they always remained vulnerable to deportation and had few legal rights.

At the beginning of the 1990s the economic priorities were beginning to change. The growing prosperity of populations in Europe, linked to the impoverishment of Third World countries and starvation in Africa, gave rise to fears (and their political exploitation) that Europe might be about to experience an invasion of poor people seeking a share in the prosperity. As a result immigration policies began to use the category of 'economic refugees' to distinguish this group of people from political refugees and asylum-seekers on the one hand and from (contracted) migrant workers on the other, ultimately in order to dispute their claims to residence in Europe. In autumn 1992 some seven hundred French police broke up a makeshift camp in the Paris suburb of Vincennes which had accommodated 683 immigrants from Mali. The action was designed to demonstrate the government's determination to deter more migrants from entering France. A report by the organisation *Intégration* showed that 'famine was having a growing impact on immigration. The main factor for the growth in numbers was poverty in sub-Saharan Africa where some villages depended for up to 80 per cent of their income on remittances by immigrants' (*Guardian* 1/11/1992: 9). If their desire to enter Europe can be portrayed as a matter of economic opportunism rather than a result of actual threats to their lives (and the starving masses of north-east Africa are unlikely to reach Europe anyway) it becomes easier to refuse entry while maintaining a humanitarian appearance. In any case, the political systems, with reference to the labour requirements of industry, want to keep their options open for 'spare labour power'.

The criteria used for the selection of 'welcome' migrant groups are, on the one hand, the level of training and skills migrants might already possess, and on the other hand the 'ability to integrate smoothly' which is traditionally assumed to be higher in white than in black migrating populations. On both counts selected groups of East Europeans are being targeted. Germany lifted visa restrictions on people from Poland, Hungary and former Czechoslovakia and issues special work permits to workers from those countries in limited numbers (*Financial Times* 12/2/1991: 7). Of particular interest are groups of East Europeans who are descendants of German settlers and are now presented as ideal candidates. There are approximately 4 million people in Eastern Europe who consider themselves of German lineage. Three million live in Russia and of these one million have declared their intention to migrate to Germany (Köhler 1992: 38). These selective immigration and recruitment policies are based on a spurious (but in the case of Germany legally supported) notion of ethnicity and national identity and contribute to the *de facto* formulation of a European 'ethnic identity': Europe for the Europeans.

VISIBLE RACISM

While all these distinctions and policies imply racist assumptions, overt racism by organised groups further exploits this political ambivalence. It also thrives on the new wave of nationalism gripping Europe with the ending of the East–West polarisation. Outright war has erupted in many parts of Eastern Europe, unleashed by nationalist 'ethnic' policies and in pursuit of blatantly racist objectives, with probably the most notorious being the 'ethnic cleansing' through mass murder and expulsion inflicted by Serbians on the Muslim community in Bosnia. Organised pogroms against Romanies, one of the gypsy groupings of continental Europe, have again been reported in Romania where the wartime Romanian dictatorship had once collaborated with Hitler in the deportation of gypsies to concentration camps. Between 1990 and 1992 about 57,000 Romanies fled to Germany to seek asylum there (*Guardian* 2/10/1992: 23). There they have become the prime targets of attacks by organised neo-Nazi groups who terrorise them with the use of established fascist anti-gypsy sentiments. The tightening of the asylum law means that their status as refugees from persecution is unlikely to be recognised and that the overwhelming majority will be deported back to Romania and other East European countries of origin. There, nationalism contests their right of residence even though most of them have not lived a nomadic life for generations.

But neo-Fascism is by no means confined to Germany. A report by the European Parliament (European Parliament 1991) found active extremist right-wing groupings present in all European countries, including East European countries, with violence against foreign people and minorities reported from everywhere. Parties similar to the National Front in the UK achieved electoral successes under proportional representation systems in France (Le Pen and nine other *Front National* candidates first won European Parliament seats in 1984 and polled 14 per cent in the presidential elections of 1988; Lloyd and Waters 1991: 61) and Belgium (FN and *Forces Nouvelles* gained little in the French-speaking parts, but the Flemish *Vlaams Blok* polled 21 per cent in Antwerp in the 1988 EC elections; Merckx and Fekete 1991: 78), while the northern Italian 'leagues' (*Lega Lombarda*), which foster anti-southern and anti-immigrant sentiments dominated the 1992 elections in Northern Italy (*Guardian* 15/12/1992: 6).

Though relatively small in numbers and in parliamentary seats (but holding the balance of power in, for instance, the Swedish coalition government of the early 1990s) these extreme right-wing parties began to exert pressure and take the initiative in political issues during the 1980s, forcing (or facilitating) governments to accommodate populist demands for greater restrictions and cultural homogeneity, particularly in relation to the treatment of ethnic minorities, refugees and other foreign nationals. Shortages of housing and jobs were the issues setting off racial attacks which scapegoat and victimise immigrants. It is tempting to divert attention away from restrictive fiscal policies which had largely contributed to housing and job shortages by scapegoating foreign nationals together with other 'scroungers'. In addition, restrictive changes in asylum-granting practice were justified as a means of preventing a further escalation of right-wing extremism.

INITIATIVES AGAINST RACISM

According to the above-mentioned 1991 report by a committee of inquiry of the European Parliament, approaches to anti-racism and anti-discrimination in the EC countries vary widely, a fact that is reflected in an uneven legal picture (European Parliament 1991). Most member states, with the exception of Ireland, are party to the UN Convention on the Elimination of

All Forms of Racial Discrimination, but explicit legislation prohibiting racial discrimination and racism only exists in Belgium, France, Portugal and the UK. Irish legislation of 1989 specifically targets expressions of racism with the Prohibition of Incitement to Hatred Act, and Greece and the Netherlands rely on general anti-discrimination legislation. The remaining countries, Denmark, Germany, Italy, Luxembourg and Spain, refer to the UN Convention and various articles in their constitutions guaranteeing freedom and liberty to all their citizens (which tends to make the protection of non-citizens precarious).

At the EC level the 1986 Joint Declaration against Racism and Xenophobia by Council, Commission and Parliament 'was significant in that it was only the second time since the signing of the Treaty of Rome in 1957 that a solemn declaration was made which would enable organizations or individuals in any Member State to urge their government to abide by the spirit of the Joint Declaration and implement measures to combat racism and xenophobia' (European Parliament 1991: 98), but alas its effect as a declaration without recommendations was minimal. After four years of intense internal wrangling a Council Resolution finally emerged in 1990 on the Combating of Racism and Xenophobia (90/C 157/01) in which, at the insistence of the UK, all references to non-EC nationals had been deleted and which in the opinion of the European Parliament 'signifies a step backward since it clearly goes against not only the spirit but also the contents of the June 1986 Joint Declaration against Racism and Xenophobia' (European Parliament 1991: 107). The Resolution advocates the use of education and information to combat racism and mentions the important role of the media and the education systems in advancing 'pluralism and tolerance', but fails to come to grips with any deeper analysis of racism and its causes.

Although the deportations and new barriers against refugees were being condemned by Amnesty International and Helsinki Watch there were few signs at the beginning of the 1990s of a concerted anti-racism movement in Europe. Indeed the anti-racist organisations which had formed during the 1970s, especially in Britain and the Netherlands, never commanded the open support of main political parties and did not have a strong political impact. Weakened by the general ideological disorientation of the Left in the wake of the collapse of communism and geared mainly to localised issues in line with other social movements, the anti-racism movement gained little media attention and failed to network successfully across Europe. The European Parliament made several efforts in the late 1980s to bring together 'institutions and associations opposed to racism, and immigrants' organizations, trade unions, professional organizations and other bodies concerned', but got bogged down in the diversity of the groups and the complexity of the task (European Parliament 1991: 103). A mass rally of 350,000 people in Berlin on 8 November 1992, called by the German President as a symbolic act to show Europe and the world that Germany was aware of the danger of repeating the tacit acceptance of Fascism which had precipitated the Nazi rise to power in 1933, did not generate a sustained political momentum for the protection of foreign nationals through improved rights.

The most systematic opposition to discriminatory policies in relation to foreigners seems to come from the churches. Through their extensive involvement in front-line services and shelters for refugees, church members have become sensitised to their plight and legal insecurity. Many local churches all over Europe have given sanctuary to asylum-seekers threatened with deportation and expressed their opposition to state policies through acts of civil disobedience (Weh 1987: 54). The churches in Sweden were at the forefront of protest against restrictions in immigration rules, offering the ancient right of asylum in some of the churches, and the Catholic Hierarchy in Austria openly criticised the country's grand-coalition government for pandering to populist right-wing demands for a 'defence of Austrian identity against foreign influences' (*Der Standard* 24/10/1992: 1).

FROM MULTICULTURALISM TO ANTI-RACISM

Social workers, especially in continental Europe, are understandably reluctant to take up the concept of 'race' and to base their practice on anti-racist principles. They abhor the crude biologism usually associated with race as a means of classification, and their traditional values emphasise the dignity of 'individuals' rather than focusing on collective identities. Where structural disadvantage is prevalent, social workers, in trying to avoid the pitfall of 'pathologising' the disadvantaged, tended to relate it to poverty or class, and latterly to gender, probably because of the pervasiveness of these categories among their cases. If anything, social workers refrained from letting race come into their decisions, assuming that it should not matter to them whether a case of child abuse occurred in a black or a white family or if an offence was committed by a black or a white youngster. Indeed, social workers would usually be critical of news reporting that highlights the ethnic identity of suspects and perpetrators of crimes in order not to be playing into the hands of racist stereotypes. It has now been recognised, at least in the UK, that this 'universality of treatment' approach constituted social work's 'colour-blindness' (Dominelli 1988: 36, Ballard 1989: 127). Values of tolerance and of cultural pluralism might actually add to the oppression experienced by black people. 'Ethnicism, which is inherently part of the processes of cultural or ethnic differentiation within a pluralist model, represents a shift from "race" hierarchies to "ethnic" hierarchies and from race and class exploitation to ethnic marginalisation through social, economic and political disempowerment' (Essed 1991: 15).

Europeans are generally reluctant to see themselves involved in racism; most assume that, with the defeat of Nazism and the end of colonial rule, racism has disappeared from the agenda of 'respectable politics'. This adds to the difficulty of making racism visible particularly in societies which regard themselves as 'homogeneous' or indeed as the victims of racism. The historical experience of victimisation, however, is in itself no safeguard against these societies themselves developing racist practices. Irish people have been traditionally and still are being discriminated against in Britain and are victims of racist stereotypes alleging backwardness, laziness and proneness to alcoholism. Yet the largest minority grouping within Ireland, the 'travellers', are labelled by Irish people in the same way, and are discriminated against in social life and in some official policies. For instance, they are 'racially segregated' when claiming welfare benefits, which are paid at an exact specified time all over the country separate from the benefit payments to the rest of the population, even when the claimants are well 'settled'. In fact Ireland is an example where the ideological notion of an already established 'homogeneous society' produces its own racist practices. 'Racialised "outsiders" have come to represent the presumed chaos which lies outside the protection of the community in Ireland. In this context, "community" is not simply a warm and embracing notion, but rather a central element in communal repression' (McVeigh 1992: 42).

The same stereotypical prejudices that used to confront migrant workers from Italy and Spain in North European countries in the 1970s and 1980s are now being reproduced within those South European countries against black migrants; this is particularly striking in Spain as that country's specific version of Fascism under Franco did not contain racism as a significant ideological component which could now be referred back to and politically exploited by right-wing groups (Carr 1991: 93). But these different historical experiences in various parts of Europe make it all the more necessary to detach the issue of racism from traditional prejudices based on colour and other physical characteristics and to focus instead on the systems of power in social relations.

Essed elaborated on this in a study of 'everyday racism' in the Netherlands. The Dutch ideological tradition of pluralism is rooted in the tolerance and institutionalisation of religious diversity, hence the perception of Black groups, who form 5 per cent of the population, has been framed in terms of 'ethnic diversity' rather than 'racism'. Tolerance and pluralism presuppose an acceptance of the 'overall context' in which such toleration is supposed to apply, deny the existence of conflict and also imply limits of toleration as measured against the (paternalist) norms of the dominant group.

> The norm of cultural tolerance has two sides. The dominant group is expected to be tolerant. Therefore, the dominated must believe in the 'goodwill' of the dominant group. Obviously, the idea that both parties must be equally tolerant ignores the power differences involved.
>
> (Essed 1991: 210)

Within this framework high unemployment among blacks, for instance, (up to 45 per cent compared to 14 per cent nationally) can then be interpreted as a result of unwillingness to integrate or even as a result of positive discrimination measures having 'pampered' blacks and thereby made them unfit for the harsh reality of competition on the labour market.

In the light of this analysis social workers in the Netherlands and in all European countries have to examine very carefully whether their approaches are appropriate – not so much by the criteria of their own professionalism, but against the background of a wider political agenda – particularly where that agenda is one of cultural 'pluralism' at national or European level. This can lead to acute dilemmas in everyday situations, as Essed illustrates: a black social worker found herself working at a Dutch hostel for runaway girls, where it was a rule that there should be no contact with the parents. This arises from the distinct (White) precepts of feminism, which emphasise the independence of daughters from the oppression they might experience at home. For Black daughters, however, the family might be a form of protection against racism. Is the worker likely to add to the oppression of the girl by following the dominant standards (even if they are 'anti-repressive' in feminist terms)?

> The application of White norms and values to Blacks contains marginalizing and repressive elements. There is only a thin line between the use of dominant norms, rejection of 'ethnic' behaviour, and coercion to adapt.
>
> (Essed 1991: 196)

Basically, a framework of multiculturalism and of pluralist tolerance falls short of creating the conditions and the need for understanding the world from the other person's point of view if it does not challenge and question the unequal power structure within which this communication takes place. The situation for social workers in this regard is precarious. It is tempting at least to hold on to liberal notions of tolerance and pluralism when official politics sees the answer to overt racism and xenophobia as lying in ever more restrictive measures against foreign nationals. Valid and valuable though this position is in itself, the experience of multicultural projects in all European countries shows that it can become a barrier that prevents minority groups from stating their demands in the manner and form they choose. As a member of the immigrant groups attending a major Italian conference on immigration observed (CNEL 1990: 347), multiculturalism puts pressure on them to be content with a few tokenistic appointments of their representatives to positions of public visibility and influence.

In contrast to the attempts at tackling discrimination within the framework of multiculturalism which prevail on the continent, social work in Britain towards the end of the 1980s made a determined effort to address anti-racist and anti-discriminatory practices explicitly. CCETSW took a decisive lead in this regard with the regulations for the new Diploma in Social Work.

> Social workers need to be able to work in a society which is multiracial and multicultural. CCETSW will therefore seek to ensure that students should be prepared not only for ethnically sensitive practice but also to challenge and confront institutional and other forms of racism.
>
> (CCETSW 1991: para. 1.20)

This meant a long overdue acknowledgement that racism is a reality in British society which social work cannot ignore. Apart from changes in curricula and regulations this also stimulated a move towards anti-discriminatory recruitment policies and towards forms of practice that emphasise rights as a corrective to the individualism implied in casework. But it still begged the question of how 'ethnically sensitive' practice could be taught, tested and delivered. The strategy implies an expectation that social workers can resolve problems of racial discrimination and inequality through their practice.

In addition, the high visibility of ethnic diversity in terms of skin colour in Britain, encapsulated in the term 'black', may actually make other areas of racism less accessible. 'Turkish and Greek Cypriots, for example, Jewish people and the Irish have been unable to find a voice within a political and cultural space marked out as "black"' (Rattansi 1992: 40). It is precisely here that a widening of the discourse to other parts of Europe would help to lay bare the many facets of racism and oppression, the social mechanisms, processes and structures which combine to construct racism, and the way in which day-to-day social work practices interact with them. A cross-national perspective would also underline how these discourses vary from context to context and, through this context dependence, rule out any possibility of a universally appropriate terminology. It is and must remain an open question for social work: in what 'language' can differences be properly articulated? Stuart Hall suggests that the term 'ethnicity' can be re-appropriated from the racist misuse it received in the dominant discourse which equated it with nationalism and imperialism.

If the black subject and black experience are not stabilized by

Nature or by some other essential guarantee, then it must be the case that they are constructed historically, culturally, politically – and the concept which refers to this is 'ethnicity'. The term ethnicity acknowledges the place of history, language and culture in the construction of subjectivity and identity, as well as the fact that all discourse is placed, positioned, situated, and all knowledge is contextual.

(Hall 1992: 257)

The analysis of racism and its diverse, constantly changing manifestations leads back to the shifting sands of a historical understanding of discriminatory processes. It is impossible and dangerous to assume that racism can be tackled and associated conflicts and dilemmas resolved by, for instance, isolated and fixed policy changes such as the switch to 'same-race' adoption and fostering. The British experience with that policy shows that the

inflated rhetoric and culturalist orthodoxies of antiracism have borne some peculiar fruit [leading to the] idealisation of black family norms. . . . 'same-race' adoption and fostering for 'minority ethnics' is presented as an unchallenged and seemingly unchallengeable benefit for all concerned. It is hotly defended with the same fervour that denounces white demands for 'same race' schooling as a repellent manifestation of racism . . . The pathological imagery has simply been inverted so that it forms the basis of a pastorial view which asserts the strength and durability of black family life and . . . retreats from confronting the difficult issues which result in black children arriving in care in the first place . . . The contents of the racist pathology and the material circumstances to which it can be made to correspond are thus left untouched.

(Gilroy 1992:58)

SOCIAL WORK WITH PERPETRATORS OF RACIAL VIOLENCE

Working within and yet challenging a framework of racism means accepting that the whole structure of social relations is implicated and needs to change. It means taking the risk that the direction this change will take cannot be determined from within the premises of the dominant discourse. At the same time it cannot mean a facile version of multiculturalism which eliminates all discomforting conflict. In other words, facing up to racism and oppression means taking risks. Experience with such risk-taking at the limits of 'acceptable social work practice' is now accumulating from the other front-line, normally studiously avoided by social work, i.e. work with potential and actual perpetrators of racist violence.

In the light of growing right-wing extremism in Germany, which has manifested itself in orchestrated attacks on refugee hostels, and in the light of findings which confirm that a substantial proportion of young people – up to one-third of sixteen to seventeen year-old school pupils – subscribe to an ideology of inequality and some 15 per cent tolerate acts of racist violence (Heitmeyer 1987), German social youth work has had to re-examine its traditional approaches. These either suggested that youth workers stay 'neutral' and avoid becoming involved in any ideological polarisations, or that workers try to counter racism in a youth group by confronting the young people with historical facts from Germany's past in the hope that this would lead to a rational rejection of extremism. Both approaches, though ethically 'correct', have proved utterly ineffective in reaching those groups of Skinheads, Hooligans and Badboys, as they call themselves, who are at the forefront of racial violence and are often used by organised extremist groups to 'stir up trouble'.

First studies of the growing tide of right-wing extremism among young Germans indicate that there is a complex but intricate connection between this type of group behaviour and macro-social processes. One explanatory model, put forward by Heitmeyer, suggests that young people react to the insecurity created by the accelerating modernisation of society by compensating for their powerlessness with a greater acceptance of violence, for growing social isolation with nationalist collectivism and for the general absence of role models with preferences for authoritarian dogmas (Heitmeyer 1990: 24–7). Another group of researchers (Held and Horn) attribute the phenomenon to sharper competition in the world of work that weakens cooperative values and behaviour, which would account for the violence erupting in the midst of affluence. The feminist contribution to the German debate put forward by Rommelsbacher and Holzkamp develops this analysis further and links right-wing extremism with the prevailing male culture of dominance which tends to treat all other cultures and value systems as inferior. Those who are convinced of their own superiority still precieve 'alien' cultures as threats and provocations to their own dominance because they represent the suppressed sides of their own psyche (Schumann 1992: 188).

But these analyses offer little in the way of practical proposals for youth and community workers on the ground, who have to decide, for instance, whether to exclude an extremist group from the use of a youth centre. One approach, developed by students and staff in Bremen, set up a youth project that avoids excluding those gangs of youngsters whose behaviour is most provocative (Heim *et al.* 1991). Based on the American 'street work' approach, this type of 'accepting youth work' does not set conditions for the contact between workers and youth group. They simply 'hang around' with them, sharing their general boredom but refraining from making direct suggestions for activities which would only trigger rejection. Project workers acknowledge that they come from a different world, that they have difficulties in accepting violent behaviour, uncontrolled drinking and drug-taking, that they disagree with the blatant racism (and often sexism) in the groups' behaviour, but they make no attempt to control that behaviour. They present their job as an attempt to understand, asking to be allowed in on the groups' terms, as having nothing to offer but themselves. On the whole they were surprised by the readiness of those 'way-out' youngsters to talk, engage in interactions, and recognise their powerlessness. 'Actual changes cannot be didactically programmed, they only unfold as self-motivated learning processes which are aimed at a more satisfying immediate reality' (Heim *et al.*1991: 473). Only on the basis of this acceptance were they able to make limits visible, limits not as abstract moral dogmas, but as subjective statements, such as 'I cannot go along with this'. This type of work involves risks, misunderstandings, and conflicts with authorities, but it also creates a better understanding of the structural origins of racist behaviour on both sides (Krafeld *et al.* 1993: 91).

This approach, pioneered, for example, in projects for football hooligans in several European countries, has since become more widely established in Germany. It derives its legitimation from the consideration that if the experience of powerlessness, isolation and alienation forms the basis for the violent, racist behaviour of these youth groups, control through further exclusion from society, through arrests and prosecutions will alienate them further and in a sense mirror their own reliance on power assertions and violence. Social work has a mandate to offer differentiated alternatives to the simplifications and falsifications of group identity put forward by neo-fascist organisations. Its only chance of achieving this is by creating a space in society for these youngsters, by seeking to encounter them, understand their situation and developing with them non-violent forms of excitement, role models and rallying points for group identity. 'We concentrate on the problems which these younsters have, not on those which they create' (Krafeld *et al.*: ibid.). Essentially, the approach claims to represent not a new type of work, but an extension of the generally accepted principles of 'good youth work' towards groups that have been written off as 'beyond reform'. All forms of social and youth work have to confront and alter existing power relations, and most resort to offering new opportunities for unpicking the socialisation process and for working on new forms of identity. The rehabilitative work with youth who show racist tendencies is, however, no substitute for, and needs to be paralleled by, political changes concerning inequality and exclusion in society at large (Möller 1991: 321).

This is exactly what critics of the approach point out: that this pedagogical focus might lead once again to the redefinition of political issues in terms of behavioural problems. It could also be seen as unacceptable because it implies a hidden agenda ('bringing those youngsters back to normality') under the mantle of acceptance. And it could give ambivalent signals to the public about social workers (yet again) condoning unacceptable behaviour. The Federal Ministry for Women and Youth, alarmed by the rise in racist violence recorded in eastern Germany, launched a 'special action programme against aggression and violence' which may promote this type of approach 'officially' in those parts of the united Germany, and questions have already been asked about the implications of such methods setting a 'standard' and about giving youth in eastern Germany such focused, and possibly stigmatising, attention (Schumann 1992: 187).

This controversial example points at the dilemmas faced by

social workers once again. Like these German youth workers they are under increasing pressure to respond to a crisis, which is structural in essence, with therapeutic means. By intervening where crises become manifest and trying to understand the social causes of violent behaviour they might inadvertently contribute to the perversion of cause and effect that regards migrants and asylum-seekers as the 'cause' of right-wing extremism. While gangs of hooligans engaged in violent attacks against foreigners might well act out the violence implied in forced deportations, military border controls and refugees being left to their destiny outside the borders (Scherr 1992: 394) they also have a personal responsibility for their behaviour. Anti-racist practice could start by exposing the symmetry between deviant and officially sanctioned aggression, but it must proceed to challenge actors at the various levels of the social system to respect in their behaviour human and democratic rights, precisely because these rights may have been so far denied to them.

One classical explanation for the association between nationalism and violence may become highly relevant again in today's situation and offer indications as to how small projects and political campaigns have to relate to each other. It goes back to the application of psychoanalytic concepts to authoritarianism and Fascism in entire societies by exponents of the Frankfurt School of Critical Theory (Adorno, Horkheimer, Marcuse) and by Erik Erikson, Erich Fromm and Bruno Bettelheim (Held 1980: 138–147). Just as secure individual identity is acquired through the successful resolution of crises, societies need to be able to experience divergent cultural and political interests and find ways and means of sustaining and integrating the ensuing conflicts constructively. A lack of control over this process creates fear and anxiety, and this anxiety can be projected onto external objects, aliens, who as scapegoats become carriers of one's own fears and one's own aggression. By portraying ethnic minorities or groups of foreign nationals as a threat to national stability and identity, by imputing to them acts of violence, attention can be diverted from one's own inability to deal with the lack of identity and with one's own aggressive tendencies. In order to develop an integrated and integrative identity one must learn how to handle power issues and resources and have ideas that help overcome one's own impotence.

This perspective adds further weight to the conclusion that it is not primarily the organised neo-fascist groups that constitute 'the problem', however much destruction and suffering they cause, but the resonance their sentiments and simplifications show in broader sections of the population in terms of their own (suppressed) difficulties over national identity. Social workers meet pensioners resentful of foreigners who receive assistance 'without having worked for it', people desperate for housing who blame the housing shortage on immigrants, parents who attribute the bad reputation of a school to the high number of children for whom the native language is their second language, and in all such encounters uncertainty about national identity features, as do unresolved historical issues and unfulfilled personal aspirations. The ways in which these resentments and uncertainties are articulated are not side-issues but central to the interaction with social workers and as such they are an important contribution to wider political developments. In these encounters issues of personal and national identity are intricately linked, and they therefore require of social workers a thorough understanding of the political and historical contexts in which they take place.

A similar explanation has been put forward by Šiklová in relation to the rise in nationalism in former communist countries. In her view people under the old regimes could only survive by bartering or in other ways breaking official rules which the authorities largely tolerated in return for small favours by the 'culprits' (information, support, acquiescence). Unable now to face up to the support they had thus given the system they 'are looking for an ideology which does not constitute a threat to them: they are finding it in nationalism. Clearly, the only thing they can own up to without a sense of shame is their primary, inherited, social status, i.e. their generation, their gender, their race, and their nationality' (Šiklová 1991: 770). Hence nationalism is prevalent among 'groups of the culpable . . . who had allowed themselves to be oppressed' (Šiklová 1991: 771).

CONFRONTING SECTARIANISM

The most intractable form in which the discrepancy and the contradictions between a professional and a political framework of action, between the need to maintain neutrality and the impossibility of remaining neutral, present themselves anywhere in the UK and perhaps in Europe is in Northern Ireland. Social workers there operate literally on the front line of sectarian divides, often at enormous risk to their personal safety, and yet they cannot even debate their dilemmas openly and freely nor are there agreed conceptual frameworks which could give them reference points for their actions. The moral uncertainty over whether they should let sectarianism affect their work at all (although it is in practice only too obvious that it does have a pervasive impact) relates to the 'under-theorised' status of sectarianism compared with racism (Brewer 1991: 96). It seems impossible to subsume it totally and meaningfully under the categories of race, ethnicity or class, although it shares aspects with all three. It also feeds on the same structural inequalities and psychological mechanisms as racism, which is why it seems important to discuss it in this overview.

In fact Rolston analysed the introduction of a British community development approach to Northern Ireland in terms of an attempt to subsume it under a 'racial model' as it was being practised in Britain during the 1970s. The assumption was that if 'responsible leaders' outside the sectarian organisations could be identified and supported they would become an educational influence which would eventually win over the community from divisive affiliations (Rolston 1980: 150). In the course of events not only the naïveté of this approach was exposed but also the political misuse of categories of race when they serve to simplify and objectify complex social conflicts.

It is perhaps significant that British official policies later retreated from that position and never extended the British Race Relations Act of 1976 to Northern Ireland although the 1987 Northern Ireland (Public Order) Order legislates against incitement to racial hatred. The justification given in a British report to the UN committee monitoring the application of the International Convention on the Elimination of All Forms of Racial Discrimination was that 'there has been no race relations problem to date in Northern Ireland. There have been few immigrants in Northern Ireland and no urban concentrations of immigrant groups' (quoted in Oyediran 1992: 39). The ideological framing of the conflict follows political expediency – all the more reason for social workers to develop their own frameworks with due regard to specific situations of inequality and through interaction with the people most immediately affected.

Moreover, the dilemmas of social workers and of social work educators in Northern Ireland illustrate very sharply how facile the 'value talk' in social work is, with its abstract insistence on equal treatment for each individual and respect for cultural diversity. 'The values of the social work profession already conform to these principles; the problems arise when attempts are made to translate them into objectives and practices in the workplace and apply them in a climate where people kill for their beliefs' (Brewer 1991: 110). When confidentiality can be a life and death issue, when violent threats can be made against oneself or members of one's own family over the disclosure or the inadvertent passing of confidential information, something more than ethical purity is at stake (Darby and Williamson 1978: 95).

Social workers in Northern Ireland are frequently caught in such a dilemma. They have to decide situation by situation whether, for instance, to work with community groups known for their links with para-military organisations and thereby risk denying their own beliefs and principles. On the other hand if they take a principled stand they risk being drawn into the politics of polarisation (Darby and Williamson 1978: 84). Neutrality and credibility with both sides of the community are extremely hard to maintain, although the emotional stress caused by the immediacy of violence makes it important that workers detach themselves to some extent (Downey 1992: 14). When most clients are alienated from the political system, either through becoming welfare recipients as a direct or indirect result of 'the troubles', as people dependent on public housing in segregated housing estates, as victims of politically motivated violence or as offenders against laws whose legitimacy they dispute, their social workers cannot help but become affected by those politics, by the constant framing and re-framing of problems.

Nevertheless, courageous and imaginative initiatives have developed despite, or in some people's view because of, 'the troubles'. At the statutory level the Probation Service was probably most directly affected by the political conflicts as nearly half the prison population of convicted prisoners serve sentences for 'prescribed offences', i.e. terrorist and para-military offences. Despite the stark sectarian polarisation of their clientele and the prestige para-military organisations attach to setting up their own welfare structures, the Probation Service steadfastly continued to negotiate a professional role for itself with prisoners and their relatives, acknowledging its social control but refusing to accept a political control mandate. 'Eventually prisoners and their outside representatives recognized the professionalism of the service, the strengths in *not* being members of the community, the importance of the ethic of confidentiality; and the ability to negotiate within and between formal systems' (Caul and Herron 1992: 159). The voluntary sector in Northern Ireland, though affected by polarisation, has also shown some remarkable user-centred initiatives with community advice centres, adult and community education initiatives and self-help groups in the health area. Since the removal from the local authority of the majority of traditional local responsibilities in housing, health and education, community groups, both civilian and para-military led, have been engaged in recreating structures to fill that vacuum (Griffiths 1978: 191). But civilian voluntary groups face similar dilemmas to those of social workers and some saw their official funding under threat when their activities were deemed 'political' (which can mean teaching the Irish language to adults and pre-school children).

Social work at the front line of sectarianism in Northern Ireland demonstrates that discrimination is not a matter that can be delegated to a specialised social work department in the way that 'work with migrants and refugees' can be set aside from the mainstream of statutory social work. Anti-discrimination is a central, not a specialised, task for social work in all settings and all national contexts.

Social workers in Northern Ireland have a lot of experience to contribute to a better understanding of discrimination as it operates elsewhere in Europe and might in turn be helped to see new perspectives and new ways of operating through exchanges with colleagues who operate on different front lines where discrimination becomes visible, such as social workers in the Basque region of Spain, in mixed language communities in Belgium, or those working in predominantly Turkish neighbourhoods in Germany or in Slovenian minority areas in Austria. All these 'transfers' will have contentious implications:

similarities are not parallels, and specific forms of discrimination on sectarian grounds differ from racial discrimination,
from cultural marginalisation, and from exclusion on the
grounds of poverty or disability. But the point of widening the
discourse to contacts across Europe would be to bring those
differences to the surface, to interrupt the flow of taken-for-
granted assumptions and to highlight that these boundaries and
divisions are social creations, not facts of nature. The boundary-
making as such must be reclaimed as a matter of democratic
discourse and in this task social work can apply its core skills,
the ability to sustain and to negotiate differences.

ANTI-RACIST SOCIAL WORK – SOME CONCLUSIONS

Racism and aggression against foreign and against marginalised
national citizens are a feature of all European countries, albeit
to varying degrees. The rise in such hostilities is to some extent
related to the project of economic and political integration
which occupied the EEC from its inception, but it also relates
more broadly to the difficulties and uncertainties surrounding
individual and national identity under the conditions of modernity which were themselves brought about by Europe. At the level
of individual experiences, modernity brought first of all the
close proximity of very different life styles placed seemingly
within reach of everybody through the media, through overlapping 'sub-cultures', through concentrations of wealth and
through the quickening pace of change itself. Modernity means
secondly that individuals are coming under increasing pressure
to be responsible for the choosing of their individual life style as
conventions and traditionally patterned expectations lose their
validity and authority. At the same time the growing complexity
of society and its management through technological means
offers individuals fewer chances to influence developments and
to exercise political choices (Grymer 1992: 192–195). 'The
market', 'forces of progress' and other 'external factors' have
become powerful arguments driving not least the process of
European integration.

But the negative effects of that 'progress' are also becoming
more oppressively obvious and add to the confusion, fear and
anxiety experienced by people on this rollercoaster of change.
Hopes of reconstructing the old certainties through the applic-

ation of reason and the continuing faith in the project of modernity are fading quickly in an era hailed as post-modern which is intent on reducing all differences to a matter of taste. This taxes the self-creative capacities of human beings even further and paves the way for naked power and force 'settling', *de facto*, the disputes over differences.

In most European nation states after the Second World War the question of national identity has never been settled satisfactorily, or at worst only in terms of temporary historical compromises which can break up under the strain of new developments. This was demonstrated most violently and tragically in the break-up of the Yugoslav Republic and the series of wars that erupted once the collective national identity imposed by the former communist government had lost its legitimacy and relevance. By contrast the former Czechoslovakia managed to cope with the split into two nation states by peaceful means. Nevertheless, historical resentments formed a large part of the desire to separate and largely fictitious images of national characteristics had to serve as reference points for the creation of political realities.

At the time of writing (1992) there are unresolved aspects to the national identity of other European countries. Germany has recently experienced unification, with all the associated conflicts both internally and in relation to the rest of Europe where memories of the previous 'Greater Germany' proved to be more vivid than anticipated in Germany. This was one factor in Denmark's rejection of the Maastricht Treaty in 1992 which stalled the entire process of political integration, calling into question the dominant role played by powerful nations within the EC. Belgium is sitting uneasily on the compromise of two cultural traditions which could come in for questioning in the context of other regions asserting their autonomy in Europe. Spain's attempts at delegating greater powers to its provinces was successful in the Catalan region but failed to appease the Basque demands for separate status. Italy's notorious political stalemate was made even more precarious through the strong showing of a separatist party in Lombardy, the prosperous north, which called into question the uneasy solidarity that had existed with the impoverished south of the *mezzogiorno*. In Greece the intention of its neighbouring state and former part of Yugoslavia to call itself 'Macedonia' raised fervent national feelings as there is a Macedonian part to Greece, and again images of the rather distant past (Macedonia as the cradle of Greek nationhood under Alexander the Great) were utilised to 'defend' Greek identity against any presumed incursion by a neighbour. And while talks are going on between the governments of the Republic of Ireland and Britain, and political representatives of Northern Ireland to explore terms under which negotiations over the political future of Northern Ireland could be conducted, the answer to Irish national identity seems still as far off as it did when Ireland (or parts of it) achieved political independence in 1921. These talks may well have implications for Great Britain as well, where nationhood appears so neatly resolved by the geographical shape of the island and yet where the plurality of nationalities is becoming ever more apparent, both geographically in Scotland and Wales and ethnically in the greater assertiveness of minority populations. Finally, applications for membership of the EC have been submitted or are being prepared by Austria, Norway, Sweden and Switzerland, and these considerations trigger deep divisions in each of these countries, as every opinion poll and referendum has shown.

This chapter has attempted to show how vital it is for social workers to understand the link between individual psychological processes and the dynamics of social and political change and to keep abreast of European and global political developments in the constant framing and re-framing of conflicts and problems. Without this knowledge and its critical application to daily decisions their interventions can be made to serve unintended political purposes. The political temptation will always be to deploy social workers 'strategically' in situations where crises have already erupted or are about to erupt, i.e. in urban areas of high immigrant concentration, in youth work projects with skinheads, in hostels for asylum-seekers, in refugee camps; at best they might be granted marginal preventative scope to develop for instance multi-cultural pre-school initiatives, stimulate self-help and advice centres among ethnic minorities, and create work opportunities for re-settled young people, etc. But such work, important though it is, will not be sufficient, will not redeem the general social mandate placed on social work to contribute to social solidarity and may even unwittingly play into the hands of deep-seated prejudices against minority groups as unworthy of such 'special treatment'.

As the process of European integration and the ensuing questioning of national and personal identity are beginning to encroach on all aspects of life, social workers must refuse to treat the issues of racism and discrimination against 'outsiders' as marginal and additional to the core of social work concerns and must place it at the centre of their work. Their work puts them in a particularly sensitive position in society, where their way of intervening in situations deemed 'problematic' can either reduce these problems to the level of individual pathology or help to articulate them as issues of social injustice. Social workers therefore have a responsibility to press for the full implementation of international conventions aimed at securing the rights of refugees, migrants and ethnic minorities such as the Helsinki Accords, which commit signatories to respect human rights regardless of race and to guarantee the rights of 'national minorities', the European Convention on Human Rights and the UN International Convention on the Elimination of All Forms of Racial Discrimination (ICERD). At the same time, their own actions need to be based on human rights and promote the implementation of rights in the very important sphere of social welfare as a continuous process. The history of modern Europe has shown that 'making the solutions of all social issues conditional on a particular set of institutional changes is either illusory or deliberately misleading' (Heller and Fehér 1988: 116). In other words, social work needs to approach anti-racism at the level of and in conjunction with social movements. More important than the change of political structures is the strengthening of solidarity at the level of civil society, so that it can accept and deal with its diversity without resorting to violence and exclusion.

The legitimacy and force of such demands would be further enhanced by pro-active policies of professional training and career opportunities in social work for members of ethnic minorities. This is an essential, though often neglected, aspect of internationalising social work which is usually concerned with contacts across national boundaries. Internationalising social work means critically questioning the conventional boundaries of solidarity, questioning the ideological assumptions, dressed up as economic arguments, behind measures of exclusion, pushing out the boundaries of solidarity beyond the European to a global perspective and ultimately contributing to a shift from the welfare discourse to one on human rights.

Chapter 8

Emerging issues and conclusions

In the light of profound changes in European and global political structures social work can no longer afford either to limit itself to national social policy reference points or to withdraw into the seeming neutrality of traditional professionalism. To do so would mean a dangerous detachment from history, a denial that social work is rooted not in scientific constructs but in historical and political processes, and a reneging on its claims that it can effect changes in society. The internationalisation of social problems has become inescapable, not just in inner-city areas which experience the effects of international crises more immediately in the encounter with refugees and migrants, but also in remote rural areas where economic survival is dependent on international trade deals, stock exchange fluctuations and subventions from transnational bodies, to say nothing of the universal fear of ecological doom. People's own awareness of global processes has been immensely heightened through the impact of the media and they plan their lives more and more with reference to international dimensions, be that in relation to holidays, employment considerations or consumption behaviour.

Just as the political process of European integration is inevitably a challenge to the concept and the contents of 'national identity', so the closer proximity to other forms of social work practice, the emergence of European social policies and the encounter with international service users challenges social work to examine its own identity. What forms of social work make sense in these changed conditions, what types of practice are appropriate and legitimate, what distinguishes social work from other professional activities and indeed from voluntary and informal activities?

The sometimes considerable differences that exist between neighbouring welfare services and policies can affect areas of social work practice very tangibly. Some problems would not be problems if they presented themselves on the other side of the border, or at least they might be problems of a different kind. These differences also develop their own momentum for change, if brought into the public limelight, as happened in early 1992 in the case of a fourteen-year-old girl in Ireland who had been abused and raped by a man known to the family. The sexual abuse resulted in her becoming pregnant and in the parents seeking to prosecute the perpetrator, who denied the allegations. After careful consideration of all the options, the family decided to arrange for the termination of the girl's pregnancy, which had to be done in Britain as the Irish constitution does not allow for any kind of abortion. They thought that under European Community law they were entitled to receive medical treatment in another member state without being subject to restrictions according to Council Directive 73/148 EC (the European Court of Justice had upheld this right in the case of Luisi and Carbone v. Ministero del Tesoro 1 ECR, p. 377 and p. 403). However, police investigations into the rape led to the reporting of intended abortion to the Director of Public Prosecutions, which in turn caused the Attorney General to issue an injunction against the girl and her parents prohibiting her from leaving the country for nine months. This ruling was at first upheld by the High Court even though evidence was produced that the girl was acutely suicidal as a result of her ordeal and at the prospect of having to give birth to a child under these circumstances. But later the Supreme Court interpreted the amended Irish constitution in the sense that as the mother's life was in danger, in her case from suicide, the abortion could be legally carried out even in Ireland and the prohibition on her freedom to travel abroad for this purpose had to be lifted (*Irish Times*, 6 March 1992: 5–10).

This case throws into sharp relief the uncertainties faced by the counselling professionals caring for this family and many women in similar situations: what are the ultimate reference points for their interventions? Are they bound by national law or can their professional judgement and concern go beyond the advice that is legally permitted, particularly if a neighbouring country has removed these legal obstacles? The High Court Judge in his judgement explicitly stated that European Community law must be enforced by Irish courts and that it has priority over Irish law. But he referred to Article 8 of the relevant Council Directive 73/148 which allows for member states to derogate from the principle of free access to provisions 'on grounds of public policy', i.e. in matters considered to be moral and ethical issues. Previous European Court decisions had allowed national states (or their competent authorities) a degree of discretion in the interpretation of what constitutes 'public policy' at the time and the judge, Mr Justice Costello, interpreted the moral stance the Irish electorate had taken in 1983 when they amended their constitution to include the ban on abortion as being grounds for such 'discretion'.

> Community law already recognises that within the Community wide cultural differences exist and has permitted derogations which flow from such differences. I can see no reason why it should refuse to do so when the derogation by a member-state arises because of deeply held convictions on moral issues. I think the attainment of the fundamental objectives of the Treaty is enhanced by laws which assist in the development of a Community in which legitimate differences on moral issues are recognised and which does not seek to impose a spurious and divisive uniformity on its members on such issues.
>
> (*Irish Times*, 18 February 1992: 6)

As a result of this case, in November 1992 three further referenda for constitutional amendments were placed before the Irish electorate, dealing with the right to travel (which was endorsed), the right to abortion information (also accepted) and a new version of the prohibition of abortion in Ireland in all circumstances except life-threatening physical medical conditions (which was rejected). This result signalled the end of moral certainty even in Ireland, though not the end of oppression. For people working in the counselling field these tensions and contradictions over European unity, over the balance between harmonisation and national autonomy, equality or cultural diversity are not abstract issues but affect their work directly.

Living in a wider European community *is* about diversity and not uniformity, no matter how many regulations on harmonisation come into force, and this diversity will also accentuate the diversity within national communities. But it is also about justice and equality, and 'public policy' is not solely defined by judges and articulated through referenda. Public policy gets made and defined in the daily decisions of social service personnel, of counsellors and of community workers who see policy as an evolving process, not as a static framework of given laws. Their decisions are limited by national law and this can increasingly lead to conflicts when their own sense of justice and their knowledge of conditions in other countries point at possibilities not realisable within given national conditions. It is of course not social workers and counsellors on whom dissemination of information on services available in a neighbouring country depends – users of services themselves are increasingly aware of national differences and seek to use the opportunities of greater mobility and of greater equality promised by EC regulations.

Uncertainties and conflicts similar to those created over abortion relate to the treatment of illegal immigrants or refugees and are uncomfortable and confusing for social workers. The preceding chapters were an attempt at preparing the ground for answers (in the plural), based on the assumption that different answers will be appropriate in different circumstances and that this diversity by no means diminishes social work's professional and ethical standing. Social work competence will increasingly depend on practitioners being able to account for their answers to these questions not with reference to a formula devised by academics or professional bodies but with reference to their own understanding as to where the profession has its place in society and how this came about, what its limitations are and where its opportunities for changing and transforming these limitations lie.

To summarise the main ideas brought together here: as indicated in Chapter 1, social work is bounded by the welfare state and has always played an important part in 'fine-tuning' welfare provisions. This constitutes both its humanitarian commitment and its social control function within every national welfare system. However, the current changes in the nature of all types of welfare regimes are triggered by economic pressures and could increase the discriminatory aspects of welfare and of social work. Once again, the solidarity and commitment of certain sections of the population take priority over those of others, and the privatisation of social work in terms of its disengagement from the welfare state could play into the hands of those divisions.

The origins of social work and particularly of social work education do not, however, lie within state structures but within the domain of civil society. The various starting positions were concentrated in a band of middle-class concerns, religious renewal, philanthropy and women's emancipation; working-class and socialist ideas of self-help and solidarity did not normally translate into social work training. Nevertheless, these value positions did create a space around social work within which the demands of the various state systems could be modified and re-interpreted and a professional profile of social work could develop across the divergent value positions.

However, just at the crucial time when social workers in Europe and all over the world were beginning to claim this space by organising themselves internationally, when they hoped to be able to rise above the narrow confines of state welfare policies and the charitable aims of private agencies by formulating methods and techniques which apply to human beings regardless of the political system, the profession became totally subjected to state ideology in Germany. The various value positions from which the prevailing social work principles were derived proved a weak defence and in some regards even a facilitator of the rise to power of Fascism. This experience had a lasting effect on the profession's relationship with value positions. The era after the Second World War emphasised democratic principles and self-determination as a central defence against such ideological misuse. Internationalism had at first also been dealt a blow by National Socialism, but through the persecution of Jewish social workers the transfer of concepts and methods between countries was actually enhanced. After the war different forms of social work took on a much more visible and expanded function in the different welfare systems, converging on a secular, functional mandate yet still very much concerned with the mediation between individuals and the state in a manner parallel to the mediation of citizenship through political and legal structures.

The chances of social work deriving a greater degree of autonomy not just from 'value positions' but from distinct intellectual and scientific traditions was examined in Chapter 4.

The 'intellectual homelessness' of most social work practice traditions, with the exception perhaps of that of social pedagogy, indicates on the one hand the limits of the profession in ever achieving high status and autonomy, but it is on the other hand keeping the profession intellectually and conceptually open. The theme which all approaches pursue, albeit by emphasising the two poles differently, is how collective and individual needs for belonging, identity and cohesion can be reconciled within modern societies. Behind this quest lies the problem of norms and normality of whose relativity social workers have always been aware. The basic tenets of psychodynamic psychology, of the various paradigms of social science and of pedagogy consistently point social work towards having to start from the person as an active, creative subject if change in the direction of stability and identity is to be achieved, both in the individual person and in the wider society. People cannot be engineered or manipulated into solutions, they have to be involved in the problem-solving themselves.

In the closing decades of the twentieth century this theme echoed back to social workers very loudly, though from very different directions, from the range of social movements all across Europe which were explored in Chapter 5. At first dismissed by official established powers as a freak phenomenon they have become a political and historical force themselves, whose most visible testimony was the fall of the Berlin Wall and the Iron Curtain in the middle of Europe. The movements are in one sense a sign of the political systems of all different persuasions being in crisis, and with them the credibility of established political processes. In the wake of these challenges they exacerbated the crisis of the welfare state, which was revealed to be not just a fiscal crisis but also a crisis of the legitimacy of the kind of social solidarity the state welfare provisions represent. Liberation movements, self-help initiatives and public awareness campaigns all questioned the authority of experts and people in political power to speak and act on their behalf and through their actions exposed the gaps in civil, political and social citizenship gaping in the systems which welfare measures had often papered over. In another sense social movements represent a new, not yet fully elaborated way of conducting politics and representing interests and needs which places personal aspects at the centre, very much in the way all forms of social work had always sought to do in their practice.

Above all, new social movements drew attention to the infinite diversity of interests, tastes and styles, to the resourcefulness of individuals, groups and communities once they have seized their potential power. This in turn tempts the state to exploit those resources and to transfer its costly responsibilities to the private sphere which began to organise itself again so conveniently. Thus social work becomes embroiled in a double dilemma. In terms of its own hard-won professionalism the rise of volunteers and self-help groups appears as a threat, especially when it is being exploited for political ends and could translate into job losses and a lowering of standards of services. And yet the challenges have laid bare some of the oppressive and discriminatory structures operating in society to which social workers have – often unwittingly – been party. This makes it imperative for the profession to question its own elitism, power and oppressive practices and to seek ways of participating in the transformation of civil society which social movements are potentially engaged in.

These developments occurred in all parts of Europe with striking similarity, as if to indicate that the initiative in political processes was shifting from the top to the bottom. Indeed, contacts between groups in different European countries had been facilitated by the cultural initiatives contained in the EC integration programme such as youth exchanges, partnerships and educational and professional cooperation. But, as Chapter 6 tried to explain, this cosy arrangement – which had sought to contain participation, cultural diversity and consumer choice at the private level – got disturbed when the dominance of the economic agenda in European integration was becoming ever clearer. Yes officially European integration was about pluralism and choice, but in very tightly controlled parameters. The section of the population best protected through rights of mobility within the EC, social protection, equality legislation and in that sense EC citizenship were the economically active and useful group. The rest enjoy far less protection, and the position of non-EC nationals is as vulnerable as ever, or in the case of refugees more vulnerable. This indicates that whilst national boundaries between EC countries assume less importance so as to give the appearance of a process of greater inclusion, measures of exclusion accompany this process. And it is with the latter processes that social work is directly implicated. Measures of exclusion cause instability and protest in societies which base themselves on liberal ideals and which are keen to maintain the high moral ground in the global arena of politics, condemning political regimes which violate civil and human rights through blatant acts of discrimination. Welfare measures soften this appearance and are therefore framed by such political considerations, which means that exclusions from jobs, housing, educational opportunities, rights of residence and liberty must be seen to be legitimate, either by due process of law, or in the subtleties of decisions the law can never reach and are hence left to the discretion of experts. Deficits in 'adjustment' come to indicate 'pathology' and hence require treatment and therapy, and since welfare personnel cannot offer rights they make the best use of the limited means they can utilise.

The realisation that these structural constraints spell racism in essence is only gradually dawning within the much more widespread discourse of 'multiculturalism' in Europe. But facing up to racism is the crucial precondition for social workers if they want to make a positive contribution to the transformation of national civil societies and to the formation of a European civil society, as Chapter 7 tries to argue. Official policies by the European countries are designed to 'externalise' the problem of racism, to portray it as a problem caused by extremist groups, in close parallel to the externalisation of the problem of political and 'economic' refugees. But the tightening of asylum legislation and the increase of the controls on external EC borders are the outward signs of a concealed process which defines European identity, the outlines of European nationhood, in a manner reminiscent of the building of national identities in several European countries during the nineteenth century: partly by external exclusion of 'others' as potential threats or even enemies against whom the national boundaries afford protection, partly also by substantiating the national solidarity with welfare measures and other benefits and rights for its own citizens.

It is to be expected that social work will be, and has already been, drawn into this project of European nation-building. At national level, social workers find themselves often called upon to create conditions in which extremist violence is less likely to occur, either by improving the integration of groups of foreign nationals or increasingly also by working directly with the perpetrators of violence. At the European level, despite the rudimentary state of a European social policy as such, a growing number of workers in all countries are now employed in projects financed partly from the EC Structural Funds or the Combat Poverty Programme. The rationale for these funds is that they have a vital contribution to make to counteract the adverse effects on particular regions and employment sectors of the Single European Market. The objective of integration is written into their conditions.

This highlights the precarious nature of the European integration project. The exclusion of refugees and asylum-seekers, as well as the selective treatment of migrant workers, have been presented not as a matter of political choices but as one of economic necessity, depending on the capacity of the economy to 'absorber' non-nationals. This is reminiscent of the dominance of economic arguments produced by National Socialism in justifying the sterilisation, exclusion, detention and extermination of people labelled as 'parasites', and as illustrated in Chapter 3, workers in the social professions were drawn into this racist spiral because they failed or refused to recognise its racist nature and its catastrophic consequences.

What gives equal cause for alarm is the dominance of economic reference points in the process of European integration as such. The separation of political from economic integration seems to imply the safeguarding of national sovereignty, which remained a deep-felt concern not only from the British point of view but was also mirrored in the referenda results in Denmark and France in 1992. But it means in reality that transnational market considerations, albeit steered and tempered to some extent by the European Commission and by the Council of Ministers, are beyond the direct controls (such as they are) of national political processes. The often stated 'democratic deficit' of the EC, whose parliament has a very marginal function, is going to worsen as European citizens' lives are going to be affected more and more directly by EC regulations whilst they have still only very limited means of participating in and influencing these developments.

What interests me is the question whether this disparity is just a passing imbalance that can be set right by the parliamentarization of the Brussels expertocracy or whether these suprastate bureaucracies with their orientation towards sheer economic criteria of rationality merely highlight a general trend that has for a long time also been gaining momentum within the nation states. I am thinking of the fact that economic imperatives have gradually become independent of all else, and that politics has gradually become a matter of administration, of processes that undermine the status of the citizen . . .

(Habermas 1992: 10)

This would amount to a gloomy, even frightening outlook if it was not juxtaposed with that other contemporary experience of equally momentous proportions, the disintegration of systems which had had a disproportionally higher democratic deficit and had kept the civil societies of their citizens in a virtual stranglehold. Although the final verdict on the causes of the collapse of communist regimes is still outstanding, the events certainly add credence to the general observations of the history of modern states that the quest for citizenship has gathered an irreversible momentum. If such citizenship is being denied, or indeed if it becomes reduced to the participation in abstract voting procedures, and particularly if large sections of the population are again visibly excluded from enjoying the rights of full citizenship or demonstrate the meaninglessness of the implied obligations through crime, violence and vandalism, the process of society-building must somehow start afresh.

And this appears to be the hopeful side of the present crisis and the perspective which affords social work an historic chance to make a positive contribution and apply the lessons of its short but eventful history. The fact that it proved impossible to detach social work from history, despite all efforts at giving it a timeless, objective character, might be of far-reaching importance now. 'History has become mobilized; it is accelerating, even overheating. The new problems are shifting old perspectives and, what is more important, opening up new perspectives for the future, points of view that restore our ability to perceive alternative courses of action' (Habermas 1992: 1).

It is not just the case that European national identities are in the melting pot as a result of the economic integration, of the opening of borders towards the East and of immigration; individual identities share these uncertainties, and with often tragic consequences. But within the confrontations and struggles over identity a theme is once more sounding through, the theme that people have to carry out these struggles themselves, that democracy can only be achieved 'from below' and only through structures in which people recognise themselves in a correspondence between the personal and the political. This is a theme social work in all its intellectual traditions and forms of practice across Europe keeps coming back to. There are grounds therefore to assume that social work does have a good deal of experience to offer in this 'melting-pot' situation.

But the particular ambivalence of social movements, of renewed signs of the growth of voluntarism and the emergence of self-help initiatives points towards a central ingredient in this process 'from below'. These movements become divisive and oppressive themselves if their actions are divorced from a central concern for human rights as the inalienable precondition for diversity. 'The social rights of citizenship unite those whom the market inevitably divides' (Alcock 1989: 37). If voluntary groups become drawn into a 'zero-sum game' where the gain of one group is linked to the loss of another group, where self-help becomes the mirror of official discriminatory policies, they will not only damage their 'competitors' but will eventually destroy their own legitimation and thereby their own purposes.

From a positive viewpoint, while the outlines of a new civil society are by far not visible yet, there are experiences and principles which give the tentative new beginnings a definite direction. The restructuring and dismantling of existing welfare states is likely to continue and there is no new blueprint appearing on the political or the academic horizon or contained within the campaigns of any of the social movements. But the erupting conflicts and divisions set some parameters, and the task is now laid down for professionals and service users to explore the possibilities jointly.

For social work more specifically this fragmentation, both of the 'welfare scene' and of political goals, has several far-reaching implications. First, it has to examine more carefully its mandate for intervention to ensure that it is democratically derived. It is no longer sufficient to be acting on the authority of the state and within a secure legal framework, to be 'sticking to regulations'; social workers will have to check out directly with the users of services whether they authorise their actions. This might be extremely difficult in the area of work that certainly dominates British community care – the field of statutory child protection – but the fact that it is so difficult to raise the possibility of having service users and indeed 'perpetrators' of violence against children involved in the planning and development of appropriate services might indicate how much social workers have become boxed into their statutory roles. Social workers in other European countries have been far less directly in the firing line of public criticism, as protection work is shared by a greater range of agencies and of professional groups.

Second, social workers at the 'private' end of the spectrum equally have to guard against reneging on a societal mandate for their work. Private social work practice has not taken off on any larger scale anywhere in Europe, and where social workers are attached to small projects and sectional action groups 'networking' has been recognised as a vital aspect of such work, not only to increase the effectiveness of the projects but very much also as an expression that the action needs to encourage solidarity and lead to equity and justice.

The third implication is that there is unlikely to be a convergence towards one internationally recognised form of social work and a unified profession, despite all efforts at harmonising curricula and qualifications. The European Directives on the mutual recognition of qualifications very wisely refrain from laying down prescribed contents and leave it instead up to national recognition bodies to decide on equivalence and on deficits. This is bound to lead to dilemmas and inconsistencies, for instance when British-trained youth workers could obtain certain social work posts in Germany which are closed to them in their own country. But the warning of a 'dilution of standards' often issues from quarters least prepared to be exposed to a radical examination of these standards from the position of other intellectual and practice traditions. The coexistence of several, often exchangeable or overlapping qualifications in social professions, certainly in Belgium, Denmark, France, Germany, Italy and the Netherlands, has not only mutually enriched those fields but has also kept social work from becoming closed and exclusive.

To ask the question as to the nature of 'culture-specific' social work means also asking the question of how racism might have become institutionalised in the arena of social work methods. A model of social work that is assumed to apply universally is likely to be oppressive in the sense that it claims to derive its criteria from a level 'above' the traditions of practice, personal preferences and cultural norms which prevail in specific local contexts. The diversity of social work approaches which, despite all efforts at international harmonisation has not been levelled to one standard norm, might turn out to be one of the profession's greatest assets in facing up to the diversity of the newly emerging welfare scenario. Above all it might be a crucial factor in allowing the profession to examine critically its own racist tendencies, which can show itself for instance in a fixed boundary towards the work of volunteers and towards the inherent methodology of spontaneous social action campaigns and self-help initiatives, which mostly involve more members of minority groups than can be found in the ranks of the profession. The systematic comparative analysis of internationally used social work methods, which has barely begun (Kreidenweis and Treptow 1990: 36), would neglect this political dimension at its peril. The lessons of the contradictions in which the 'multicultural' social work project became entangled before the hidden pervasiveness of racism was realised would be well applied in the examination of the profession's internationalism and interculturalism.

The fourth implication seems to contradict the previous one, but in recognising the diversity of social work models and of localised forms of practice a new, transformed sense of the unity of the profession emerges. Academics perhaps need to be far less concerned about establishing this unity by trying to formulate the definitive unitary approach and would do better by listening to the common concerns being dealt with by practitioners in very different circumstances and by paying attention to the common themes which their work articulates. Taking again the experience of social movements, particularly the feminist movement, as an indication it is becoming quite clear that despite the very different manifestations of feminism in different countries, in different ethnic contexts and at different class levels it makes sense to subsume this diversity under the heading of feminism. The equivalent term that could symbolise the unity of the social work field could be 'the social', in all its meanings (including, hopefully, the celebratory ones). Social work is one of the many threads that weave the texture of a social fabric. It constitutes a set of practices and skills derived from conscious reflection on the making of this fabric, on the processes and actions between individuals and social structures. It operates not in isolation from other social professions, such as teachers or lawyers, but with a vaguer brief that necessitates going back to the foundations of those processes, not their institutional manifestations.

This is not to subscribe to the post-modern vision of social work that is content with stating diversity and fragmentation as the fate of the post-modern age. While the fragmentation of the welfare state might succeed, the 'privatisation of the social' will not succeed because individual identity is socially constructed and, as Kant has shown, we can extricate ourselves from a fundamental ethical responsibility for others only by declaring them sub-or non-human, i.e. by drawing on racist principles. And yet this unity cannot be achieved by a return to the ethical, rationally grounded certainties of the 'classical' social work period, since those failed to recognise their own subjective biases. Between those equally deceptive poles (McBeath and Webb 1991) a European dimension of social work suggests unity of the profession as a 'communicative community'. Despite the different languages in which social work is being conducted (literally and metaphorically), possibilities exist not just for sharing concerns, but much more importantly for arguing with each other, disagreeing over aims and assumptions, criticising each other vehemently and thereby influencing each other's practice. 'We have to become aware that a multi-racial society is in fact full of vitality and turmoil, but also because of that it is a society that is potentially highly conflictual' (De Rita 1992: 12). This applies also to social work's diversity. The unity consists not in social workers all learning the one language (or, in McBeath and Webb's terms that they should 'learn the unitary Esperanto'), but in realising that they can somehow come to terms with their differences through communication, through taking partners in this dialogue seriously and through recognising themselves at times in what the partner expresses.

This opens up the possibility of integrating the three reference points which seem to determine the variety of social work practice in Europe: the politics of welfare as part of the state and nation-building project, the intellectual traditions, concepts and scientific resources which informed social work education, and the expressions of consumer demands to which social work has always remained at least nominally responsive. So far the different forms of social work tended to define themselves by drawing the line between professional autonomy and social policy dictates on the one hand and voluntary initiatives on the other. But practically it is quite evident that the interplay of these factors is a source of creative possibilities, though not without its dangers. But the integration of all three dimensions might become all the more relevant now that both state welfare and voluntarism are in transition. The forms of social work that could emerge from this process will not be categorised neatly any longer according to methods and theories, as these categories are already becoming obsolete. Their unifying element, however, will have to be the principle of citizenship which is the central value social work has to serve.

Europe *is* an issue for social work even if European political integration does not happen; or rather, it becomes an even more acute and urgent issue for social work if European integration were to fail and Europe became torn apart in festering nationalist feuding. The fact that almost all European nation states are showing problems with national integration indicates that linking integration with differentiation is the crucial task facing European societies at all levels, from the personal to the European. In this process, which takes place primarily at the level of civil society, social work can make an important contribution as long as social workers see their actions as a part of the transformation of civil society towards one in which rights prevail.

Bibliography

Achterhuis, H. (1980), *De markt van welzijn en geluk*, Baarn: Ambo-Herdruk.

Adams, R. (1990) *Self-help, Social Work and Empowerment*, London: Macmillan.

Alcock, P. (1989) 'Why citizenship and welfare rights offer new hope for new welfare in Britain', *Critical Social Policy* 9, 2: 32–43.

Alexander, L.B. (1972) 'Social work's Freudian deluge: myth or reality?', *Social Service Review* 46, 4: 517–38.

Althaus, H. (1936) *Soziale Arbeit und Gemeinschaft: ein Beitrag zur III. Internationalen Konferenz für soziale Arbeit, London 1936*, Karlsruhe: Braun.

Altmeyer, A. (1955) 'Training for international responsibilities', in Myrdal, A., Altmeyer, A.J. and Rusk, D., *America's Role in International Social Welfare*, New York: Columbia University Press.

Anderson, J. (1978) '"GER": A voluntary Anglo-German contribution', in A. Hearnden (ed.), *The British in Germany: Educational Reconstruction after 1945*, London: Hamish Hamilton.

Ariés, P. (1962) *Centuries of Childhood*, London: Cape.

Armstrong, H. and Hollows, A. (1991) 'Responses to child abuse in the EC', in M. Hill (ed.), *Social Work and the European Community*, London: J. Kingsley.

Ascoli, U. (1987) 'The Italian welfare state: between incrementalism and rationalism', in R.R. Friedmann, N. Gilbert, M. Sherer (eds), *Modern Welfare States: A Comparative View of Trends and Prospects*, Brighton: Wheatsheaf.

Astier, P. (1985) 'Animation et/ou travail social', in U. Menzemer and A. Moreau (eds), *L'emprise du social: perspectives françaises et allemandes sur la jeunesse et le travail social*, Paris: Armand Colin.

Austin, D.M. (1983) 'The Flexner Myth and the history of social work', *Social Service Review* 57, 3: 357–77.

Baine, S., Benington, J. and Russell, J. (1992) *Changing Europe*, London: NCVO Publications.

Bakker, B. and Karel, M. (1983) 'Self-help – wolf or lamb? The Netherlands', in D. Pancoast, P. Parker and C. Froland (eds), *Rediscovering Self-Help*, London: Sage.

Ballard, R. (1989) 'Social work with black people: what's the difference?, in C. Rojek, G. Peacock and S. Collins (eds), *The Haunt of Misery*, London: Routledge.

Bauer, C. and Ritt, L. (eds), (1979) *Free and Ennobled. Source Readings in the Development of Victorian Feminism*, Oxford: Pergamon.

Bauer, R. and Thränhardt, A.-M. (1987) *Verbandliche Wohlfahrtspflege im internationalen Vergleich*, Opladen: Westdeutscher Verlag.

Baumann, Z. (1992) 'Soil, blood and identity', *Sociological Review* 40, 4: 675–701.

Bäumer, G. (1929), 'Die historischen und sozialen Voraussetzungen der Sozialpädagogik und die Entwicklung ihrer Theorie', in H. Nohl, L. Pallat (eds), *Handbuch der Pädagogik: Sozialpädagogik*, Berlin–Leipzig: Beltz.

Beale, J. (1986) *Women in Ireland*, London: Macmillan.

Becker, S. (1987) 'How much collaboration?', *Community Care* 26 March: 23–4.

Bernardi, L. *et al.* (1985) *Professionalità sociale e innovazione*, Bologna: Cappelli.

Bernfeld, S. (1969) Kinderheim Baumgarten: Bericht über einen ernsthaften Versuch mit neuer Erziehung', in S. Bernfeld, *Antiautoritäre Erziehung und Psychoanalyse*, Darmstadt: März.

Birnbaum, L. C. (1986) *Liberazione della donna: Feminism in Italy*, Middletown, Connecticut: Wesleyan University Press.

Blankenburg, M. (1988) *Internationale Wohlfahrt: Ursprünge und Entwicklung des ICSW*, Berlin: Deutsches Zentralinstitut für soziale Fragen.

Bluhm, S. (1971) 'Friedrich Froebel', in L.C. Deighton (ed.), *The Encyclopedia of Education*, New York: Free Press and Macmillan.

Bono, P. and Kemp, S. (eds), (1991) *Italian Feminist Thought: A Reader*, Oxford: Basil Blackwell.

Bosanquet, H. (1914) *Social Work in London 1869–1912: A History of the Charity Organisation Society*, London: J. Murray.

Boulding, E. (1977) *Women in the Twentieth Century World*, London: Sage.

Boyd, N. (1982) *Josephine Butler, Octavia Hill, Florence Nightingale*, London: Macmillan.

Branckaerts, J. (1983) 'Belgium', in D. Pancoast, P. Parker and C. Froland (eds), *Rediscovering Self-Help*, London: Sage.

Brauns, H.-J. and Kramer, D. (1988) *Social Work Education in Europe: A Comprehensive Description of Social Work Education in 21 European countries*, Frankfurt: Deutscher Verein für öffentliche und private Fürsorge.

Brauns, H.-J. and Kramer, D. (1991) 'Social work education and professional development', in M. Hill (ed.), *Social Work and the European Community*, London: J. Kingsley.

Brenton, M. (1982) 'Changing relationships in the Dutch social services', *Journal of Social Policy* 11: 59–80.

Brewer, J. (1991) 'The parallels between sectarianism and racism: the

Northern Ireland experience', in CCETSW, *One Small Step towards Racial Justice*, London: Central Council for Education and Training in Social Work.

Brinker-Gabler, G. (1983) 'The women's movement in the German empire: the revolution dismisses her children', in I. Drewitz (ed.), *The German Women's Movement*, Bonn: Hohwacht.

Brubaker, W.R. (1989) *Immigration and the Politics of Citizenship in Europe and North America*, New York/London: University Press of America.

Bunyan, T. (1991) 'Towards an authoritarian European state', *Race and Class* 32,3: 19–27.

Burmeister, W. (1978) 'Adult education for a new society', in A. Hearnden (ed.), *The British in Germany: Educational Reconstruction after 1945*, London: Hamish Hamilton.

Canevini, M.D. (1991) 'L'assistente sociale' in R. Maurizio and D. Rei (eds), *Professioni nel sociale*, Turin: Gruppo Abele.

Cannan, C. (1991) 'Seine Policies', *Social Work Today*, 14 March 1991: 25–26.

Cannan, C. Berry, L. and Lyons, K. (1992) *Social Work and Europe*, London: Macmillan.

Castle-Kanerova, M. (1992) 'Social policy in Czechoslovakia', in B. Deacon *et al.*, *The New Eastern Europe: Social Policy Past, Present and Future*, London: Sage.

Carr, M. (1991) 'Spain: racism at the frontier', *Race and Class* 32, 3: 93–97.

Caul, B. and Herron, S. (1992) *A Service for People: Origins and Development of the Personal Social Services of Northern Ireland*, Belfast: December Publications.

Cavallone, A. (1986) 'Social work education in Italy' in Brauns, H.-J. and Kramer, D., *Social Work Education in Europe: A Comprehensive Description of Social Work Education in 21 European Countries*, Frankfurt: Deutscher Verein für öffentliche und private Fürsorge.

CCETSW (1991) *Rules and Requirements for the Diploma in Social Work* (Paper 30, second edition), London: Central Council for Education and Training in Social Work.

CEC (Commission of the European Communities) (1990) *The Community Charter of Fundamental Social Rights for Workers*, European File, June 1990.

CENSIS (Centro Studi Investimenti Sociali) (1989), *Italy Today: Social Picture and Trends 1989*, Rome: F. Angeli.

Chamberlayne, P. (1992), New directions in welfare? France, West Germany, Italy and Britain in the 1980s, *Critical Social Policy* 11, 3: 5–21.

Cigno, K. (1985) 'The other Italian experiment: neighbourhood social work in the health and social services', *British Journal of Social Work* 15: 173–186.

CNEL (Consiglio Nazionale dell'Economia e di Lavoro) (1990), *Riconoscere e riconoscersi: il senso delle società locali e il vissuto dei soggetti migranti in dieci incontri territoriali da Como a Palermo*, Rome: CNEL.

Constable, R. and Przybylska, B. (forthcoming) *The Context for Practice and Education in Polish Social Work*, Chicago: Lyceum Press.

Corby, B. (1991) 'Sociology, social work and child protection', in M. Davies (ed.), *The Sociology of Social Work*, London: Routledge.

Courtioux, M., Jones, H.D., Kalcher, J., Steinhauser, W., Tuggener, H., and Waaldijk, K. (1986), *The Social Pedagogue in Europe: Living with Others as a Profession*, Zurich: FICE Verlag.

Dahrendorf, R. (1992) 'The new Europe', *Journal of European Social Policy*, 2, 2: 79–85.

Dal Pra Ponticelli, M. (1985) *I modelli teorici del servizio sociale*, Rome: Astrolabio-Ubaldini.

D'Anieri, P., Ernst, C. and Kier, E. (1990) 'New social movements in historical perspective', *Comparative Politics* 22,4: 445–58.

Darby, J. and Williamson, A. (1978) *Violence and the Social Services in Northern Ireland*, London: Heinemann.

Darling, V. (1972) 'Development of social work in the Republic of Ireland', *Social Studies* 1,1: 24–37.

Davies Jones, H. (1986) 'The profession at work in contemporary society', in M. Courtioux, H. Davies Jones, J. Kalcher, W. Steinhauser, H. Tuggener, and K. Waaldijk, *The Social Pedagogue in Europe: Living with Others as a Profession*, Zurich: FICE Verlag.

Deacon, B. (1991) Book review of R. Mishra, The Welfare State in Capitalist Society, *Journal of European Social Policy* 1,1: 75–7.

Deimer, K. (1992) 'Kontakt- und Informationsstellen für Selbsthilfegruppen', in R. Bauer (ed.), *Lexikon des Sozial- und Gesundheitswesens*, Munich: Oldenbourg.

Deneke, C. (1983) 'West Germany: how professionals view self-help' in D. Pancoast, P. Parker and C. Froland (eds), *Rediscovering Self-Help*, London: Sage.

De Rita, G. (1992) 'Introduzione', in F. Bentivogli et al., *Costruire la società multirazziale – appartenenze e identità a confronto*, Genoa: Marietti.

Diehm, I. (1992) 'Nationalitätenbilder und interkulturelles Lernen', in R. Brähler and P. Dudek (eds), *Fremde – Heimat: Neuer Nationalismus versus interkulturelles Lernen*, Frankfurt: Verlag für Interkulturelle Kommunikation.

Donati, P. (1987) 'Traditional political theories and new social options: replies to the crisis of the Welfare State', in A. Evers, H. Novotny, and H. Wintersberger (eds), *The Changing Face of Welfare*, Aldershot: Gower.

Donati, P. (1988) 'Il futuro dello stato sociale: continuità e discontinuità', *Annuali di Sociologia* 2,3: 171–212.

Donati, P. and Colozzi, I. (1988) 'Institutional reorganisation and new shifts in the welfare mix in Italy during the 1980s', in A. Evers and H. Wintersberger (eds), *Shifts in the Welfare Mix: Their Impact on Work, Social Services and Welfare Politics*, Vienna: European Centre for Social Welfare Training and Research.

Downey, R. (1992) 'In the firing line', *Social Work Today*, 20 February 1992: 13–14.

Duran, M.A. and Gallego, M.T. (1986) 'The women's movement in Spain and the new Spanish democracy', in D. Dahlerup (ed.), *The New Women's Movement: Feminism and Political Power in Europe and the USA*, London: Sage.

Dyson, K.H.F. (1980) *The State Tradition in Western Europe*, Oxford: Martin Robertson.

Eckstein, R. (1966) 'Bernfeld 1892–1953', in F. Alexander et al. (eds), *Psychoanalytic Pioneers*, London: Basic Books.

Ellemers, J. E. (1984) 'Pillarization as a process of modernization', *Acta Politica* 19, 1: 129–144.

Ergas, Y. (1982) 'Allargamento della cittadinanza e governo del conflitto: le politiche sociali negli anni settanta in Italia', *Stato e Mercato* 6: 429–464.

ERGO (1990) 'Museo vivo: saving the past to build a future', *Newspaper of the European Community Programme to Combat Long-Term Unemployment* 5.

Esping-Andersen, G. (1990) *The Three Worlds of Welfare Capitalism*, Cambridge: Polity Press.

Essed, P. (1991) *Understanding Everyday Racism: An Interdisciplinary Theory*, London: Sage.

European Parliament (1991) *Report drawn up on behalf of the Committee of Inquiry into Racism and Xenophobia*, Luxembourg: Office for Offical Publications of the European Communities.

Evers, A. and Wintersberger, H. (eds), (1988) *Shifts in the Welfare Mix: Their Impact on Work, Social Services and Welfare Politics*, Vienna: European Centre for Social Welfare Training and Research.

Fasheh, M. (1990) 'Community education: to reclaim and transform what has been made invisible', *Harvard Educational Review* 60, 1: 19–35.

Ferge, Z. (1979) *A Society in the Making: Hungarian Social and Societal Policy 1945–75*, Harmondsworth: Penguin.

Ferrand-Bechmann, D. and Murswieck, A. (1987) 'Zur Rolle privater Verbände in der französischen Sozialpolitik', in R. Bauer and A.-M. Thränhardt (eds), *Verbandliche Wohlfahrtspflege im internationalen Vergleich*, Opladen: Westdeutscher Verlag.

Field, M. H. (1980) 'Social casework practice during the "psychiatric deluge"', *Social Service Review* 54,4: 482–507.

Filtzinger, O. and Johann, E. (1992) *Interkulturelle Pädagogik im Elementarbereich*, Koblenz: Schäfer Verlag.

Finch, J. (1984) 'The deceit of self help: preschool playgroups and working class mothers', *Journal of Social Policy* 13,1: 1–20.

Fischer-Defoy (1933) 'Deutsche Aufartungsgesetzgebung', *Deutsche Zeitschrift für Wohlfahrtspflege* 9, 6: 241–8.

Fletcher, C. (1987) 'Developments in community education: a current account', in G. Allen et al. (eds), *Community Education*, Milton Keynes: Open University Press.

Flora, P. (1986) *Growth to Limits: The Western European Welfare States since World War II*, Vol. 1, Berlin: de Gruyter.

Floris, F. and Pollo, M. (1992) 'Concetti di animazione', *Animazione sociale* 22,5: 25–46.

Freire, P. (1972) *Pedagogy of the Oppressed*, Harmondsworth: Penguin.

Friedlander, W. (1949) 'Some international aspects of social work education', *Social Service Review* 23,2: 204–10.

Friedlander, W. (1955) *Introduction to Social Welfare*, Englewood Cliffs, N.J.: Prentice-Hall.

Friesenhahn, G. (1988) *Zur Entwicklung interkultureller Pädagogik*, Berlin: Express Edition.

Fröbel, F. (1910) *The Education of Man*, London: Appleton and Co..

Garrett, A. (1949) 'Historical survey of the evolution of casework', *Journal of Social Casework* 30,6: 219–29.

Giddens, A. (1991) *The Consequences of Modernity*, Cambridge: Polity Press.

Gilligan, R. (1989) 'Policy in the Republic of Ireland: historical and current issues in child care' in P. Carter, T. Jeffs and M. Smith (eds), *Social Work and Social Welfare Yearbook* 1, Milton Keynes: Open University Press..

Gilroy, P (1992) 'The end of antiracism', in J. Donald and A. Rattansi (eds), *'Race', Culture and Difference*, London: Sage.

Griffiths, H. (1978) 'Community reactions and voluntary involvement', in J. Darby and A. Williamson, *Violence and the Social Services in Northern Ireland*, London: Heinemann.

Gruber, H. (1984) Reflections on the problematique of socialist party culture and the realities of working-class life in Red Vienna', in H. Konrad and W. Maderthaner (eds), *Neuere Studien zur Arbeitergeschichte, 3: Beiträge zur Kultur- und Geistesgeschichte*, Vienna: Europaverlag.

Grunow, D. (1986) 'Debureaucratisation and the self-help movement: towards a restructuring of the welfare state in the FRG?' in E. Øyen (ed.), *Comparing Welfare States and Their Futures*, Aldershot: Gower.

Grymer, H. (1992) 'Die Angst, der Feind, die Deutschen und ihre Ausländer', *Neue Praxis* 22,3 :181–206.

Gstettner, P. (1988) *Zwanghaft Deutsch?*, Klagenfurt/Celovec: Drava.

Gulick, C.A. (1948) *Österreich von Habsburg zu Hitler* (2 vols.), Vienna: Danubia.

Habermas, J. (1987) *The Theory of Communicative Action, 2: Lifeworld and System*, Cambridge: Polity Press.

Habermas, J. (1992) 'Citizenship and national identity: some reflections on the future of Europe', *Praxis International* 12, 1: 1–19.

Hall, S. (1992), 'New ethnicities', in J. Donald and A. Rattansi (eds), *'Race', Culture and Difference*, London: Sage.

Hämäläinen, J. (1989) 'Social pedagogy as a meta-theory of social work education', *International Social Work* 32,2: 117–28.

Hamburger, F. (1991) 'Interkulturelle Erziehung: Pädagogik zwischen Selbstüberforderung und Bedeutungslosigkeit' in D. Kiesel and R. Wolf-Almanasreh (eds), *Die multikulturelle Versuchung: Ethnische Minderheiten in der deutschen Gesellschaft*, Frankfurt: Haag und Herchen.

Hamburger, F. (1992) 'Interkulturelle Pädagogik' in R. Bauer (ed.), *Lexikon des Sozial- und Gesundheitswesens*, Munich: Oldenbourg.

Harmsen, H. (1935) 'Bericht über den Internationalen Strafrechts- und Gefängniskongress', *Soziale Praxis* 44, 42: 1205-29.

Harris, R. (1990) 'Beyond rhetoric: a challenge for international social work', *International Social Work* 33: 203-12.

Harvey, E. (1989) 'Die Jugendfürsorge in der Endphase der Weimarer Republik', in H.-U. Otto and H. Sünker (eds), *Soziale Arbeit und Faschismus*, Frankfurt: Suhrkamp.

Havel, V. (1988) 'Anti-political politics', in Keane, J., *Civil Society and the State*, London: Verso.

Heim, G. et al. (1991) 'Jugendarbeit mit rechten Jugendcliquen – Handlungsansätze aus der Praxis', *Deutsche Jugend* 11: 471-81.

Heitmeyer, W. (1987) *Rechtsextremistische Orientierungen bei Jugendlichen: Empirische Ergebnisse und Erklärungsmuster einer Untersuchung zur politischen Sozialisation*, 3rd edn 1989, Weinheim: Beltz.

Heitmeyer, W. (1990) 'Jugend auf dem Weg nach rechts?', in D. Kollmann, J. Kollmer, K. Rees, H.-P. Steffen (eds), *Neofashismus: (k)ein langfristiges Problem?*, Bielfeld: K. Böllert - KT-Verlag.

Held, D. (1980) *Introduction to Critical Theory*, London: Hutchinson.

Heller, A. and Fehér, F. (1988) *The Postmodern Political Condition*, Cambridge: Polity Press.

Hering, S. and Kramer, E. (eds) (1984) *Aus der Pionierzeit der Sozialarbeit: Elf Frauen berichten*, Weinheim: Beltz.

Hernes, H.M. (1984) *The Situation of Women in the Political Process in Europe, Part III: The Role of Women in Voluntary Associations and Organisations*, Strasbourg: Council of Europe, Directorate of Human Rights.

Hildeng, B. (1986) 'Social work education in Norway', in Brauns, H.-J. and Kramer, D., *Social Work Education in Europe: A Comprehensive Description of Social Work Education in 21 European Countries*, Frankfurt: Deutscher Verein für öffentliche und private Fürsorge.

Hildeng, B. (1991) 'The Norwegian welfare state: its aims and organization, in Ø. Tutvedt and L. Young (eds), *Social Work and the Norwegian Welfare State*, Norwegian State College of Local Government Administration and Social Work, NotaBene Report No. 91:4, Oslo.

Hilgenfeldt, E. (1937) *Die Idee der Nationalsozialistischen Wohlfahrtspflege*, Munich/Berlin: Zentralverlag der NSDAP.

Hill, Octavia (1883) *Homes of the London Poor,* London: Macmillan.

Hobsbawm, E.J. (1977) *The Age of Revolution: Europe 1789-1848*, London: Sphere Books.

Hollis, E.V. and Taylor, A. L. (1951) *Social Work Education in the United States: Report of a Study Made for the National Council on Social Work Education*, New York: Columbia University Press.

Hudson, A. (1985) 'Feminism and social work: resistance or dialogue?, *British Journal of Social Work* 15,4: 635-55.

Humphries, B. (1988) 'Adult learning in social work education:

towards liberation or domestication?' *Critical Social Policy* 8, 2: 4–21.

Ion, J., Tricart, J.-P. (1984) *Les travailleurs sociaux*, Paris: Éditions La Découverte.

Janssen, K. (1959) "Kinderfürsorge" in *Die Religion in Geschichte und Gegenwart, 3*, 3rd edn. Tübingen: Mohr.

Johnson, N. (1990) *Reconstructing the Welfare State*, London: Harvester Wheatsheaf.

Jouhy, E. (1984) 'Diachrone und synchrone . . .' in U. Menzemer and A. Moreau, *L'emprise du social: Perspectives françaises et allemandes sur la jeunesse et le travail social*, Paris: A. Colin.

Kalcher, J. (1986) 'Professional nomenclature', in M. Courtioux, H. Davies Jones, J. Kalcher, W. Steinhauser, H. Tuggener, and K. Waaldijk, *The Social Pedagogue in Europe – Living with Others as a Profession*, Zurich: FICE Verlag.

Karlusch, H. and Rössler, E. '"Sozio-Animation": Anstiftung zur Selbstorganisation im Rahmen amtlicher Sozialarbeit?' *Soziale Arbeit*, 41, 9: 310–13.

Keane, J. (1988) *Civil Society and the State*, London: Verso.

Kelleher, C. and Kennedy, S. (1988) 'Co-operative action as a means of community development', *Exchange* 7, January: 5–6.

Kennedy, S. (1981) *Who Should Care? The Development of Kilkenny Social Services 1963–1980*, Dublin: Turoe Press.

Keupp, H. (1992) 'Das Subjekt und das Soziale sind auch nicht mehr das, was sie einmal waren! Aber. . .' in H.-U. Otto et al. (eds), *Zeit-Zeichen sozialer Arbeit*, Neuwied: Luchterhand.

Klee, E. (1985a) *"Euthanasie" im NS-Staat: Die 'Vernichtung lebensunwerten Lebens'*, Frankfurt: Fischer.

Klee, E. (ed.), (1985b) *Dokumente zur 'Euthanasie'* , Frankfurt: Fischer.

Knowles, M. S. (1985) *Andragogy in Action: Applying Modern Principles of Adult Learning*, San Francisco: Jossey-Bass.

Knüppel-Dähne, H. and Mitrovic, E. (1989) 'Helfen und Dienen: die Arbeit von Fürsorgerinnen im Hamburger öffentlichen Dienst während des Nationalsozialismus', in H.-U. Otto and H. Sünker (eds), *Soziale Arbeit und Faschismus*, Frankfurt: Suhrkamp.

Köhler, G. (1992) 'Das "Peitzer Modell" – Ein Beispiel der Integration von Aussiedlern im neuen Bundesland Brandenburg', *Soziale Arbeit* 41, 2: 38–43.

Kolarska-Bobinska, L. (1992) 'The changing face of civil society in eastern Europe', in Z. Ferge and J.E. Kolberg (eds), *Social Policy in a Changing Europe,* Frankfurt: Campus.

Konopka, G. (1953) 'The application of social work principles to international relations', *Social Welfare Forum* 1953: 279–88.

Konopka, G. (1982) 'Selbstdarstellung' in L. Pongratz (ed.), *Pädagogik in Selbstdarstellungen*, Hamburg: Meiner.

Konrad, G. (1977) *The Case Worker*, London: Hutchinson.

Krafeld, F., Lutzebäck, E. Schaar, G. Strom, C. and Welp, W. (1993) 'Akzeptierende Jugendarbeit mit rechtsextremen Jugendlichen?', in

H. Heil, M. Perik and P.-U. Wendt (eds), *Jugend und Gewalt*, Marburg: Schüren.

Kramer, D. (1983) 'Das Fürsorgesystem im Dritten Reich', in R. Landwehr and R. Baron (eds), *Geschichte der Sozialarbeit*, Weinheim: Beltz.

Kreidenweis, H. and Treptow, R. (1990) 'Internationalität: Fragen an eine vergleichende Sozialarbeit/Sozialpädagogik', *Neue Praxis* 20, 1: 36–49.

Kronen, K. (1978), 'Sozialpädagogik: Zu Entstehung und Wandel des Begriffs', *Sociologia Internationalis* 16: 219–34.

Ksiezopolski, M. (1987) 'Polish social policy in a situation of economic crisis: is there a choice of alternatives?', in A. Evers, H. Nowotny and H. Wintersberger, *The Changing Face of Welfare*, Aldershot: Gower.

Ksiezopolski, M. and Sienko, I. (1988) 'Between state and society: the impact of traditional and new forms of volunteering in Poland', in A. Evers and H. Wintersberger (eds), *Shifts in the Welfare Mix: Their Impact on Work, Social Services and Welfare Politics*, Vienna: European Centre for Social Welfare Training and Research.

Kuper, B.O. (1990) 'Economie sociale: eine europäische Herausforderung an die Freie Wohlfahrtspflege?' *Nachrichtendienst des Deutschen Vereins* 70, 9: 307–9.

Kwhali, J. (1991) 'Assessment checklist for DipSW External Assessors', in CCETSW, *One Small Step towards Racial Justice*, London: Central Council for Education and Training in Social Work.

Langen, M. (1990) 'Community care in the 1990s: the community care White Paper "Caring for People"', *Critical Social Policy* 10, 2: 58–70.

Lavan, A. (1991) *Report 1990: Expert Network European Community Qualifications*, Dublin: Social Science Research Centre, University College Dublin.

Lee, J.J. (1989) *Ireland 1912–1985: Politics and Society*, Cambridge: Cambridge University Press.

Leibfried, S. (1992), 'Towards a European welfare state: on integrating poverty regimes into the European Community', in Z. Ferge and J. K. Kolberg (eds), *Social Policy in a Changing Europe*, Frankfurt: Campus.

Leibfried, S. and Pierson, P. (1992) 'Prospects for Social Europe', *Politics and Society* 20, 3: 333–66.

Lichtenberg, E. (1932) 'Ein Tag aus dem Leben einer Fürsorgerin', *Österreichische Blätter für Krankenpflege und Fürsorge* 8, 3: 33–39

Lifton, B.J. (1988) *The King of Children: A Biography of Janusz Korczak*, New York: Farrar, Straus and Giroux.

Lister, R. (1989) 'Defending the cash/care frontier: social work and the Social Fund', in P. Carter, T. Jeffs and M. Smith (eds), *Social Work and Social Welfare Yearbook, 1*, Milton Keynes: Open University Press.

Loescher, G. (1989) 'The European Community and refugees', *International Affairs* 65, 4: 617–36.

Lorenz, W. (1991a) 'The new German Children and Young People Act', *British Journal of Social Work* 21: 329–39.

Lorenz, W. (1991b) 'Social work practice in Europe: continuity in diversity', in M. Hill (ed.), *Social Work and the European Community*, London: J. Kingsley.

Lorenz, W. (1991c) 'Merger or takeover? East German social workers facing unification,' *Social Work Today*, 22 (2/5/1991), 19–20.

Lovett, T. (1987) 'Adult education and community action: the Northern Ireland experience', in G. Allen et al. (eds), *Community Education*, Milton Keynes: Open University Press.

Lucassen, L. (1991) 'The power of definition: stigmatisation, minorisation and ethnicity illustrated by the history of gypsies in the Netherlands', *Netherlands Journal of Social Sciences* 27, 2: 80–91.

X McBeath, G.B. and Webb, S. A. (1991) 'Social work, modernity and post modernity', *The Sociological Review* 39, 4: 745–62.

McConnell, C. (1991) 'Community Development in Europe', in M. Hill (ed.), *Social Work and the European Community: the Social Policy and Practice Contexts*, London: J. Kingsley.

McLeod, H. (1980) 'The dechristianisation of the working class in western Europe (1850–1900)', *Social Compass* 27, 2/3: 191–214.

McVeigh, R. (1992) 'The specificity of Irish racism', *Race and Class* 33, 4: 31–45.

Marcon, P. (1988) *Educators in the Europe of 1992*, Proceedings of the seminar on the EC recognition of diplomas of special/professional/ social educator/youth and community workers, Rome: Università 'La Sapienza'.

Marcon, P. (1991) 'L'educatore', in R. Maurizio and D. Rei (eds), *Professioni nel sociale*, Turin: Gruppo Abele.

X Marshall, T.H. and Bottomore, T. (1992) *Citizenship and Social Class*, London: Pluto Press.

Maurizio, R. (1991) 'L'animatore', in R. Maurizio and D. Rei (eds), *Professioni nel sociale*, Turin: Gruppo Abele.

Mayer, K.U. and Müller, W. (1984) 'The state and the structure of life course' in A.B.Sorensen, F. Weinert and L. Sherrod, *Human Development: Interdisciplinary Perspectives*, New York: Academic Press.

Medical Post-graduate Education Center in Warsaw (1978) *Social Workers, their Skills, Effectiveness of Work and Training in the Polish People's Republic*, 1, Warsaw.

Melucci, A. (1988) 'Social movements and the democratization of everyday life', in Keane, J., *Civil Society and the State*, London: Verso.

Miller, C. and Bryant, R. (eds), (1990) 'Community work in the U.K.: reflections on the 1980s', *Community Development Journal* 25, 4: 316–25.

X Mills, C.W. (1943) 'The professional ideology of social pathologists', *American Journal of Sociology* 49: 165–180.

Möller, K. (1991) 'Bedürfnisorientierung statt "Abschreckungsdidaktik"' *Deutsche Jugend* 7–8: 311–21.

Mullender, A. and Cox, B. (1992) *Role and Significance of the Voluntary Sector in the Development of the Diploma in Social Work*, London: CCETSW.

Müller, C.W. (1988) *Wie Helfen zum Berufe wurde: eine Methodengeschichte der Sozialarbeit 1945–1985*, Weinheim: Beltz.

Münz, R. (1992) 'Integration als einzige Alternative', *Steirische Erwachsenenbildung Informationen*, 50, 5: 37–8.

Myrdal, A. (1955) 'A scientific approach to international welfare', in Myrdal, A., Altmeyer, A.J. and Rusk, D., *America's Role in International and Social Welfare*, New York: Columbia University Press.

Neate, P. (1992) 'Splintering the service', *Community Care* 24 September 1992: 14–15.

Nederveen Pieterse, J. (1991) 'Fictions of Europe', *Race and Class* 32, 3: 3–10.

Neises, G. (1968) *Christian Jasper Klumker*, Frankfurt: Deutscher Verein.

Niebuhr, R. (1948) *Moral Man and Immoral Society: A Study in Ethics and Politics*, New York: C. Scribner and Sons.

Nilsson, I. and Wadeskog, A. (1988) 'Local initiatives in a new welfare state: a fourth sector approach', in A. Evers and H. Wintersberger (eds), *Shifts in the Welfare Mix: Their Impact on Work, Social Services and Welfare Politics*, Vienna: European Centre for Social Welfare Training and Research.

Nohl, H. (1926a) 'Die Einheit der Pädagogischen Bewegung', in H. Nohl (1949), *Pädagogik aus Dreissig Jahren*, Frankfurt: Schulte-Bulmke.

Nohl, H. (1926b) 'Gedanken für die Erziehungstätigkeit des Einzelnen mit besonderer Berücksichtigung der Erfahrungen von Freud und Adler', in H. Nohl (1949), *Pädagogik aus Dreissig Jahren*, Frankfurt: Schulte-Bulmke.

Nokielski, H. (1987) 'Strukturwandel organisierten Helfens in den Niederlanden', in R. Bauer and A.-M. Thränhardt (eds), *Verbandliche Wohlfahrtspflege im internationalen Vergleich*, Opladen: Westdeutscher Verlag.

Noonan, P. (1922) 'Racism against the traveller community', in Committee on the Administration of Justice, *Racism in Northern Ireland*, Belfast: CAJ.

Nowak, J. (1988) *Soziale Probleme und soziale Bewegungen*, Weinheim/Basel: Beltz.

Nowotny, H. (1984) 'Social concerns for the 1980s: act locally and think complex' in H. Nowotny (ed.), *Social Concerns for the 1980s*, Vienna: European Centre for Social Welfare Training and Research.

Oelschlägel, D. (1992) 'Umerziehung', in R. Bauer (ed.), *Lexikon des Sozial- und Gesundheitswesens*, Munich: Oldenbourg.

Offe, C. (1984) *Contradictions of the Welfare State*, London: Hutchinson.

Offe, C. (1985) 'New social movements: challenging the boundaries of institutional politics', *Social Research* 52, 4: 817–68.

Olk, T. and Otto, H.-U. (1989) *Soziale Dienste im Wandel, 2: Entwürfe sozialpädagogischen Handlens*, Neuwied and Frankfurt: Luchterhand.

Oppl, H. (1992a) 'Künftige Entwicklung von Sozialarbeit/Sozialpädagogik und Konsequenzen für Lehre und Studium', *Soziale Arbeit* 41, 3:92–8.

Oppl, H. (1992b) 'Zur "Marktposition" der Freien Wohlfahrtspflege', *Soziale Arbeit* 41, 5: 152–8.

Oyediran, J. (1992) 'The application of UK's obligations under international law to Northern Ireland', in Committee on the Administration of Justice, *Racism in Northern Ireland*, Belfast: CAJ.

Pankhurst, K.P. (1954) 'Anna Wheeler: a pioneer socialist and feminist', *Political Quarterly* 25, 2: 132–43.

Paul, R. (1991) 'Black and Third World people's citizenship and 1992', *Critical Social Policy* 11, 2: 52–64.

Peillon, M. (1987) 'State and society in the Republic of Ireland: a comparative study', *Administration* 35, 2: 190–212.

Pelczynski, Z.A. (1988) 'Solidarity and the "rebirth of civil society" in Poland, 1976–81', in Keane, J., *Civil Society and the State*, London: Verso.

Philp, M. (1979) 'Notes on the form of knowledge in social work', *Sociological Review* 27, 1: 83–111.

Pierson, C. (1991) *Beyond the Welfare State? The New Political Economy of Welfare*, Cambridge: Polity Press.

Pilley, C. (1990) 'Scotland: older people take action', in Poster, C. and Krüger, A. (eds), *Community Education in the Western World*, London: Routledge.

Pinker, R. (1990) *Social Work in an Enterprise Society*, London: Routledge.

Pius XI (1931) *Encyclical Letter (Quadragesimo Anno) on Reconstructing the Social Order and Perfecting it Conformably to the Percepts of the Gospel in Commemoration of the Fortieth Anniversary of the Encyclical "Rerum Novarum"*, Oxford: Catholic Social Guild.

Placier, A. (1989) *Les carrières sociales*, Paris: L'Etudiant.

Pollo, M. (1991) *Educazione come animazione*, Turin: Libreria Dottrina Cristiana.

Poster, C. and Krüger, A. (eds), (1990) *Community Education in the Western World*, London: Routledge.

Pullan, B. (1976) 'Catholics and the poor in early modern Europe', *Transactions of the Royal Historical Society* Series 5, 26: 15–34.

Rattansi, A. (1992) 'Changing the subject? Racism, culture and education', in J. Donald and A. Rattansi (eds), *'Race', Culture and Difference*, London: Sage.

Rauschenbach, T. (1991) 'Sozialpädagogik: eine akademische Disziplin ohne Vorbild?', *Neue Praxis* 21, 1: 1–11.

Reithofer, R. (1992) 'Flüchtlingslos', *Steirische Erwachsenenbildung Informationen* 50, 5: 3–6.

Richmond, M. (1917) *Social Diagnosis*, New York: Russell Sage Foundation.

Ricknell, L. (1986) 'Social work education in Sweden', in Brauns, H.-J. and D. Kramer, *Social Work Education in Europe: A Comprehensive Description of Social Work Education in 21 European Countries*,

Frankfurt: Deutscher Verein für öffentliche und private Fürsorge.

Rimbau Andreu, C. and Rossell Poch, T. (1986) 'Social work education in Spain', in Brauns, H.-J. and D. Kramer, *Social Work Education in Europe; A Comprehensive Description of Social Work Education in 21 European Countries*, Frankfurt: Deutscher Verein für öffentliche und private Fürsorge.

Roebroek, J.M. (1989) 'Netherlands', in J. Dixon and R.P.Scheurell (eds), *Social Welfare in Developed Market Countries* London: Routledge.

Rohde, B. (1989) *Sozialpädagogische Hochschulausbildung: Eine vergleichende Untersuchung von Studiengängen an Fachhochschulen und wissenschaftlichen Hochschulen*, Frankfurt: P. Lang.

Rojek, C. (1986) 'The "subject" in social work', *British Journal of Social Work* 16, 2: 65–77.

Rojek, C., Peacock, G. and Collins, S. (eds) (1988) *Social Work and Received Ideas*, London: Routledge.

Rolston, B. (1980) 'Community politics', in L. O'Dowd, B. Rolston and M. Tomlinson (1980) *Northern Ireland between Civil Rights and Civil War*, London: CSE Books.

Ronge, V. (1991) 'Social change in eastern Europe: implications for the western poverty agenda', *Journal of European Social Policy* 1, 1: 49–56.

Room, G. (1989) 'Key issues in action to combat poverty: the relevance of the European action-research projects', *Exchange* 10 January: 6–7.

Room, G. (1990)'*New Poverty in the European Community*', Basingstoke: Macmillan.

Rosanvallon, P. (1988) 'The decline of social visibility', in J. Keane (ed.), *Civil Society and the State*, London: Verso.

Rose, H. (1986) 'Women and the restructuring of the welfare state, in E. Oyen (ed.), *Comparing Welfare States and Their Futures*, Aldershot: Gower.

Rossell, T. (1987) *L'entrevista en el treball social*, Barcelona: Colleció Euge, Publicaciones de l'Escola Universitària de Treball Social.

Rusk, D. (1955) 'Peace, freedom, and social welfare', in Myrdal, A., Altmeyer, A.J. and Rusk, D. *America's Role in International Social Welfare*, New York: Columbia University Press.

Rusk, R.R. (1965) *The Doctrines of the Great Educators*, London: Macmillan.

Sablik, K. (1983) *Julius Tandler: Mediziner und Sozialreformer*, Vienna: A. Schendl.

Sachße, C. and Tennstedt, F. (1980) *Geschichte der Armenfürsorge in Deutschland: Vom Spätmittelalter bis zum 1. Weltkrieg*, Stuttgart: Kohlhammer.

Sachße, C. and Tennstedt, F. (1988) *Geschichte der Armenfürsorge in Deutschland: Fürsorge und Wohlfahrtspflege 1871 bis 1929*, Stuttgart: Kohlhammer.

Salomon, A. (1917) *Soziale Frauenbildung und Soziale Berufsarbeit*, Leipzig/Berlin: Teubner.

Salomon, A. (1919) *Die deutsche Frau und ihre Aufgaben im neuen Volksstaat*, Leipzig/Berlin: Teubner.

Salomon, A. (1926) *Soziale Diagnose*, Berlin: Heymanns Verlag.

Salomon, A. (1937) *Education for Social Work: A Sociological Interpretation based on an International Survey*, Zurich/Leipzig: Verlag für Recht und Gesellschaft.

Salomon, A. (1983) *Character ist Schicksal*, Weinheim/Basel: Beltz.

Saraceno, C. (1987) 'Between state intervention, the social sphere and private life: changes in the family's role', in A. Evers, H. Nowotny and H. Wintersberger, *The Changing Face of Welfare*, Aldershot: Gower.

Schendelen, M. van (1984) 'Consociationalism, pillarization and conflict management in the Low Countries', *Acta politica* 19 (special edition).

Scherr, A. (1992) 'Anforderungen an professionelle Jugendarbeit mit ausländerfeindlichen und gewaltbereiten Jugendszenen', *Neue Praxis* 22, 5: 387–95.

Schmid, C.L. (1981) *Conflict and Consensus in Switzerland*, Berkeley: University of California Press.

Schriewer, J. (1983) 'Pädagogik: ein deutsches Syndrom?', *Zeitschrift für Pädagogik* 29, 3: 359–89.

Schumann, M. (1992) 'Rechtsextremismus, Jugendbiographie und Jugendhilfe', *Soziale Arbeit* 41, 6: 186–92.

Seliger, M. and Ucakar, K. (1985) *Wien: Politische Geschichte 1740–1934*, Vienna: Jugend und Volk.

SFS 1980/620 *Social Services Act (Sweden)*, Stockholm: Ministry of Health and Social Affairs, International Secretariat, July 1990.

Shanks, M. (1977) *European Social Policy, Today and Tomorrow*, Oxford: Pergamon Press.

Sielert, U. (1985) *Zwischen Basisbewegung und staatlichem Zugriff: Sozialpädagogik/Sozialarbeit in den Niederlanden*, Frankfurt: Campus.

Sieveking, K. (1992), 'Amalie Sieveking', in R. Bauer (ed.), *Lexikon des Sozial- und Gesundheitswesens*, Munich: Oldenbourg.

Šiklová, J. (1991) The solidarity of the culpable', *Social Research* 58, 4: 765–73.

Stathopoulos, P. (1986) 'Social work education in Greece', in Brauns, H.-J. and D. Kramer, *Social Work Education in Europe: A Comprehensive Description of Social Work Education in 21 European Countries*, Frankfurt: Deutscher Verein für öffentliche und private Fürsorge.

Stathopoulos, P. (1991), 'Community development in rural areas of Greece', in M. Hill (ed.), *Social Work and the European Community: The Social Policy and Practice Contexts*, London: J.Kingsley.

Stewart, G. (1992) 'The Social Fund and social work', in R. Davidson and A. Erskine (eds), *Poverty, Deprivation and Social Work*, London: J. Kingsley.

Stjerno, S. and Seltzer, M. (1991) 'Social work practice in the welfare state: a Norwegian example', in Ø. Tutvedt and L. Young (eds),

Social Work and the Norwegian Welfare State, Norwegian State College of Local Government Administration and Social Work, NotaBene Report No. 91:4, Oslo.

Svenson, M. and MacPherson, S., (1988) 'Real issues and unreal figures: the impact of the 1986 Social Security Act', in S. Becker and S. Macpherson (eds), *Public Issues, Private Pain*, London: Insight.

Svensson, T.G. (1976) *Ethnicity and Mobilization in Sami Politics*, Stockholm: University of Stockholm Department of Anthropology.

Talos, E. (1984) 'Sozialpolitik im Austrofaschismus', in E. Talos and W. Neugebauer, *Austrofaschismus*, Vienna: Verlag für Gesellschaftskritik.

Tampke, J. (1981) 'Bismarck's social legislation: a genuine breakthrough?', in W. Mommsen (ed.), *The Emergence of the Welfare State in Britain and Germany 1850–1950* , London: Croom Helm.

Tandler, J. (1927) 'Städtisches Gesundheitswesen', in Städtewerk der Gemeinde Wien, *Das Neue Wien*, 2: 339–400.

Tausz, K. (1990) 'Why community development still has to find a role in Hungary', *Community Development Journal 25*, 4: 300–6.

Taylor, P.V. (1993) *The Texts of Paulo Freire*, Buckingham: Open University Press.

Tent, J.F. (1982) *Mission on the Rhine: Reeducation and Denazification in American-Occupied Germany*, Chicago: University of Chicago Press.

Thiersch, H. (1986) *Die Erfahrung der Wirklichkeit: Perspektiven einer alltagsorientierten Sozialpädagogik*, Weinheim/Munich: Beltz.

Thiersch, H. (1988) 'Theorie der Sozialarbeit/Sozialpädagogik', in D. Kreft, I. Mielenz (eds), *Wörterbuch Soziale Arbeit*, Weinheim/Basel: Beltz.

Tophoven, K. (1992) 'Pädagogik und Sozialpädagogik', *Neue Praxis* 22, 1: 52-67.

Townsend, P. (1989) 'And the walls come tumbling down', *Poverty 75*: 8–11.

Tranchina, P. and Serra, P. (1983) 'Community work and participation in the new Italian psychiatric legislation', in H. Stierlin et al. (eds), *Psychosocial Intervention in Schizophrenia*, Berlin: Springer.

Tschmelak, A. (1992) 'Deutschstunden', *Steirische Erwachsenenbildung Informationen 50*, 5: 71-4.

Tuggener, H. (1986) 'Social Pedagogics as a profession: a historical survey', in M. Courtioux, H. Davies Jones, J. Kalcher, W. Steinhauser, H. Tuggener and K. Waaldijk, *The Social Pedagogue in Europe: Living with Others as a Profession*, Zurich: FICE Verlag.

United Nations (1958) *Training for Social Work* : Third International Survey, Department of Economic and Social Affairs, New York: United Nations Publications.

U.S. Department of Health, Education, and Welfare (1955) *Social Workers Abroad Assess their Training in the United States*, Washington D.C., Government Printing Office International Service.

Waaldijk, K. (1985) 'Korczak's realism and its importance for the training of educators', Driebergen: unpublished manuscript.

Wallimann, I. (1986) 'Social insurance and the delivery of social services in France', *Social Science and Medicine* 23, 12: 1305–17.

Ward, D. and Mullender, A. (1991a) 'Empowerment and oppression: an indissoluble pairing for contemporary social work', *Critical Social Policy* 11, 2: 21–30.

Ward, D. and Mullender, A. (1991b) *Self-Directed Groupwork: Users Take Action for Empowerment*, London: Whiting and Birch.

Weh, L. (1987) 'Recent tendencies in the evolution of national law and practice in the field of asylum and refugees', in Council of Europe, *The Law of Asylum and Refugees: Present Tendencies and Future Perspectives*, Strasbourg: Council of Europe.

Wendt, W.R. (1985) *Geschichte der sozialen Arbeit*, 2nd edn., Stuttgart: Ferdinand Enke.

Wieler, J. (1987) *Er-Innerung eines zerstörten Lebensabends: Alice Salomon während der NS-Zeit (1933–1937) und im Exil (1937–1948)*, Darmstadt: Lingbach.

Wieler, J. (1989) 'The impact of Alice Salomon on social work education', in Fachhochschule für Sozialarbeit und Sozialpädagogik Berlin, *60 Jahre International Association of Schools of Social Work*, Berlin: FHSS.

Willenberg, U. (1992) 'Kirchliche Sozialeinrichtungen bangen um Freiräume in den neuen Bundesländern', *Sozialmagazin* 92, 1: 58–60.

Wolins, M. (ed.), (1967) *Selected Works of Janusz Korczak*, Springfield: Virginia.

Zaragozà, J.-V. (1991) 'Gesetzliche Grundlagen sozialer Arbeit in Spanien', in F. Hamburger (ed.), *Sozialarbeit in Deutschland und Spanien: Vergleichende Analysen und lokale Fallstudien*, Rheinfelden: Schäuble.

Name index

Subject index